THE GRIERS

Upper and Lower Canada, c. 1852

THE
GRIERS

PIONEERS IN AMERICA
AND CANADA
1816-1991

WILLIAM M. GRIER, JR.

DENVER

GRIER & COMPANY

Library of Congress Catalog Card Number: 91-075928

ISBN 0-9623268-1-X

Printed in the United States of America

For

my wife

JOAN GRAFMUELLER GRIER

ABOUT THE AUTHOR

Born in Oakland, California, Bill was raised in nearby
Piedmont and San Francisco and educated at the
University of California at Berkeley and Columbia
University Business School. He also studied at the
University of Oslo and the Sorbonne. His biography—
*Grier of San Francisco: Builder in the West and His Family,
1878–1988*—was published in 1989. Bill is married,
with a son by his first wife, and lives with his second
wife in Denver, Colorado. He is president of Grier &
Company, management consultants and publishers,
and founder in 1976 of *Real Estate West*, a newspaper
serving the commercial real estate industry from the
Midwest to the Pacific Coast.

History is the essence of innumerable biographies.

—Thomas Carlyle

CONTENTS

PART THREE

THOMAS JOHNSTON GRIER BRANCH

PART FOUR

WILLIAM JOHN GRIER BRANCH

ILLUSTRATIONS

xvi

xviii

PREFACE

The first volume of this series, *Grier of San Francisco: Builder in the West and His Family, 1878–1988*, covered the major events in my father's life—his childhood in San Francisco; his service in the Philippines during the Spanish-American War; his early career in real estate development, oil exploration, and gold mining; and his extensive work in railroad contracting, civil engineering, and construction across the American West. Sketches were also included on allied families and his Scot forebears, who settled in Upper Canada (now Ontario) after the War of 1812 and emigrated to the American West after the Civil War, during the burgeoning westward movement spurred by the Union Pacific Railroad.

This book is a succession of biographies. My paternal great-great-grandparents, the Pattersons—Scot-born George (1782–1862) and English-born Anne Merrigold (1791–1867)—settled in Perth, Upper Canada, in 1816. A sea captain who served seven years in the British Army, George saw combat on two continents: He fought on Gibraltar during the Peninsular War (1808–1814); in Upper Canada in the War of 1812; and at Waterloo in 1815, in the last epic battle of the Napoleonic Wars, which witnessed the routing of the French and the final abdication of Napoleon I.

After capturing Quebec in 1760, Britain had acquired the Canadas, Upper and Lower (so named because, though Upper Canada is actually "lower" than Lower Canada, travel to both was via the St. Lawrence River, and Upper Canada was further upstream). Between 1800 and 1875, seven and a half million people—my ancestors among them—crossed the ocean from Britain to make their homes in the Canadas. In fact, the population of Upper Canada increased seven-fold in the first third of the century. Thus, British Canada was settled in the nineteenth century, much later than the United States where the Puritans had arrived some two centuries earlier.

My great-grandfather James Grier (1818–1892), born in Northern Ireland of Scot descent, emigrated to Pakenham, Upper Canada, in the late 1830s and worked initially as a carriage- and sleighmaker. In 1844, he married the Pattersons' younger daughter, Eliza Anne (1825–1884). They had ten children and settled in Iroquois, Ontario. There, James became a member of the first town council and postmaster.

Like the first- and second-generation Griers, the eight survivors of the third soon showed they had the stamina and resilience of pioneers. They left home with diplomas from Iroquois High School, bookkeeping and telegraphy skills honed in their father's office, and inborn enthusiasm and fortitude. Four remained in Canada: J.R. Henry (1845–1911), George E. (1846–1925), Eliza Victoria (1855–1941), and Georgina Clara (1864–1946). The other four emigrated to the American West from 1870 to 1882. Anne (1848–1935) and husband Gilbert Fell moved to Ogden, Utah, where, after being a Central Pacific superintendent, a banker, and a businessman, he xxiv

was elected a two-term mayor. Thomas Johnston (1850–1914) settled in the Black Hills, Dakota Territory, where he directed Homestake Mining Company. William John (1853–1909), my grandfather, resided in San Francisco, where he was supervisor of telegraphers with the Central Pacific Railroad Company and, later, a land manager in Butte County, California. Albert E. (1859–1907), who had attended Osgoode Hall in Toronto (North America's oldest law school), became an attorney in Denver, Colorado.

The period from 1870 to 1990, when members of the fourth to seventh generations of Griers were born in Canada and the American West, was one of vast social and economic change, of prodigious growth, and of dramatic scientific and technological advances. It marked the gradual transition from a stable agricultural and commercial frontier to a modern, postindustrial society. Between the horse-and-buggy years and the age of space travel were the traumas of five wars, the 1929 Crash, the Great Depression, the cold war, and the sudden collapse of communism.

The careers of the Griers were multifaceted, involving aspects of politics, art, law, music, and business. Lastly, this volume profiles six other Griers in North America, not directly related to my family, whose distinguished lives honor our Scot heritage and clan, the Macgregors: an associate justice of the United States Supreme Court; a general of the army; a Canadian portrait painter; an art director of the Frick Collection in New York City; the founder of The Grier School for young girls in Tyrone, Pennsylvania; and a founding partner and first president of Edgerton, Germeshausen, and Grier, Inc. (now EG&G, Inc.), a major supplier of engineering and technical services to U.S. governmental agencies.

Denver, Colorado
July 1991

William M. Grier, Jr.

ACKNOWLEDGMENTS

For original material, pictures, help, and advice, I am indebted to Elo Lannon Grier, my mother; Eloyd John Grier, my brother; cousins David D.E. Grier, George Ann Palmer, Victoria ("Muddie") Grier Nelsen, and Dorothy Withycomb Miller (Mrs. A. Pirie Miller); Kathleen Zwicker Grier (Mrs. C. Denham Grier); Raymond Fell Lillie, grandson of Anne M. Grier (Mrs. A. Gilbert Fell); Donald H. McLaughlin, late president of Homestake Mining Company; Mildred Fielder, author of *The Treasure of Homestake Gold;* Madge Ferrie Christie; Virginia Havens Gowing; John H. Nopel, historian of Butte County, California; and Donald D. Toms, co-director of the Black Hills Mining Museum in Lead, South Dakota.

I appreciate the assistance of William P. Banning, Jr. (Muddie Grier's son by her first husband); Joan Taylor Grier Bird (adopted daughter of Ormonde Palethorpe Grier); and John S. Mead (son of Winfield Scott Mead, partner in Grier and Mead).

For information and insight on George and Anne Patterson (nee Merrigold) and on the Allan family, I thank Eleanor Grant (Mrs. Will Brewer Grant).

My gratitude, too, to the librarians at the following institutions: *in the United States*—California State Library (California Section) in Sacramento; Sutro Library, a branch of the C.S.L. in San Francisco; California Historical Society Library in San Francisco; Bancroft Library at University of California, Berkeley; Natural History Museum of Los Angeles County; Meriam Library Special Collection, California State University at Chico; Oregon State Historical Society Library in Portland; Genealogical Library of the Church of Jesus Christ of Latter-Day Saints in Salt Lake City, Utah; and New York Genealogical and Biographical Society in New York City; *in Canada*—Anglican Church of Canada, Dioceses of Ottawa, Montreal, and Ontario; Public Archives Canada in Ottawa; the Archives of Ontario in Toronto; National Postal Museum in Ottawa; Iroquois Public Library in Iroquois, Ontario; National Library of Canada in Ottawa; Stormont, Dundas and Glengarry Historical Society in Ontario; and Glengarry Genealogical Society in Ontario.

The staffs at several main public libraries were most helpful: in San Francisco, Oakland, Sacramento, and Oroville, California; Portland, Oregon; Ogden and Salt Lake City, Utah; Helena, Montana; Lead and Deadwood, South Dakota; Denver, Colorado; and New York City, New York.

Special thanks are due to the staff of the *Lead Daily Call* in Lead, South Dakota, who provided me with editorials regarding T.J. Grier and the Homestake Mining Company; to John D. Russell, director emeritus of Menlo College, for his reading and thoughtful suggestions on the Menlo xxvi

text; and to Laura E. Vance, who, in staying the course through two manuscripts, deftly typeset the many revisions.

Finally, words are inadequate to express the author's appreciation for the skill and dedication of his editor, Joan W. Sherman, without whose guidance this book would not have been possible.

PART ONE

JAMES GRIER BRANCH

GRIER COAT OF ARMS

The Grier coat of arms illustrated above was drawn by a heraldic artist from information officially recorded in ancient heraldic archives and documented in Burke's General Armory. Heraldic artists of old developed their own unique language to describe an individual coat of arms. In their language, the arms (shield) is as follows:

> Az. a lion ramp. or, armed and langued gu. betw. three antique crowns of the second, on a canton ar. an oak tree eradicated, surmounted by a sword in bend cinister, ensigned on the point with a royal crown all ppr.

Above the shield and helmet is the crest which is described as:

> An eagle displayed ppr. charged on the breast with a quadrangular lock ar.

When translated, the blazon also describes the original colors of the Grier arms and crest as they appeared centuries ago.

Family mottos are believed to have originated as battle cries in medieval times. The motto recorded with this Grier coat of arms was: *Memor Esto.*

1

SCOT FOREBEARS

The Grier family roots can be traced back to the Middle Ages, that period in western Europe preceding the formation of nation-states. The surname Grier is an abbreviation of Grierson, both names having been a "sept," or division, of the Scottish Macgregor clan, which was considered one of the purest of all Celtic tribes.[1] Its members were direct descendants of the Albanich or Alpinian aboriginal inhabitants of Scotland.

THE MACGREGOR CLAN

The Macgregors' original territory is believed to have covered the Scottish district of Glenurchy in Lorn, a portion of the Argyll region which was granted by King Alexander II to his military chiefs after their conquest of the area in the early thirteenth century. The family held this land until the late 1400s, though they did so by "right of the sword," rather than actual title.

The tenacious and rebellious Macgregors alienated their neighboring clans, particularly the Campbells, who possessed feudal rights to the Glenurchy territory and actively sought the annihilation of the "Clan Griogair" (the Macgregors' Gaelic name). The Campbells succeeded in diminishing the Macgregors to "tenants at will" on their lands and oppressed their rivals on all possible fronts.

In an effort to survive the often violent repression they faced, the Macgregors were forced to resort to a life of crime—most often victimizing those who had stolen their lands from them. Clan leaders became known as free-booters—men who plundered and pillaged. (The notorious Rob Roy, a seventeenth-century descendant of these men, is perhaps the most

---

1.   The Celts originated in Middle Europe. Before the birth of Christ, they moved westward into France and later swept across Britain. The Celts were conquered by the Romans, re-established themselves, and eventually had to fight off the invading Angles and Saxons. At its height, Celtic civilization covered a large area of Europe and produced epic literature, as well as beautiful jewelry and artifacts.

famous free-booter of all.)

In time, their enemies decided to destroy the Macgregors completely and used every legal means to do so. Allying themselves with the government, they eventually forced the Macgregor families into the Highland mountains, where the beleagured clan continued its fierce resistance.

After the Macgregors slaughtered the much larger Colquhouns tribe in 1603, the government of King James VI enacted a series of severe "acts of proscription" against the clan. Its members were ordered, under penalty of death, to change their surnames, often adopting Campbell, Stewart, Drummond, or Graham. They were forbidden to carry any weapons, and clan members assembling in groups of five or more were subject to death. An Act of Parliament in 1607 extended these proscriptions to members of the clan's younger generation as well, in an effort to dominate this rebel tribe in years to come.

It is believed that Grier's Scot forebears first settled in Dumfrieshire, coming from the Highlands of Scotland at the beginning of the 1400s. Two centuries later, when the persecution of the Macgregors was at its worst, many Griers emigrated to Northern Ireland and, eventually, to Canada and the United States.

The Scottish estate of Straharlie was owned by one line of the Grier family. The original owner's eldest son became a Knight Banneret and was granted the title of Sir James Grier, Knight. In time, James's son Henry migrated to Ireland, where he lived in County Tyrone at Radford near Grange and became the ancestral head of the family of Greer of Grange MacGregor.

Other Griers settled in Ireland's County Antrim, where the 1669 Hearth Money Roll includes: Ffranc Greer, Dreen Townland, Parish of Craigs; Thomas Greer, Ballee Townland, Parish of Connor; and William Greer, Craigfaddock Townland, Parish of Dunghy.

The legal repression of the Macgregors was first rescinded and then reenacted over the next 150 years, and it was not until 1784, during the reign of William and Mary, that Parliament finally revoked these excessive laws. At last, clan members could reclaim their family name and were, for the first time, accorded all the rights and privileges of British citizenship.

Map of the United Kingdom and the Republic of Ireland

Map of the Republic of Ireland and Northern Ireland

North Sea

Atlantic
Ocean

Aberdeen

SCOTLAND

Dundee

Edinburgh

Glasgow

Dumfries
and
Galloway

NORTHERN
IRELAND

Belfast

Isle of Man

Irish Sea

Map of Scotland

CHRONOLOGY OF JAMES GRIER

1818	Born in Northern Ireland
late 1830s	Emigrates to Upper Canada (later known as Ontario), settling in Pakenham; works as carriage- and sleighmaker
1844	Marries Eliza Anne Patterson in Perth, Upper Canada on July 4
1845	Son, James Richard Henry, born in Perth
1846	Moves back to Pakenham; son, George Edwin, born on October 10
1848	Daughter, Anne Marigold, born on May 27 in Pakenham
1850	Son, Thomas Johnston, born on May 13 in Pakenham
1851	Moves to Matilda Township (later renamed Iroquois); continues as carriage- and sleighmaker
1853	Son, William John, born on June 19 in Iroquois
1855	Daughter, Eliza Victoria, born on May 16 in Iroquois
1857	Appointed to first town council of Iroquois; daughter, Margaret ("Maggie")Armstrong, born on August 21 in Matilda
1859	Son, Albert Ephraim, born on July 28 in Iroquois
1860	Appointed Iroquois postmaster on March 1
1862	Son, Charles Allan, born in February in Iroquois
1864	Daughter, Georgina Clara, born on August 1 in Iroquois
1882	Son Charles dies in Toronto on September 9

1883	Retires from Canadian Postal Service on June 11; travels through American West with wife; moves to Anaheim, California
1884	Daughter Maggie dies in Anaheim during spring; moves back to Canada with wife and settles in Montreal; wife dies there on October 14
1886	Marries Susannah Allan Weatherhead in Perth on June 17
1892	Dies on May 11 in Toronto

10

The Basin in Perth, Ontario, Canada, c. 1908
(Courtesy of National Archives of Canada/PA-30949)

2

JAMES GRIER
1818–1892

Iroquois Postmaster

James Grier, a Scot descendant of the Macgregor clan, was born in Northern Ireland in 1818. In the late 1830s, he emigrated to Upper Canada (later known as Ontario) and settled in the township of Pakenham. James first worked as a carriage- and sleighmaker, a trade that took him to many nearby towns, including Perth. There he met and, on July 4, 1844, married Eliza Anne Patterson, in the Episcopal Church of St. James.

FAMILY

Born in Perth in 1825, Eliza was the second daughter of George Patterson and Anne Merrigold. (See Part One: 4) Her father was born in Perth, Scotland in 1782 and her mother, in Worcestershire, England in 1791. The Pattersons raised eight children—two daughters and six sons: Walter (birthdate unknown), Janet (b. 1817), James (b. 1819), Eliza (b. 1825), Ephraim (b. 1826), Charles, Richard, and George (dates of birth unknown).

Initially, James and Eliza Grier lived in her native city, where their first child, James Richard Henry, was born in 1845. The next year, they moved to Pakenham, thirty-two miles to the northeast.[1] Three more children were born to the couple in this village: George Edwin, on October 10, 1846; Anne Marigold, on May 27, 1848; and Thomas Johnston, on May 13, 1850.

In 1851, James, Eliza, and their four children moved to Matilda Township, fifty-five miles southeast of Pakenham on the St. Lawrence River. There James bought the title on Lot 23 from Matthew and Catherine Coons and continued in his trade of carriage- and sleighmaker until 1860, when he

---

1. Perth is about forty-five miles southwest of Ottawa. Today, the town has a population of 5,000; nearby Pakenham now has fewer than 1,000 residents.

Bird's-eye view of Pakenham, Ontario, c. 1910
(Courtesy of National Archives of Canada/PA-55783)

was appointed postmaster. In 1857, he also became a member of Matilda's first town council.

Matilda Township was settled in 1786 by six families who owned lots covering some 1,200 acres. The following year, the settlement was officially named in honor of the eldest daughter of King George III—the Princess Royal, Augusta Matilda. However, the British cut their ties with the township in its second year of existence.

Travel in those early days was rigorous. Settlers typically traveled in groups, forced to tow their boats up and down much of the river and, in winter, to haul their sleighs over ice. Given the difficulties of both travel and trade at that time, Matilda Township's growth was slow: By 1811, the population was a modest 111.

During the War of 1812, a group of American soldiers landed at Point Iroquois. In response, the British government ordered that a fort be built on that site, but it was never completed. A second fort, however, was finished on the river just below Point Iroquois, in hopes of thwarting an invasion by American troops. The much-prophesied invasion never took place, and the outpost was soon christened Fort Needless.

Growth in Matilda Township was stimulated by the completion of the Point Iroquois Canal in 1847, followed by the opening of the Grand Trunk Railroad in 1859. During this period, the town became increasingly important as a center of trade. Farmers opened stores along the waterfront and exchanged their butter, eggs, and honey for other necessities, while settlers from as far away as Kemptville, Chesterville, and Winchester were drawn to these small shops to replenish their food supplies. The farmer/store-keepers soon prospered and became Matilda's respected leaders.

CIVIL SERVANT

By 1857, Matilda's residents sought an independent government. Because the town lacked the requisite population of 750, a specific law was passed to permit its incorporation, under the name of Iroquois.[2] George Brouse, a former member of Parliament (MP) and a leading pioneer, was influential in obtaining this incorporation and became the first "reeve," or elected president, of the town council. Other councilmen included James Grier, J.S. Ross (MP), William Elliot, and Philip Carman.

---

2.   When the St. Lawrence Seaway was constructed in the 1950s, the town of Iroquois was moved some distance from its original site, which is now under water. Today, the town's population is less than 1,000.

All of the council members held other important positions and were active in community life. Grier, for example, was appointed postmaster on March 1, 1860, only the second man to fill that position. He succeeded his old friend George Brouse, who had died three weeks earlier. (Brouse had begun his service as postmaster sometime prior to 1832, when the town was still known as Matilda.) Brouse and Ross also served as members of Parliament for one- and three-year terms, respectively, and Elliot and Carman were elected wardens—officials in charge of the port and market at Iroquois.

As postmaster, one of James's responsibilities was to deliver Iroquois mail to the Grand Trunk Railway Company's station half a mile away. As of May 3, 1860, the contract called for twenty-four trips per week, for which Grier was paid $70. However, he relinquished this contract in 1864, as his other responsibilities had grown considerably.

Two years after the Griers' move to Matilda, Eliza gave birth to her fifth child, William John, on June 19, 1853. Following William came five other children: Eliza Victoria, born on May 16, 1855; Margaret ("Maggie") Armstrong, on August 21, 1857; Albert Ephraim, on July 28, 1859; Charles Allan, in February 1862; and Georgina Clara, on August 1, 1864. All of the children were baptized in St. John's Episcopal Church in Iroquois.

As the Grier children grew up, they shared household chores and clerked in their father's post office. There they sorted and delivered mail, learned bookkeeping, and became telegraph operators. These skills later proved invaluable to the careers of several of the Grier boys.

From 1850 to 1900, Canada suffered much political unrest and experienced little economic growth, thereby providing limited employment opportunities for the younger generation.[3] As a result, four of James and Eliza's ten children emigrated to the American West: Anne Marigold, Thomas Johnston, William John, and Albert Ephraim. Three others settled in Montreal: James Richard Henry (known as Henry Grier), Eliza Victoria, and Georgina Clara. Maggie, who suffered from tuberculosis, remained with her parents in Iroquois, while her brother George Edwin initially made Iroquois his home, but later moved to Kemptville in Grenville County. The

---

3.   A contributing factor and an issue very much in the forefront at the time was that of the Clerical Reserves. This system, in effect since 1791, set aside one-eighth of all land in each county to provide revenue for the Protestant clergy and had a profoundly depressing effect on the economic development of the province for more than half a century. The Clerical Reserves Secularization Act of 1854 ameliorated the situation, but not before life had been lost over the issue.

Griers' youngest son, Charles Allan, was studying at Osgoode Hall Law School in Toronto when he died of tuberculosis at twenty, on September 9, 1882.[4]

RETIREMENT YEARS

After twenty-three years in the Canadian Postal Service, James retired on June 11, 1883.[5] Before moving to California with their ailing daughter Maggie, James and Eliza put their home and additional lot up for sale with an Iroquois broker. Traveling westward by train, they stopped in the Black Hills of the Dakota Territory to see their son Thomas Johnston, then a bachelor and bookkeeper for Homestake Mining Company. En route, they also visited Albert Ephraim, an attorney in Denver; their daughter Anne and son-in-law A. Gilbert Fell in Ogden, Utah; and, finally, their son William John in San Francisco, along with his wife Georgie, children Milt and May, and Georgie's parents, Joseph Milton and Martha Whitney Orr.

In choosing a place to retire, James and Eliza were seeking a mild climate where Maggie might recover from tuberculosis. After visiting William John and his family, they settled in Anaheim, California, in the heart of the citrus groves southeast of Los Angeles.[6] Despite the healthy climate, however, Maggie, never able to regain her health, died in the spring of 1884 in Anaheim and was buried there.

Although James and Eliza had sold their house and land in Iroquois, they decided nonetheless to return to Canada, for they missed their homeland, family, and friends and were deeply saddened by Maggie's death. On the return trip, they visited again with their children and grandchildren in the American West.

Shortly after the Griers settled in Montreal, Eliza died suddenly on October 14, 1884 while visiting her daughter Georgina. Two days later, she was buried next to her son Charles Allan (1862–1882), in the cemetery of St. John's Episcopal Church in Iroquois.

---

4.   Charles's brother Albert Ephraim was also a student at Osgoode Hall, the oldest law school in North America.

5.   His successor was Adam Harkness (1835–1904), an old friend and Iroquois "reeve." Harkness held the position until he died on June 24, 1904.

6.   Anaheim was settled in 1857 by a colony of fifty German immigrants who bought 1,165 acres of the Mexican land grant and rights to water from the Santa Ana River, in order to produce wine. When a disease wiped out the vines in 1888, the area was replanted with citrus and nut trees. Today, Anaheim is known as the home of Disneyland.

SECOND MARRIAGE

On June 17, 1886, James Grier married Susannah Allan Weatherhead in St. Andrew's Presbyterian Church in Perth, Ontario; the Reverend McGilvrey officiated. Susannah was fifty-nine at the time and James, sixty-eight. The couple lived on Drummond Street in Perth.

The widow of Thaddeus Weatherhead, one of Perth's early prosperous merchants who had died in 1877, Susannah Allan was born in 1826 in Kingston, the second eldest child of William "Banker" Allan. Her brother, Andrew Allan, was married to Eliza Grier's only sister, Janet. She spent her childhood in Balderson Corners where, as a young girl, she regularly rode into Perth on horseback to attend church services in the old St. Andrew's Presbyterian Church.

James Grier died suddenly of a heart attack at age seventy-two in Toronto on May 11, 1892; he was buried three days later beside his first wife Eliza and his son Charles Allan, in St. John's Episcopal Cemetery in Iroquois.

Surviving her husband by seventeen years, Susannah died on April 11, 1909; she was buried in the Elmwood Cemetery in Montreal. In the Perth *Courier* obituary, Susannah was remembered as being "philanthropic in a quiet way." She had been one of the oldest residents of Perth, having worked for years in various community and church organizations.

17

Aerial view of Iroquois, Ontario, c. 1920
(*Courtesy of National Archives of Canada/PA-30697*)

Eliza Victoria Grier and Mary Jane Palethorpe Grier, May 9, 1896

3

JAMES GRIER'S FAMILY
IN CANADA

Four of James and Eliza Grier's ten children emigrated to the United States in the 1870s and 1880s. Their eldest daughter, Anne, moved to Ogden, Utah with her husband A. Gilbert Fell in 1870. Sons Thomas Johnston and William John soon followed, first settling in Denver, Colorado in 1872. Ten years later, Albert Ephraim moved to a town in the Black Hills of the Dakota Territory, near his brother T.J., before he settled in Denver, where he would establish a legal career. (See Parts Two, Three, Four, and Five)

The majority of the Griers' children, however, chose to retain their Canadian citizenship.

J. R. HENRY GRIER
1845–1911

Bookkeeper–Treasurer

The Griers' first-born, James Richard Henry (called Henry by family and friends), was born in Perth, Ontario in the spring of 1845 and was baptized in St. James Anglican Church on August 3 of that year. When Henry was six years old, the family moved to Matilda Township, where he completed his schooling.

In 1862, following graduation from Iroquois High School, Henry moved to Montreal and began work as a bookkeeper. On August 5, 1868, he married Charlotte A. Moore in her family's home at 184 St. Constant Street. Charlotte, the second daughter of the late John Moore, would bear five children: Henriette, Caroline, Florence, Eva, and Henry, Jr.

Early in his career, Henry was bookkeeper for the City of Montreal. Then, from 1895 to 1911, the last sixteen years of his life, he was the secretary-treasurer of the Lyman Knox Company, Ltd., importers and manufacturers of drugs and chemicals, with offices at 374-8 St. Paul Street, Montreal.

He and his family lived at 522 1/2 St. Urbain Street in Montreal, where Henry died on June 11, 1911. He was buried in the Mount Royal Cemetery.

GEORGE E. GRIER
1846–1925

Bachelor

George Edwin, born in Pakenham, Upper Canada on October 10, 1846, died seventy-nine years later in Kemptville, Grenville County, Ontario on September 25, 1925. A bachelor, George left his estate to his three surviving sisters: Georgina Clara (Mrs. Charles William Withycomb), who lived at 597 Victoria Avenue, Westmount, Quebec (a Montreal suburb); Eliza Victoria (Mrs. Arthur Joseph Williams), who lived on Claremont Avenue, Westmount; and Anne Marigold (Mrs. A. Gilbert Fell), who lived at 575 25th Street in Ogden, Utah.

ELIZA VICTORIA GRIER
1855–1941

Musician–Contralto

Eliza Victoria was born on May 16, 1855 in Iroquois, Ontario, where she received her early education. As a young woman, she studied at the Royal College of Music in London, England. There, in 1884, she married Arthur Joseph Williams. Returning to Montreal, where her husband was named manager of an English tea firm, they lived at 4277 Western Avenue. They had no children.

Music and the performing arts were a vital part of Eliza's life. She played the piano and organ and was, for many years, the contralto soloist at both Christ's Church Cathedral and St. James the Apostle Church in Montreal. Eliza and Arthur regularly attended the opera, symphony, and theatre in Montreal and enjoyed trips to New York and London, where they saw friends and attended concerts and plays. While living in Montreal, they were often visited by her Denver nephew Denham Grier, sister Anne Grier Fell, and niece Goldie Fell Niehaus.

Following Arthur's retirement in 1926, the couple lived in Los Angeles, California, where they had often spent their winters, enjoying the company of Eliza's sister-in-law Mary Jane Grier (Mrs. Thomas Johnston Grier) and her children Thomas Johnston, Jr., Lisgar, Ormonde, and Evangeline Victoria ("Muddie"). Eliza and Mary Jane had been close friends for some time, sharing their interest in music and the arts.

Eliza and Arthur returned to Montreal in 1928. He died there the following year. Some thirteen years later, on April 5, 1941, Eliza died in her home at the age of eighty-five.

MARGARET A. GRIER
1857–1884

Born on August 21, 1857, Margaret ("Maggie") Armstrong developed tuberculosis as a young woman. Her parents' efforts to move with her to a temperate climate proved futile when Maggie, not yet twenty-six, died in early 1884, in Anaheim, California.

CHARLES ALLAN GRIER
1862–1882

Law Student

The Griers' youngest son, Charles Allan, a graduate of Iroquois High School, died of tuberculosis at age twenty. Charles—born February 1862 in Iroquois, Ontario—was a student at Osgoode Hall, the law school, in Toronto at his death.

GEORGINA CLARA GRIER
1864–1946

Pianist–Contralto

Born on August 1, 1864 in Iroquois, Ontario, Georgina Clara was the tenth and last child of James and Eliza Grier. She married Charles William Withycomb on her twenty-fourth birthday in 1888, at Montreal's Christ's Church Cathedral. They lived at 4069 Grey Avenue in Montreal and had six children—three daughters and three sons: Eveline Clara, Charles Robert Grier, Gwendoline, Donald, Malcolm, and Dorothy Marguerite. They also had a country home in Little Nelles on the St. Lawrence River.

Like her sister Eliza, she greatly loved music, ballet, and theatre. An accomplished contralto and pianist, she was an active member of the choir of Christ's Church Cathedral and regularly attended the Montreal opera and symphony.

Georgina, the youngest of James and Eliza Grier's children, outlived her siblings and died on November 25, 1946, at age eighty-two, having survived her husband by five years. She was buried in the Mount Royal Cemetery.

Dorothy Withycomb Miller
1894–1980

Georgina's youngest child, Dorothy Marguerite, married A. Pirie Miller; they had no children. Although she lived in Montreal all of her life, Dorothy traveled frequently to New York City and Toronto with her husband, where they attended opera, concerts, and theatre. Like her mother and her aunt Eliza, Dorothy was also a lifelong devotee of music and the performing arts.

A. Pirie Miller, an accountant, died on November 26, 1978. Two years later, Dorothy passed away in Montreal on June 4, at the age of eighty-six.

Donald and Malcolm Withycomb

Two of Dorothy's brothers, Donald and Malcolm, both became American citizens. They lived and worked in New York from the 1920s to the '50s, sharing an apartment on East 76th Street, off Fifth Avenue. Dorothy and Pirie often visited them there, staying at the Biltmore Hotel or Essex House. Donald died in New York City, Malcolm in Phoenix, Arizona.

Charles Robert Grier Withycomb

Georgine Clair Grier Withycomb and daughters Dorothy and Gwendoline

Dorothy Withycomb Miller (1894–1980)

A. Pirie Miller (1898–1978)

Anne Merrigold Patterson (1791–1867)

4

ALLIED FAMILIES
Patterson / Allan

GEORGE PATTERSON, 1782–1862

ANNE MERRIGOLD PATTERSON, 1791–1867

A native of Perth, Scotland, George Patterson, father of Eliza Patterson Grier, was a sea captain who spent seven years in the military before emigrating to Upper Canada in 1816. He began his military career at age twenty-seven by volunteering, on September 25, 1809, for service in the British 37th Regiment of Foot Soldiers. Lieutenant Patterson fought on Gibraltar in the Peninsular War, then in Upper Canada in the War of 1812, and in France in the 1815 Battle of Waterloo, where Napoleon was defeated.

George's wife, Anne Merrigold (later changed to Marigold), was born in Worcestershire, England in 1791. She accompanied her husband on his military campaigns, giving birth to two children during this period. The first, a daughter, died in infancy and was buried on Gibraltar. Their second child, Walter, was sent to live with Anne's family in London.

On June 23, 1816, George Patterson was mustered out of the 37th Regiment. Having survived three major battles on two continents, he was rewarded with a land grant in Perth, Upper Canada, where he and Anne then made their home. Son Walter joined them there when he was fourteen.

Sparsely settled when the Pattersons moved there, Upper Canada was truly a frontier to be conquered. In 1791, the country had been divided into its upper and lower provinces by the British government. Upper Canada, renamed Ontario in 1846, bordered the Great Lakes and was largely settled by United Empire Loyalists who had fled the Thirteen Colonies during the Revolutionary War. Further inland, most settlers were immigrants from Scotland and Ireland.

In this frontier of constant challenge, Anne and George Patterson raised two daughters and six sons: Walter (birth date unknown), Janet (August 29, 1817), James (1819), Eliza Anne (1825), Ephraim (1826), Charles, Richard, and George (birth dates unknown). George Patterson, Sr. died on July 20,

1862 and was buried in the Episcopal cemetery in Perth, Ontario. His wife died five years later on May 3, 1867, in the home of her daughter Janet and son-in-law Andrew Allan in Balderson Corners. She was also buried in the Episcopal cemetery in Perth.

EPHRAIM PATTERSON
1826–1892

George and Anne Patterson's son Ephraim had a distinguished career with the Episcopal church. On August 19, 1849, he was made deacon at St. George's Church, Kingston, Ontario by the Right Reverend John Strachan, Bishop of Toronto. On November 17, 1850, he was ordained a priest by the same bishop at Holy Trinity Church in Toronto. Ephraim also served as curate to Dr. Bethune at the Church of England Theological College in Cobourge, Upper Canada from 1849 to 1850. He then served as a missionary in Portsmouth and on Wolfe Island from 1850 to 1851. For the next forty years, Ephraim was rector of St. James Parish in Stratford, Ontario.

While in this post, Patterson earned two university degrees at Trinity College in Toronto—a B.A. in 1859 and an M.A. in 1861.

During this period, Ephraim married Jane Wanchope Mackenzie. The ceremony took place in Perth on October 22, 1852 at St. James's Anglican Church, officiated by the Reverend M. Harris. Ephraim and Jane had fourteen children, only seven of whom survived infancy: Frederick William, Anna Maria, Wilhelmina Ashley, Edith Beatrice, Maud Mary, Henry Strachan, and George Mackenzie.

As rector, Ephraim was an innovator who contributed significantly to the development of education in the Stratford area and witnessed many changes in the community. When he arrived there in 1851, it was a rough frontier town of 400 inhabitants, but at his death in 1892, the population had increased to 10,000.

JANET PATTERSON, 1817–1901

ANDREW ALLAN, 1826–1907

Janet Patterson, the second child of George and Anne Patterson, married Andrew Allan in 1848. Nine years her junior, Andrew was born on Wolfe Island on July 31, 1826, the son of William and Eleanor Davis Allan. Andrew had six sisters: Eleanor, Jane, Hannah, Margaret, Anne, and Susannah (who married James Grier in 1886).

Andrew's father, William Allan, a veteran of the Napoleonic Wars, fought in 1815 under the Duke of Wellington at the Battle of Waterloo. After the war, he settled on Wolfe Island near Kingston, Lake Ontario. A stonemason by trade, William helped build Fort Henry at Kingston, near the United States border.

Andrew Allan lived near Perth with other British soldiers and later moved to Balderson Corners, where he became a charter member of the Presbyterian church. For a time, he taught in the community and was also a member of the Freemasons.

Janet and Andrew owned a farm where they lived in a large, red-brick house that he built himself. The Allans had three daughters and four sons: Annie Marigold (January 30, 1849–August 9, 1930), William Hiram (September 29, 1850–August 9, 1936), Eleanor Davis (March 18, 1853–1910), George Constantine (January 19, 1855–May 5, 1931), Marshall Henry (May 12, 1857–September 29, 1923), Norman Grier (March 21, 1859–April 23, 1936), and Adaline Eliza (July 21, 1862–July 30, 1862).

Janet Patterson died on January 23, 1901 in Balderson Corners, Ontario. Andrew died six years later in August 1907 and was buried in the Elmwood Cemetery in Perth, Ontario.

ELIZA ANNE PATTERSON
1825–1884

George and Anne Patterson's youngest daughter, Eliza, married James Grier, a native of Northern Ireland who had emigrated to Upper Canada in the late 1830s. The wedding took place at Perth's Episcopal Church of St. James on July 4, 1844. (See Part One: 2) After two years in Perth, the young couple moved to Pakenham, some thirty miles northeast. By 1851, they had relocated to Matilda Township, a small town on the St. Lawrence River which was later renamed Iroquois. James was elected to the community's first town council and became the Iroquois postmaster in 1860, a position he would hold for over twenty-three years.

Eliza and James had ten children: James Richard Henry (1845–1911), George Edwin (1846–1925), Anne Marigold (1848–1935), Thomas Johnston (1850–1914), William John (1853–1909), Eliza Victoria (1855–1941), Margaret Armstrong (1857–1884), Albert Ephraim (1859–1907), Charles Allan (1862–1882), and Georgina Clara (1864–1946).

Eliza Patterson Grier died at age fifty-nine on October 14, 1884; she was buried in St. John's Episcopal Cemetery in Iroquois. Her husband died nearly eight years later on May 11, 1892 in Toronto and was buried next to Eliza and their son Charles Allan, who had died of tuberculosis at twenty.

PART TWO

ANNE GRIER BRANCH

32

THE GRIER FAMILY

Genealogical Trees of Anne M. Grier
(Mrs. A. Gilbert Fell) and C. Denham Grier

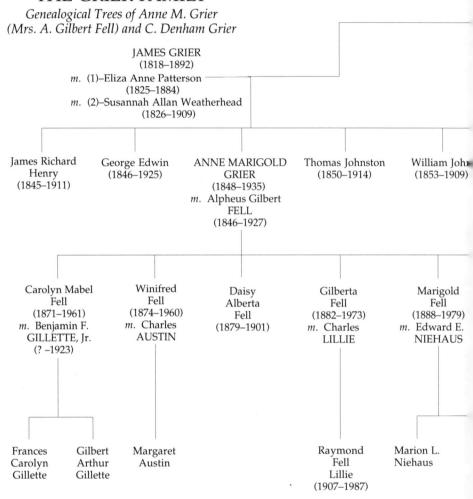

JAMES GRIER
(1818–1892)
m. (1)–Eliza Anne Patterson
(1825–1884)
m. (2)–Susannah Allan Weatherhead
(1826–1909)

James Richard
Henry
(1845–1911)

George Edwin
(1846–1925)

ANNE MARIGOLD
GRIER
(1848–1935)
m. Alpheus Gilbert
FELL
(1846–1927)

Thomas Johnston
(1850–1914)

William John
(1853–1909)

Carolyn Mabel
Fell
(1871–1961)
m. Benjamin F.
GILLETTE, Jr.
(? –1923)

Winifred
Fell
(1874–1960)
m. Charles
AUSTIN

Daisy
Alberta
Fell
(1879–1901)

Gilberta
Fell
(1882–1973)
m. Charles
LILLIE

Marigold
Fell
(1888–1979)
m. Edward E.
NIEHAUS

Frances
Carolyn
Gillette

Gilbert
Arthur
Gillette

Margaret
Austin

Raymond
Fell
Lillie
(1907–1987)

Marion L.
Niehaus

* *Name changed to Marigold in next generation.*
** *Daughter died in infancy.*
*** *Couple has chosen to remain unmarried.*

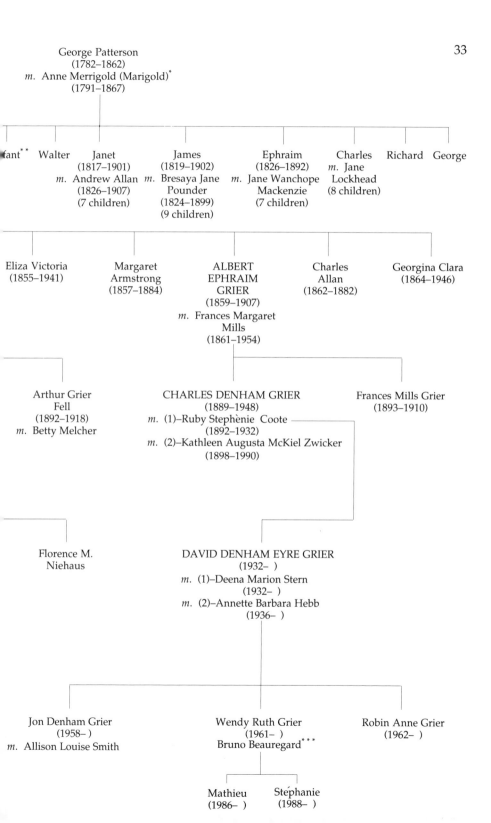

George Patterson
(1782–1862)
m. Anne Merrigold (Marigold)*
(1791–1867)

ʃant**   Walter   Janet   James   Ephraim   Charles   Richard   George
                 (1817–1901)   (1819–1902)   (1826–1892)   *m.* Jane
              m. Andrew Allan *m.* Bresaya Jane *m.* Jane Wanchope Lockhead
                 (1826–1907)   Pounder   Mackenzie   (8 children)
                 (7 children)   (1824–1899)   (7 children)
                                 (9 children)

Eliza Victoria   Margaret   ALBERT   Charles   Georgina Clara
(1855–1941)   Armstrong   EPHRAIM   Allan   (1864–1946)
                    (1857–1884)   GRIER   (1862–1882)
                                      (1859–1907)
                                    m. Frances Margaret
                                      Mills
                                      (1861–1954)

Arthur Grier   CHARLES DENHAM GRIER   Frances Mills Grier
Fell   (1889–1948)   (1893–1910)
(1892–1918)   *m.* (1)–Ruby Stephènie Coote
m. Betty Melcher   (1892–1932)
                     m. (2)–Kathleen Augusta McKiel Zwicker
                            (1898–1990)

Florence M.   DAVID DENHAM EYRE GRIER
Niehaus   (1932–)
                     m. (1)–Deena Marion Stern
                            (1932–)
                     m. (2)–Annette Barbara Hebb
                            (1936–)

Jon Denham Grier   Wendy Ruth Grier   Robin Anne Grier
(1958–)   (1961–)   (1962–)
m. Allison Louise Smith Bruno Beauregard***

                          Mathieu   Stéphanie
                          (1986–)   (1988–)

CHRONOLOGY OF ANNE GRIER FELL

1848	Born in Pakenham, Upper Canada on May 27
1851–1870	Lives in Matilda Township (later renamed Iroquois), Upper Canada; graduates from Iroquois High School in June 1865; works in father's post office
1870	Marries A. Gilbert Fell on October 13; moves to Ogden, Utah, where husband is division superintendent for Central Pacific Railroad
1871	Daughter, Carolyn Mabel, born on September 2
1874	Daughter, Winifred, born on April 20
1879	Daughter, Daisy Alberta, born
1882	Daughter, Gilberta, born
1888	Daughter, Marigold, born
1892	Son, Arthur Grier, born on June 14
1901	Daughter Daisy dies on November 18
1911–1915	Husband serves two terms as mayor of Ogden
1918	Son Arthur Grier dies
1927	Husband dies on December 28
1935	Dies in San Francisco on October 28

Anne Marigold Grier Fell, c. 1900

5

ANNE GRIER FELL
1848–1935

Pioneering In Utah

Anne Marigold Grier was the first of James and Eliza Grier's children to leave Canada and take on the challenges of life in the American West during a period of rapid and far-reaching changes brought about by the expansion of the railroad.

Born on May 27, 1848 in Pakenham, Ontario, Anne was the Griers' third child and oldest daughter. She was educated at the Iroquois elementary and high schools and, like her brothers and sisters, became a skilled telegrapher while working in the Iroquois office of her postmaster father. Fondly called "Annie" by friends and family, she was bright, energetic, and gregarious, traits that would help her adjust easily to a pioneering life in Utah.

MARRIAGE TO GILBERT FELL

Anne married her childhood friend Alpheus Gilbert Fell (known as "A.G." or "Gilbert") on October 13, 1870 in St. John's Episcopal Church in Iroquois. The autumn wedding was attended by many members of both the Grier and Fell families.

Gilbert, born to James and Sarah Fell on March 13, 1846 in Prescott, Ontario, grew up in nearby South Mountain and in 1863 graduated from Iroquois High School. Like the Grier children, he clerked and operated the telegraph in James Grier's post office while still a student.

Ambitious and hardworking, Fell began a long and successful career with the railroads as a train dispatcher in Iroquois on the Grand Trunk Railroad, from 1864 to 1866. Then, seeking new challenges, he moved to Carlin, Nevada, where he worked as a freight agent and dispatcher for the Union Pacific Railroad Company. In 1868, he accepted a position as chief dispatcher with rival Central Pacific.

OPENING THE WEST

With the discovery of gold at Sutter's Mill on January 24, 1848, the California gold rush was on, and thousands of treasure hunters poured into the state by three routes. The fastest (and most expensive) way west was via ship to Panama, across the isthmus and the "transit route" that Commodore Vanderbilt had opened through the rivers and jungles of Central America, then up the Pacific Coast. The entire journey took only three to four months, but travelers on this route risked their lives with hostile Indians and tropical diseases in the jungle areas.

There was also an all-water route to California, leaving an eastern seaport, sailing around the southernmost tip of South America, then heading northward. Covering 10,000 nautical miles, the trip took five to eight months; though considerably longer than the Panama route, this journey was far safer and drew the largest volume of traffic.

The third route west—an overland route—followed the Oregon Trail from the Missouri River across Nebraska and Wyoming to Idaho, where travelers picked up the California cut-off heading southwest. The trip took six months or more and entailed a number of hazards—Indian raids, water shortages, weather extremes, disease, and the ever-present danger of running short on vital supplies.

Although California became a state two years after the discovery of gold, the area remained relatively isolated from the rest of the union. However, the advent of the transcontinental railroad, together with the Homestead Act of 1862, would change that.[1] The legislation provided vast land grants to the Union Pacific and Central Pacific Railroads for each mile of track they laid. These tracks were built by construction companies owned by the railroads themselves (a gross, but overlooked, conflict of interest) which were paid exorbitantly for work that had to be redone within a generation. (In fact, the first railroad tycoons made their fortunes through this construction, not from revenues provided by the railroad services.)

Central Pacific's "Big Four," all Sacramento merchants in the 1850s, were: Leland Stanford, president; Collis P. Huntington, vice president; Mark Hopkins, treasurer; and Charles Crocker, superintendent of construction. A fifth member of the management team was a brilliant construction engineer named Theodore D. Judah.[2] These five men each subscribed for

1.   Construction on the Central Pacific Railroad began in Sacramento, California on January 8, 1863, at the foot of K Street; two years later, crews in Omaha, Nebraska began laying tracks for the Union Pacific, moving westward.

2.   In 1854, Judah, who had a greater knowledge of railroads than any man in the country at the time, had been brought from New York to California by the promoters of the Sacramento

150 shares of Central Pacific Railroad stock at $100 per share; others subscribed for 830 additional shares. A mere ten percent was required as a down payment; thus, the CPRR began construction with only $15,800 in its coffers.

Almost immediately, Judah differed with his partners.[3] His goal was to build a great railroad, but the priority for the "Big Four" was amassing huge profits. And profit they did; the fortunes they derived from this construction totaled $200 million.

A self-dealer, Leland Stanford, who was governor of California at the time, obtained additional land grants from the state to maximize the railroad's profitability. He also appointed Charles Crocker's brother Edward to an unexpired term as a judge of the California State Supreme Court, despite the fact that Edward was simultaneously serving as Central Pacific's corporate counsel. (The riches Edward Crocker accumulated from the CPRR and the State of California are on display today in his Sacramento home—the E.B. Crocker Art Gallery—near the levee at the foot of K Street, where the Central Pacific construction began in early 1863.)

After the completion of the transcontinental railroad, pioneering in the West was never the same. Settlers, including a number of the Griers, now arrived by train after a journey of a few short days—a stark contrast to the months of hardship and peril facing newcomers just a few years earlier. Transcontinental rail service was heralded as an industrial revolution, as well, enabling goods and mail to move cross-country in days, not months.

FELL'S CAREER

By 1869, Fell had advanced to the position of division superintendent for the Central Pacific in Utah. His tenure there coincided with the completion of the transcontinental railroad, as the last of the track was laid by the Central Pacific through a gap to Promontory Point, Utah. (Fell supplied his construction crew with ample materials, and the final ten miles of track were laid in the record-breaking time of one day.)

To celebrate the historic connection of the nation's first coast-to-coast

---

Valley Railroad to build a line from Sacramento to Folsom, the first railroad on the Pacific Coast.

3.   In 1863, after the "Four" awarded a lucrative construction contract to Charles Crocker & Co., a dummy firm they owned themselves, Judah protested and broke with them completely. En route to New York, he contracted yellow fever in Panama; he died on November 2, 1863, shortly after his arrival in New York.

railroad, officials had decided to "broadcast" via telegraph the exact moment when the east- and west-bound tracks were joined on May 10, 1869. To accomplish this, one telegraph line was attached to the last spike on the track and another to a silver sledgehammer. Leland Stanford, Central Pacific's president, was given the honor of hammering in that last spike. Amidst great fanfare, he stood by the track, raised the hammer, swung down, and completely missed his mark. Fortunately, a quick-witted Gilbert Fell simulated the blow with his telegraph key, thereby notifying President Ulysses Grant in the White House that the joining by rail of the East and West Coasts had been completed.[4]

The dream of spanning the continent had finally come true. In cities across the nation, church bells chimed and factory whistles announced the news. The inscription on the last golden spike, which had been entrusted to Gilbert Fell before its use, expressed the country's sentiment: "May God continue the unity of our country, as the railroad unites the two great oceans of the world."

The ceremony at Promontory Point marked not only a revolution in transportation but the beginning of a significant period of growth in the national economy. As auxiliary lines expanded into all parts of the West, the railroads quickened the pace of the country's industrialization.

After the excitement and feverish pitch of work on the transcontinental railroad subsided, Gilbert returned to Iroquois in the summer of 1870 to see his family and Anne Grier, with whom he had kept in touch after moving to America. On this occasion, Anne accepted his marriage proposal, and after their marriage and honeymoon in Canada, they emigrated to Ogden, Utah.

At that time, Ogden was a thriving Mormon community.[5] As in other farming communities around Salt Lake Valley, the earliest settlers had lived

---

4.   When the two locomotives, "Number 119" of the Union Pacific and "Jupiter" of the Central Pacific, touched noses on that date, the race between the two lines was over. The Union Pacific had laid greater mileage—1,086 miles compared to the Central Pacific's 689. However, the Union Pacific's track from Omaha, Nebraska was laid through flat, prairie terrain; Central Pacific's line was built across the rugged, high Sierra Nevada.

5.   First established as Brownsville, Ogden was settled in 1848, two years after the pioneers arrived in Salt Lake Valley. Captain James Brown of the Mormon Batallion (young Latter-Day Saints called to fight in the Mexican War) had been authorized to buy the Miles Goodyear claims on the Weber River. Brownsville was established on this land.

in rough, temporary frame dwellings until substantial homes could be completed. But by the fall of 1870, Ogden was a well-established and prosperous town, largely because it had become a railroad terminus for the Union Pacific, Central Pacific, Utah Central, and Utah Northern Railroad lines.[6] These rail connections provided an important outlet for the agricultural produce of area farmers, thus contributing considerably to the health of the local economy.

LIFE IN OGDEN

Gilbert and Anne Fell prospered in this bustling community. The couple had five daughters and one son. Carolyn ("Carrie") Mabel was born on September 2, 1871; Winifred ("Winnie"), on April 20, 1874; Daisy Alberta, in 1879; Gilberta, in 1882; Marigold ("Goldie"), in 1888; and Arthur Grier, on June 14, 1892.

Like other women of that period, Anne devoted her time to raising her children and tending her home and family. In contrast to her somewhat stern countenance in photographs, family members recall her being lively, fun-loving, and strong.

Gilbert Fell worked for the railroads from the 1860s to 1888. When he retired after a quarter of a century of service, he traveled for a while with his family in the United States and Canada, visiting relatives en route.

Upon his return to Ogden, Gilbert turned his energies to a variety of enterprises, including wool-growing, banking, livery (he was fond of raising and racing horses), and real estate. For many years, he was vice president and director of Ogden's Commercial National Bank and a partner in the livery company of Nelson & Fell. A popular and esteemed member of the Ogden community, Gilbert was an Episcopalian, a Republican, and a member of the Chamber of Commerce and the Weber Club.

---

6. This is in contrast to the so-called "hell-on-wheels" town of Corinne, Utah, the last of the lawless transcontinental railroad camps. It was populated by "Gentiles" (non-Mormons) and boasted of nineteen saloons. Although Corinne had geographical advantages over Ogden in terms of facilitating a rail center, it could not compete with the overall positive environment provided by Ogden. And just five months before the transcontinental railroad was completed, Mormon leader Brigham Young managed to obtain the land needed for an Ogden depot. Urged by their prophet, individual landowners donated a 133-acre tract for the purpose, thereby persuading railroad officials to join the two lines at Ogden, rather than Corinne. Corinne languished during the 1870s and eventually became a virtual ghost town. In this period, Anne Fell's brothers T.J. and William John worked briefly in Corinne for Western Union, prior to transferring to the Salt Lake City office.

Anne and Gilbert were saddened by the premature death of their daughter Daisy, who succumbed to tuberculosis on November 18, 1901 while visiting her uncle and aunt, William John and Georgie Grier, in Palermo, California; she was just twenty-two years old.

Their four surviving daughters eventually married and had children of their own. Both Goldie and Gilberta moved to the San Francisco Bay area, while Carolyn and Winifred remained in Ogden. The Fells' only son, Arthur, also remained in his hometown. He married, but had no children before he died in an automobile accident in Ogden on March 31, 1918.

MAYOR FELL
1911–1915

At age sixty-five, retirement age for many, Gilbert Fell became an active and articulate partisan of progressive city government in Ogden. In 1911, he ran for mayor, spurred by his wife's social conscience and the desire to serve the people of his adopted city. Anne and Gilbert both believed that city government was responsible to the entire community, not merely to special interests, and Gilbert campaigned "Against the Corporation Ticket." He was elected mayor of Ogden by a comfortable margin, and his party's two candidates for commissioner, Thomas E. Browning and Carl Allison, also won easily. Two years later, in 1913, Gilbert was overwhelmingly reelected.

Water development was a major achievement of Mayor Fell's administration. He was instrumental in developing artesian wells, a source of water which continues to serve the city of Ogden today. A subterranean deposit of pure water was developed to a daily flow of six million gallons, providing one of the finest artesian water systems in the United States.

Fell's two-term administration succeeded in making government more representative and less corrupt, improving conditions, and restoring opportunities for the common man. In the first two decades of the 1900s, Fell played an active role in this spirit of reform.

LATER YEARS

After retiring from public life on December 31, 1915, Gilbert continued to speak out on public issues and to be active in business. From 1910 to 1927, he and Anne lived in their comfortable brick home at 575 25th Street in Ogden.

Gilbert Fell died at eighty-one of arteriosclerosis, on December 28, 1927; he was buried in Ogden's Mountain View Cemetery.

As a widow, Anne Grier continued to live in the family home, entertaining her friends and visiting her daughters and grandchildren in Ogden and San Francisco and Berkeley, California. Suffering from heart disease, she lived the last year of her life with her daughter, Gilberta Lillie, and grandson, Raymond Lillie, in their San Francisco apartment near Union Square. She died there on October 28, 1935, in her eighty-eighth year, and was buried next to Gilbert and their son Arthur and daughter Daisy in the Mountain View Cemetery in Ogden.

The Fell family, c. 1898: *seated, from left*: Annie, Arthur, A. Gilbert, and Goldie; *standing, from left*: Daisy, Carrie, Winifred, and Gilberta

6

FELL FAMILY

CAROLYN FELL
1871–1961

Born on September 2, 1871, Carolyn ("Carrie") Fell was Anne Grier and Gilbert Fell's oldest child. Remaining in her native town of Ogden, Utah, Carolyn married Benjamin F. Gillette, Jr. and had two children. Their daughter, Frances Carolyn, a nurse, never married; son Gilbert Arthur married and had two children. Benjamin died in 1923, and Carolyn, in November of 1961, in her ninetieth year.

WINIFRED FELL
1874–1960

Winifred ("Winnie") Fell, born on April 20, 1874, attended Utah Agricultural and Mechanical School (later renamed Utah State University) in Logan from 1896 to 1897. She married Charles Austin and had one daughter, Margaret. Winifred died on December 13, 1960.

DAISY FELL
1879–1901

Daisy also attended Utah Agricultural and Mechanical School, with sister "Winnie," then worked as a stenographer. When she became ill with tuberculosis, she was sent to her uncle and aunt, William John and Georgie Grier, in Palermo, California to recuperate. However, she died there on November 18, 1901.

GILBERTA FELL
1882–1973

Gilberta, born in Ogden in 1882, lived all of her adult life in California—in Berkeley, San Francisco, Palo Alto, and Hayward. Her husband, Charles Lillie, died many years before her death. As a widow, Gilberta shared the home of her son, Raymond Fell Lillie, who had been born in Oakland in 1907. Gilberta died in 1973, at age ninety-one.

RAYMOND FELL LILLIE
1907–1987

Raymond received his A.B. (1929) and his M.A. (1931) in Germanic languages from Stanford University. His studies and subsequent teaching enabled him to work and travel extensively in Europe.

From 1934 to '37, he taught German, English, and history at San Francisco's Lowell High School.

He completed two semesters at Ludwig Maximillian Universitat in Munchen, Germany from 1937 to 1938, then studied at the University of Berlin in the fall of 1938 and at the University of Konigsberg, East Prussia the following spring. After returning to the States, Raymond taught German and Latin at Utah State Agricultural College and worked as a librarian in Cedar City, Utah until mid-1941. He then returned to California to become a German and French teacher at Hayward Unified High School, where he remained until his retirement in 1973.

During the summers of 1945, '46, and '47, Raymond attended Mills College and worked with Madeline Milhaud, wife of the composer Darius Milhaud. He took classes with her and was chosen by her for a role in a play presented at the end of each session.

In 1952, he was one of only seventeen teachers in the United States to be chosen to go to Germany in the first group of exchange high school teachers following the war. There, he taught English and French at the Ludwig-Wilhelm Gymnasium in Rastatt/Baden.

Raymond pursued his lifelong interest in the performing arts as an active member of the Hayward Community Theater and attended the opera and concerts in San Francisco.

MARIGOLD FELL
1888–1979

Born in 1888, the fifth of Gilbert and Anne's children, Marigold ("Goldie") settled in Berkeley, California with her husband Edward E. Niehaus. After meeting in the summer of 1909 on a cruise from Seattle to Alaska, the couple married on June 29, 1910 in her parents' home in Ogden, Utah. They had two daughters, Marion L. Niehaus Wiggins and Florence ("Billie") Niehaus Glaser, both of Concord, California. Goldie died on September 12, 1979, at age ninety-one.

ARTHUR GRIER FELL
1892–1918

The youngest of the Fell children, Arthur Grier was born on June 14, 1892. He attended Boone Preparatory School and the University of California at Berkeley.

While at Berkeley, Arthur contracted spinal meningitis which left him deaf. Returning to Utah, he entered the Utah School for the Deaf, where he became proficient in lip-reading.

Arthur became a bookkeeper and entrepreneur, an owner and operator of several Ogden businesses, including an automobile agency and Murphy Wholesale Grocery Company. He married Betty Melcher, but had no children and was later divorced.

During World War I, Arthur tried to enlist in the military, but was rejected because of his deafness. He then offered his services to the Red Cross and the YMCA as a lip-reading instructor for deaf soldiers. His continuing appeal to serve in the military was eventually supported by Utah Senators Smoot and King, with an endorsement from Utah Governor Bamburger; however, before the situation could be resolved, Arthur was killed in an automobile accident in Ogden on March 31, 1918.

PART THREE

THOMAS JOHNSTON GRIER BRANCH

THE GRIER FAMILY

*Genealogical Trees of Thomas Johnston Grier, Sr. and
Eliza V. Grier (Mrs. Arthur J. Williams)*

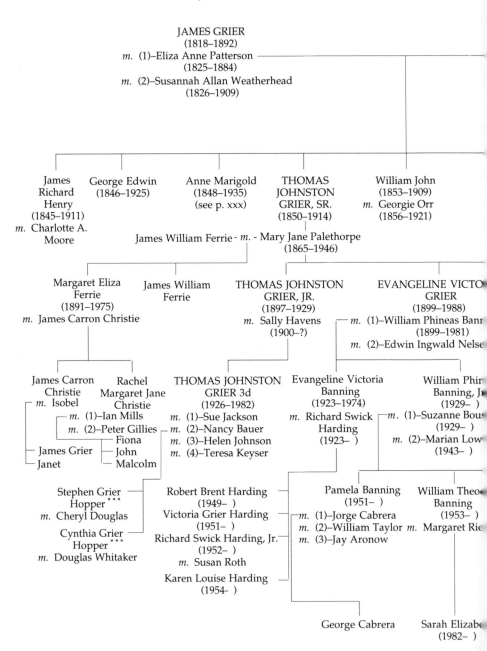

JAMES GRIER
(1818–1892)
m. (1)–Eliza Anne Patterson
(1825–1884)
m. (2)–Susannah Allan Weatherhead
(1826–1909)

James Richard Henry (1845–1911) m. Charlotte A. Moore

George Edwin (1846–1925)

Anne Marigold (1848–1935) (see p. xxx)

THOMAS JOHNSTON GRIER, SR. (1850–1914)

William John (1853–1909) m. Georgie Orr (1856–1921)

James William Ferrie - m. - Mary Jane Palethorpe (1865–1946)

Margaret Eliza Ferrie (1891–1975) m. James Carron Christie

James William Ferrie

THOMAS JOHNSTON GRIER, JR. (1897–1929) m. Sally Havens (1900–?)

EVANGELINE VICTO GRIER (1899–1988) m. (1)–William Phineas Banr (1899–1981) m. (2)–Edwin Ingwald Nelse

James Carron Christie m. Isobel — James Grier — Janet

Rachel Margaret Jane Christie m. (1)–Ian Mills m. (2)–Peter Gillies — Fiona — John — Malcolm

THOMAS JOHNSTON GRIER 3d (1926–1982) m. (1)–Sue Jackson m. (2)–Nancy Bauer m. (3)–Helen Johnson m. (4)–Teresa Keyser

Evangeline Victoria Banning (1923–1974) m. Richard Swick Harding (1923–)

William Phin Banning, J (1929–) m. (1)–Suzanne Bous (1929–) m. (2)–Marian Low (1943–)

Stephen Grier Hopper*** m. Cheryl Douglas

Cynthia Grier Hopper*** m. Douglas Whitaker

Robert Brent Harding (1949–) Victoria Grier Harding (1951–) Richard Swick Harding, Jr. (1952–) m. Susan Roth

Karen Louise Harding (1954-)

Pamela Banning (1951–) m. (1)–Jorge Cabrera m. (2)–William Taylor m. (3)–Jay Aronow

William Theo Banning (1953–) m. Margaret Rie

George Cabrera

Sarah Elizab (1982–)

* *Name changed to Marigold in next generation.*
** *Daughter died in infancy.*
*** *Adopted by Jack Hopper (Nancy B. Grier's second husband).*
**** *Adopted by Ormande P. Grier*

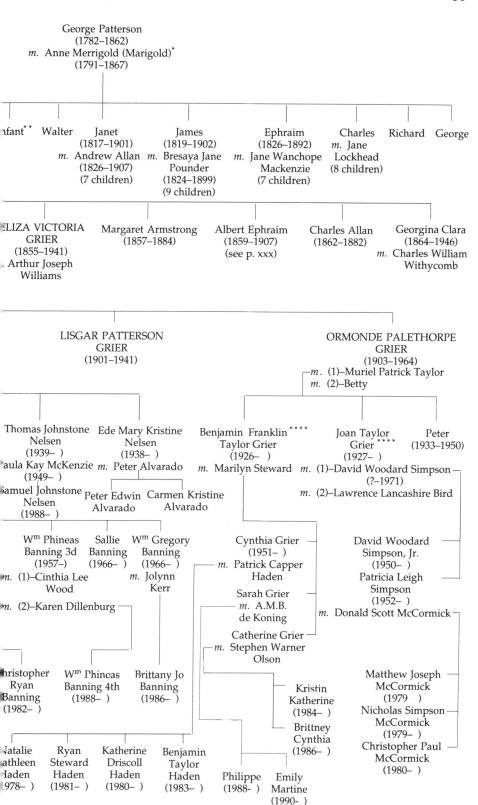

George Patterson
(1782–1862)
m. Anne Merrigold (Marigold)*
(1791–1867)

ıfant**   Walter   Janet   James   Ephraim   Charles   Richard   George
  (1817–1901)   (1819–1902)   (1826–1892)   *m.* Jane
  m. Andrew Allan   *m.* Bresaya Jane   *m.* Jane Wanchope   Lockhead
  (1826–1907)   Pounder   Mackenzie   (8 children)
  (7 children)   (1824–1899)   (7 children)
  (9 children)

ELIZA VICTORIA   Margaret Armstrong   Albert Ephraim   Charles Allan   Georgina Clara
GRIER   (1857–1884)   (1859–1907)   (1862–1882)   (1864–1946)
(1855–1941)   (see p. xxx)   *m.* Charles William
. Arthur Joseph   Withycomb
Williams

LISGAR PATTERSON   ORMONDE PALETHORPE
GRIER   GRIER
(1901–1941)   (1903–1964)
         m. (1)–Muriel Patrick Taylor
         m. (2)–Betty

Thomas Johnstone   Ede Mary Kristine   Benjamin Franklin****   Joan Taylor   Peter
Nelsen   Nelsen   Taylor Grier   Grier****   (1933–1950)
(1939–)   (1938–)   (1926–)   (1927–)
'aula Kay McKenzie   *m.* Peter Alvarado   *m.* Marilyn Steward   *m.* (1)–David Woodard Simpson
(1949–)   (?–1971)
ìamuel Johnstone   Peter Edwin   Carmen Kristine   *m.* (2)–Lawrence Lancashire Bird
Nelsen   Alvarado   Alvarado
(1988–)

Wm Phineas   Sallie   Wm Gregory   Cynthia Grier   David Woodard
Banning 3d   Banning   Banning   (1951–)   Simpson, Jr.
(1957–)   (1966–)   (1966–)   *m.* Patrick Capper   (1950–)
m. (1)–Cinthia Lee   *m.* Jolynn   Haden   Patricia Leigh
Wood   Kerr   Sarah Grier   Simpson
      m. A.M.B.   (1952–)
m. (2)–Karen Dillenburg   de Koning   *m.* Donald Scott McCormick
      Catherine Grier
      m. Stephen Warner
      Olson

ihristopher   Wm Phineas   Brittany Jo   Matthew Joseph
Ryan   Banning 4th   Banning   McCormick
Banning   (1988–)   (1986–)   Kristin   (1979)
(1982–)   Katherine   Nicholas Simpson
      (1984–)   McCormick
      Brittney   (1979–)
      Cynthia   Christopher Paul
Vatalie   Ryan   Katherine   Benjamin   (1986–)   McCormick
athleen   Steward   Driscoll   Taylor   (1980–)
Haden   Haden   Haden   Haden
1978–)   (1981–)   (1980–)   (1983–)   Philippe   Emily
        (1988-)   Martine
          (1990-)

CHRONOLOGY OF THOMAS JOHNSTON GRIER, SR.

1850	Born in Pakenham, Upper Canada on May 18
1851–1867	Lives in Matilda Township (later renamed Iroquois), Upper Canada; attends public schools there and works in father's post office
1867	Graduates from Iroquois High School; moves to Montreal to work as telegrapher with Montreal Telegraphy Company
1872	Emigrates to the American West; works as telegrapher with Western Union in Denver, Colorado and Corinne and Salt Lake City, Utah
1878–1884	Begins career with Homestake Mining Company in Lead, Dakota Territory (later known as South Dakota); advances from entry position as bookkeeper and telegrapher; becomes acquainted with Homestake co-owner and U.S. Senator George Hearst
1884	Appointed superintendent of Homestake Mining Company
1884–1914	During tenure as Homestake superintendent, develops cyanidation process to extract gold from ore, improves mining technology significantly, and invents stamp-mill ore screen (1891 patent); travels extensively in U.S. and abroad on business and with family; becomes close friend of philanthropist Phoebe Apperson Hearst
1896	Marries Mary Jane Palethorpe Ferrie, of Edinburgh, Scotland
1897	Son, Thomas Johnston, Jr., born in Lead on May 9
1899	Daughter, Evangeline Victoria, born in Lead on August 18

1901	Son, Lisgar Patterson, born in Lead on January 23
1903	Son, Ormonde Palethorpe, born in Lead on May 13
1905–1914	Addresses numerous professional conventions, universities, and other groups on mining, conservation, labor relations, and related subjects
1907	Underground fire at Homestake quenched after forty days by his bold decision to flood the mine, averting potential explosion beneath Lead
1909–1910	Severe labor disputes result in a lockout at Homestake in November 1909; recruits non-union crews and reopens mines in January 1910; initiates unique employee benefits program, including pioneering health and accident insurance package
1912	Suffers heart attack while in Chicago
1914	Testifies before the U.S. Commission on Industrial Relations in August; dedicates Homestake Opera House and Recreation Building in Lead on August 31; travels to Los Angeles with family, where, on September 22, he dies in his sleep; funeral in Lead attended by 14,000 people
1916	Bronze statue of T.J. Grier is unveiled in Lead, the memorial gift of Homestake miners and residents

Thomas Johnston Grier, Sr. (1850-1914)
(Courtesy of Homestake Mining Company, Lead, South Dakota)

7

THOMAS JOHNSTON GRIER, SR.
1850–1914

Superintendent of Homestake Gold

*"He was a forceful character and proved to be an organizer
and administrator of great ability . . . . Grier was aggressive and
far sighted and had unbounded faith in the future of the mines."*[1]
—Guy Norman Bjorge

Thomas Johnston Grier's career spanned nearly half a century of epochal development in the American West. He began working as a schoolboy in the 1850s and '60s in his father's post office, sorting and delivering mail, keeping books, and operating the telegraph. After his high school graduation in 1867, he worked in Canada and then in communities across the American West. In 1878, he accepted a position as bookkeeper and telegrapher for the Homestake Mining Company in Lead, South Dakota. Within a few years, he was promoted to the superintendency, a position he held until his death in 1914. As superintendent of the Homestake Mine, Thomas Grier, known as "T.J." by his family and friends, became one of the most powerful and celebrated men in the mining industry and, indeed, in the West.

EARLY YEARS

Born in Pakenham, Upper Canada on May 18, 1850, T.J. was the fourth of James and Eliza Patterson Grier's ten children. One year after his birth, his family moved to Matilda Township (later known as Iroquois), where he grew up, completed high school, and gained valuable practical experience

---

1. Guy Norman Bjorge, *The Homestake Enterprise in the Black Hills of South Dakota* (New York: The Newcomen Society of England, American Branch, 1947), p. 14.

working in his father's office. (James Grier was the city's postmaster and a member of Iroquois's first town council.) There, T.J. became an adept telegraph operator and bookkeeper and developed his management acumen—skills which served him well throughout his life.

Following his Iroquois High School graduation in June 1867,[2] T.J. moved to Montreal, where he became a telegraph operator with the Montreal Telegraphy Company. In 1870, he was joined by his eighteen-year-old brother, William John (1853–1909), who had just graduated from Iroquois High School.

Two years later, both young men responded to the lure of the American frontier, where opportunities seemed unlimited for enterprising settlers. The brothers emigrated to the U.S. via Detroit, then went to Denver, where they worked as telegraphers for Western Union Telegraph Company. Their departure from Canada had followed that of their oldest sister, Anne Grier (1848–1935), who had married A. Gilbert Fell and settled in Ogden, Utah in 1870.

After a brief time in Denver and in Corinne, Utah, where they continued as telegraphers with Western Union, T.J. and William John transferred to the company's office in Salt Lake City, where T.J. became the manager. While living in Salt Lake, William John met and, in 1875, married Georgie Orr; their first child, daughter May, was born there the following year.

Two years later, the brothers took different career paths: William John transferred to Western Union's San Francisco office, while T.J., attracted by the discovery of gold in the Black Hills of the Dakota Territory, became a bookkeeper and telegrapher for the newly formed Homestake Mining Company in Lead, South Dakota.

BLACK HILLS GOLD RUSH

News of the gold strikes in the Dakota Territory during the mid-1870s spread rapidly, triggering an influx of prospectors into the region and setting the stage for the ultimate defeat of the Cheyenne and Sioux Indians. The Salt Lake City *Daily Tribune* of July 9, 1876 reported: "On Monday, July 17th, Parlin & Thompson will start a six horse coach and saddle train for the Deadwood mines, and expect to make the trip in thirty days from Salt Lake."

The first discovery of gold in the Territory, however, was made four

---

2.   Iroquois High School was founded as a grammar school and opened on June 10, 1846. The building was donated by John Adams Carman.

decades earlier, in 1833, by a party of seven miners from Missouri working at the base of Lookout Mountain, near what came to be called Spearfish, South Dakota and some twenty miles northwest of the modern townsite of Lead. Had this party lived to tell of its discovery, the entire pattern of settlement of the trans-Mississippi West might well have occurred in a steadier westward movement, rather than by-passing the Great Plains as it did during the 1849 gold rush to California.

Details of the 1833 discovery were not made known until 1887, when Louis and Ivan Thoen discovered a piece of reddish sandstone near Spearfish. Inscriptions on the stone gave the names of the earlier miners and their report of finding gold. One prospector, having survived an Indian attack in the area, reported:

> Came to these hills in 1833, seven of us, De Lacompte, Ezra Kind, G.W. Wood, T. Brown, R. Crow Kent, Wm. King, Indian Crow. All ded but me, Ezra Kind. Killed by Ind beyond high hill. Got our gold June 1834. . . .Got all the gold we could carry. Our ponys all got by the Indians. I hav lost my gun and nothing to eat, and (have) Indians hunting me.[3]

This sandstone, known as the Thoen Stone, is now preserved in the Adams Museum in Deadwood, South Dakota.

In his 1895 writings, Catholic priest Peter Rosen spoke of the many traces left by prospectors in the years before the big gold rush in the Black Hills began in 1875 and 1876. And, as Mildred Fielder noted in *The Treasure of Homestake Gold:*

> On Battle Creek the '76ers found a shaft ten feet deep, and ten feet below that they found a shovel and a pick with decayed handles and rusted iron. Skulls, silver bowed spectacles, stumps of trees chopped by the axes of white men all spoke of prospectors who had been there years before the big gold rush.[4]

The first publicized discovery of gold in the Black Hills was made by miners who accompanied General George Armstrong Custer's 1874 military expedition into the area. (Custer's force included over 1,000 men and 100 wagons and was the largest such military expedition in the northwest region.) Two men in his party, Horatio Nelson Ross and William T. McKay,

---

3.   Quoted in Mildred Fielder, *The Treasure of Homestake Gold* (Aberdeen, South Dakota: North Plains Press, 1970), p. 8.
       The Black Hills are "hills" in name only; they easily qualify as mountains. Harvey Peak is an impressive 7,242 feet high, the tallest point east of the Rockies and the highest part of what is known to geologists as "the Black Hills Dome."
4.   Ibid., p. 8.

found gold on French Creek, and even before a report was issued, rumors of the strike spread. Custer's official report stated:

> While I am satisfied that gold in satisfactory quantities can be obtained in the Black Hills, yet the hasty examination we were forced to make, did not enable us to determine in any satisfactory degree the richness or extent of the gold deposits in that region. [5]

Earlier western gold rushes had been sparked by less encouragement than this. The Black Hills area was to become the newest burgeoning frontier, as mining towns appeared seemingly overnight.

Initially, intrusions by whites into this area were illegal under the provisions of the Laramie Treaty of 1868 that guaranteed the western portion of the Dakotas to the Sioux Indians in perpetuity. Nor did the encroachment of determined miners go unchallenged by the Sioux, for this land was sacred to them and constituted an important hunting ground. Several military expeditions were sent to patrol the boundary and to expel miners from the Sioux's land; however, the Army's best efforts could not curb the flow of prospectors.

In 1875, government representatives tried unsuccessfully to persuade Sioux chieftains to sell their lands. Continued incursions by whites were met with strong resistance, and the Army, in turn, sent an expeditionary force to quell the opposition. General Custer led the most famous column of a three-way pincer aimed at trapping the Sioux.[6] His subsequent defeat at the Battle of the Little Big Horn proved, however, to be a Pyrrhic victory for the Sioux. Shocked and angered, the American public cried out for revenge, overriding the objections of Quakers and other reformers who sought to protect the Indians' rights and secure for them a peaceful existence.

Negotiations for the purchase of the Black Hills were no longer at an impasse. Government representatives dictated a treaty to the Sioux leaders, who capitulated in the face of threats to cut off rations, bar warriors from tribal hunting grounds, and move the Sioux to Indian Territory where they would be surrounded by unfriendly tribes. Eighteen Sioux chieftains ultimately signed a treaty selling the Black Hills to the federal government for

---

5.   Ibid., p. 12.

6.   Custer, who was young and flamboyant, was stationed in the West primarily for political reasons. Conservative military leaders felt the young general would do less damage in the frontier, while his supporters planned to nominate him as the Republican presidential candidate for 1876. They believed they could secure such a nomination if Custer led his troops in a decisive defeat of the Indians.

$17 million. The area was officially opened to settlement following ratification of the treaty by the Senate in 1877.

HOMESTAKE APPRENTICESHIP

When Thomas Johnston Grier, a stockily built twenty-eight-year-old, stepped off the train in Lead, Dakota Territory in mid-1878, he saw a booming mining town. The local economy prospered as men, attracted by potential riches, arrived daily. Lead's growing population, a predominantly young and enthusiastic group, was offered a variety of entertainment: horse races, foot races, baseball, sparring matches, dog fights, Georgian minstrels, and theatrical troupes. As Louis Janin, a prominent mining engineer from San Francisco, was to report after a visit in 1879:

> All the conveniences, and even the luxuries of life, can be obtained in this section of the Black Hills. It is by no means the rough mining camp that exists in the imagination of many. On the contrary, it is one of the pleasantest of all mining localities I have visited; and in no district is justice more ably administered, or greater security afforded to life and property.[7]

Lead mirrored the growth and development of the mining industry, and the Homestake Mining Company was a dominant factor in that field. At the time of T.J.'s appointment as bookkeeper and telegrapher with Homestake, the mine was owned by a San Francisco syndicate consisting of George Hearst, Lloyd Tevis, and J.B. Haggin. The syndicate owned six separate mines: Homestake, Giant, Old Abe, Highland, Golden Terra, and Deadwood. These mines represented a consolidation of some of the first claims filed in the Lead area.[8]

The driving force of the syndicate was George Hearst, who had an uncanny knack for judging the merits of precious metals discoveries. Born in 1820 in St. Louis, Missouri, Hearst grew up in humble circumstances and received only a meager education. Despite this, however, he eventually

---

7.   Bjorge, p. 13.

8.   Brothers Fred and Moses Manual filed some of the first claims in the Lead area that were to become part of the Homestake mine. The Manuels filed a claim in Bobtail Gulch as early as February 21, 1876. On April 9, Hank Harney joined them and located a claim he called "the Homestake."

It is worth noting that one condition of receiving a mineral patent was that a vein or lode must first have been discovered on the property; to maintain the claim, the discovery had to be developed. Federal legislation also required that a claim to lode lands be no more than 1500 by 600 feet.

amassed a considerable fortune through his investments in gold and silver. He owned mines in Missouri and California and was one of the partners in the Ophir Mine, a property on the famous Comstock Lode near Virginia City, Nevada. In partnership with Haggin and Tevis, he also acquired an interest in the Ontario Silver Mines in Utah and in the Anaconda Copper Mine near Butte, Montana.

Hearst said that he first heard about the Homestake Mine from "a wild fellow that...used to come to me to get money to go somewhere or other."[9] After having received some $400 worth of telegrams from this "wild fellow" named Sevenoaks, Hearst sent L. D. Kellogg to the northern Black Hills in June of 1877 to investigate the potential of the Homestake and several neighboring claims. In response to a favorable report from Kellogg, the syndicate put up a $70,000 bond for the Homestake and Golden Star claims—a substantial sum of money for a plot of land totaling less than five acres. The amount, however, reflected Kellogg's belief in the richness of the mine. Before the end of June, Hearst arrived in Lead with the $70,000 and the necessary papers for transferring ownership of the Homestake claims. He also bought the Golden Terra Mine for $35,000, for it was vital to acquire all contiguous mining claims in order to fully utilize the rich Homestake claim.

On November 5, 1877, Hearst and his partners, Haggin and Tevis, incorporated their Black Hills holdings as the Homestake Mining Company. The firm's initial capitalization was $10 million, with 100,000 shares issued at $100 each. Hearst continued to bargain for claims that bordered the Homestake, encountering little difficulty since few miners could raise the amount of capital necessary to mine ore embedded in hard rock. Indeed, the equipment required to sink shafts and construct waterworks was expensive and heavy and had to be shipped great distances. It was typical, therefore, for prospectors to sell their claims to capitalists or to form partnerships. Under Hearst's direction, Homestake continued to grow and to consolidate, eventually becoming the richest gold mine in North America.

When Hearst returned to Lead in October of 1877 to organize and launch the operation of the Homestake Mining Company, he was accompanied by William A. Farish, who became superintendent, and L.J. Edelen, the company's bookkeeper. Samuel McMasters, who had worked for the syndicate for several years, was also in the group; in 1878, he replaced Farish as superintendent. It was at this time that T.J. Grier assumed his position with Homestake.

T.J. served as bookkeeper and telegrapher until 1884 when McMaster resigned due to ill health. Despite the fact that he had had no particular

9.   Fielder, p. 44.

background in mining, T.J., conscientious and responsible, had become acquainted with all phases of the firm's operations and was soon appointed the new superintendent by the Homestake board of directors.

EARLY SUPERINTENDENCY

While George Hearst exemplified the fortunes that could be made in those freewheeling, free enterprise days of the late nineteenth century, T.J. Grier exemplified the Scottish virtues of caution, responsibility, tenacity, and loyalty.

As superintendent of a large mining company, he was, of course, confronted with a wide variety of problems, many of them technical in nature. Early on, he sought a solution to mine cave-ins, utilizing the knowledge and experience of the men he supervised, as well as that of the best mining experts in the West. The subsequent introduction of innovative technology resulted in a considerable improvement in mine safety, and concomitantly, T.J. benefited from the increased loyalty and cooperation of his miners.

Another major development under Grier's management was the improvement of metallurgical processes used to extract additional quantities of gold from the ore mined. This was accomplished through the use of a small smelter with copper plates to which even the finest particles of gold would adhere.

T.J.'S MINING ADVANCES

Perhaps the most important advance in mining technology during the 1890s was the development of the cyanidation process to extract gold from ore. (Amalgamation, the process widely used to that point, enabled only seventy-five percent of the ore's gold content to be recovered.)

To investigate the feasibility of cyanidation at Homestake, T.J. hired Charles W. Merrill, a mining engineer and metallurgist, to work with the company's own metallurgist, Alan J. Clark, and its chemist, W.J. Sharwood. T.J.'s plan was achieved, giving Homestake the world's first major operating cyanidation process. At sharply reduced costs, the cyanidation of tailings from the mills now increased the recovery of gold to nearly ninety-five percent. This accomplishment brought international fame to Merrill and left a lasting imprint on hydrometallurgical practices thoughout the world. Other techniques developed during Grier's administration included the use of the hoist, which made mining possible at greater depths (up to 1,400 feet), and the use of a special ore screen, Grier's own invention. Indeed, on March 24, 1891, Thomas J. Grier was granted Letters of Patent No. 448,762 for a stamp-mill ore screen. The uniqueness of this sieve lay in its capacity to be taken apart for cleaning and repairs, thus prolonging the life of the screen material and making replacement of worn screens much easier.

Another priority for Superintendent Grier at the close of the nineteenth century was the consolidation of all Homestake mining properties, a feat he accomplished in 1901. Thus, Homestake, which began only twenty-four years before as a solitary claim on a remote mountaintop in the Dakota Territory, was fast becoming one of the largest and most productive gold mines in North America.

During this period of acquisition and consolidation, T.J. also added a large number of stamps to the various mills to process greater quantities of ore. By 1901, the company had 900 such stamps, creating "a deafening clatter that kept the air reverberating in the gulches."[10]

MARRIAGE AND FAMILY LIFE

While T.J's career with Homestake flourished in the 1890s, he began courting a young divorcee from Scotland, Mary Jane Palethorpe Ferrie.

Born on July 10, 1865 in Edinburgh, Scotland, Mary Jane was the daughter of James and Margaret Wright Palethorpe. She was educated in Scotland and received certificates in both piano and voice from the Royal Academy of Arts in Edinburgh. Her first husband was James William Ferrie, a mining engineer who was also born and educated in Scotland. Mary Jane bore him two children, James William and Margaret Eliza ("Madge"). (See Chapter 9)

Leaving the children with their Palethorpe grandparents, the Ferries traveled to the United States, where William worked for a time in Arizona and in Lead, South Dakota. While in Lead, Mary Jane divorced William, an alcoholic, and became the first librarian for the Hearst Free Library. She also taught voice and piano.

On August 8, 1896, Mary Jane and T.J. Grier were married in Lead. T.J.'s brother-in-law, Arthur J. Williams in Montreal, wrote to him on this occasion:

---

10.   Ibid., p. 157.
       Operating since 1876, Homestake is the largest underground gold mine in the world and the oldest continuous producer. In August 1990, its total production passed 36 million ounces. The diggings are now down to 8,000 feet, with indications of ore reserves nearly half a mile deeper than that.

I am sure you will find you are now beginning the happiest part of your life, for a man is no good single I think....Well—from what I know of my wife and hear of yours, I think we are both lucky men.[11]

To celebrate this new stage of his life, T.J. converted Homestake's three-story Victorian office into the superintendent's residence. The structure was further enhanced by the addition of a greenhouse and a Chinese pavilion in the garden. Staffed by a maid, chauffeur, gardener, and two English nannies, this stately hilltop home, named "Nob Hill" by T.J., overlooked the town of Lead, as well as the relocated Homestake office building on North Mill Street and the vast mining operation.

Pretty, vivacious, and intellectually curious, Mary Jane was deeply interested in music and the performing arts. A contralto, she played the piano and other musical instruments. She also arranged for musicians to give concerts and recitals in Lead and organized the Homestake Ladies Aid Association to provide care for the needy, usually the families of those who had sustained injuries in the mines and were unable to work.

During the evenings, T.J. and Mary Jane often entertained Homestake officials, friends, or out-of-town visitors with concerts by local or touring musicians, and Mary Jane herself occasionally sang classical and popular melodies for her guests.[12]

Although Lead was a small and remote town, T.J. and Mary Jane did not live a provincial life. They made annual trips to England and Scotland to visit Mary Jane's parents and children and to New York City, Chicago, and San Francisco. In Montreal, they visited T.J.'s older brother Henry, his sisters Georgina and Eliza, and their families. Homestake business took T.J. to the San Francisco office several times a year, and mining and labor matters took him to Washington, D.C., as well.

Despite his busy schedule, T.J. always took time to correspond with his wife. His letters to her, in fact, came to be called the "sweetheart letters," for they often began with "Dear Sweetheart" and their contents reflected the loving relationship that T.J. and Mary Jane enjoyed.

---

11.   Taken from a letter sent to T.J. by Arthur Williams, dated August 17, 1896. Arthur was the husband of Eliza Victoria Grier, T.J.'s sister who lived in Montreal.

12.   T.J.'s interest in music, perhaps inspired by Mary Jane, must have been the stimulus that led him to make the following comparison in a speech to members of the Lead City Hose Company No.1, on the evening of February 5, 1914: "While the strains of a siren during the still hours of the night do not sound much like Handel's *Largo in G* given by an orchestra of skilled musicians, can anyone here present, remember a time when the call of the siren was not promptly answered by the brave men of the Lead Volunteer Department no matter what the thermometer said about the weather outside?"

Palmer House, Chicago
8th January 1898

My dear wife,

This evening, we shall have been married seventeen months. I hope they have been as satisfactory to you as they have been to me. Tomorrow, our dear little boy will be eight months old. I hope I shall not forget to telegraph him my congratulations. Tell him for me that his Papa thinks he's the nicest little boy I ever saw.

I will write again upon arrival in Washington. With much love to my Sweethearts.

Your affectionate husband,
T.J.

* * *

Ebbitt House
Army & Navy
Washington, D.C.
14 January 1898

My dear sweet wife and baby boy,

Your welcome letter of 11 came this evening. We are still working quietly, and I think so effectively that satisfactory results are now expected in a very few days.

Today, Mr. Hope took us to the Bureau of Ingraving and we saw everything it contained. It was one of the most interesting visits I ever had here. After leaving the Bureau, we went to the Library of Congress. I cannot imagine a more beautiful and complete affair of that kind. It is quite beyond my powers of description. The weather is now quite pleasant, but they say here it is likely to change and become disagreeable almost any hour. We will likely visit the Treasury tomorrow.

Last night we saw "Hogans Ally" at one of the theatres. Nonsensical in a high degree. After returning, we found work to do which kept us up until nearly 3 a.m., and having an appointment for 8 a.m. I did not get much sleep. I am, consequently, very sleepy tonight, and ready for bed after taking a bath.

I send you, daily, a bill of fare & card of the music rendered during dinner.

I will telegraph you when we leave for New York and give you our address there.

Do not let a day go without writing to me. I am quite as anxious to get back as you possibly can be to have me.

With all my love and kisses to you and our dear little boy.

Your affectionate husband & father
T.J.

* * *

The Ten Eyck
Albany, New York
10th June 1899

Dear sweetheart wife & Junior,

Had a delightful sail up the Hudson today. Wish you had been with me. Was lonesome. Had no one to enjoy the trip with me, though there were three or four hundred passengers on the steamer. This is a beautiful hotel. Can only stop a few hours at it though. Have just driven though Albany's great "Washington Park," 100 acres—quite fine. Just as I was going out of the Netherland Hotel door to leave the city, was handed an invitation from Mrs. Ben Ali Haggin to call and have a cup of tea with her. Had not time to send written regrets and catch the boat—Told the messenger (female) to explain to Mrs. Haggin—Mrs. Ware's friend—Have just written a note to Mrs. Hearst.

Much love,
Papa

* * *

The Griers had four children—three sons and a daughter, all of whom were born in Lead: Thomas Johnston, Jr., May 9, 1897; Evangeline Victoria ("Muddie"), August 18, 1899; Lisgar Patterson, January 23, 1901; and Ormonde Palethorpe, May 13, 1903.

T.J. wrote the following note to Ormonde, while en route to England on board the R.M.S. *Lusitania*—the ship that would be sunk by a German submarine on May 7, 1915, killing 1,195 passengers.

5 pm at sea
21 October 1907

My dear Prodigal Son,

You're my boy—I love you.
There are many people on this boat. She is riding majestically in rough sea with a moderate gale, but the crew is preparing everything for a heavy gale tonight.

Mama has not been out of her berth yet today, but she sends love to all.

> Much love to all,
> Papa

Mary Jane's two children from her first marriage, James and Madge Ferrie, remained in Edinburgh, Scotland during these early years. On their 1908 visit to Scotland, T.J. and Mary Jane persuaded her parents to emigrate to Lead with the children, and in June 1908, daughter Madge, who was nearly seventeen years old, sailed with her grandmother, Margaret Wright Palethorpe, to New York where Mary Jane met them and accompanied them to Lead. Son James arrived later that summer, followed by his grandfather, James Palethorpe, in the fall.

Soon thereafter, the Palethorpes became naturalized citizens. Madge would later recall:

> It was in Lead that my grandparents became American citizens. (T.J. himself became a citizen in Lawrence County, Territory of Dakota, in 1880.) Father asked Grandpa if he would vote on an issue affecting Homestake. Grandpa said, "Of course I would." My grandparents were both happy in Lead (and later in Los Angeles) and never regretted leaving Scotland, although they were both in their early seventies at the time of their emigration.[13]

T.J. built his Palethorpe in-laws a house downhill from his own. He often stopped in for a chat and a drink on his way home from his office. He also had a deep affection for his stepchildren, whom he regarded as his own. Madge again recalled:

> The word "step" was never used. We were all treated alike, and when my stepfather died, he left us all equal legacies. He was a dear and wonderful man with a fine sense of humor.[14]

T.J. was remembered by his second child, Muddie, in a letter written many years after his death:

> He had a short, square shape. (Are there any tall Griers?) He carried a replaceable quill toothpick in a gold holder in his vest. I never heard him laugh out loud...only a chuckle and a broad grin. Sometimes we all went to his back office where Papa had his "key telegraph equipment," another big desk, an easy

---

13. From a letter written to William M. Grier, Jr. by Margaret Ferrie Christie in the 1970s.
14. Ibid.

chair, a sofa and a big spittoon. He was an expert! After a visit, I was kissed good-bye and sent home.

He took me everywhere about the mine, my hand held tightly in his. On tours, we went below, where the miners wore candles on their caps, and mules pulled the ore cars.

In our home, I climbed the narrow, steep stairs to the "fire walk" on the roof above the third floor playroom of our enormous brick home....I was taught to search the black mountains with binoculars, to look for smoke or a fire.[15]

PHOEBE HEARST

Among the guests at T.J. and Mary Jane's wedding was Phoebe Hearst, George Hearst's widow since 1891. The two women shared a wide range of cultural and educational interests and corresponded regularly. T.J. and Mary Jane were often guests at Phoebe's "Hacienda" in Pleasanton, California, and she, in turn, stayed at their home during visits to Lead. Over the years, Phoebe Hearst's activities were to have a considerable impact on T.J.'s family, as well as on the Griers of the next generation.

Born in Missouri, Phoebe was a schoolteacher there until she married George Hearst, then a prominent San Francisco mine owner. After her marriage, she continued her education, learning to speak Spanish, French, and German fluently.[16]

She was deeply interested in the well-being of the residents of mining towns from the Black Hills of South Dakota to California. In Lead, for example, she endowed and supported the Hearst Free Kindergarten, which was dedicated in May 1901 when T.J. and Mary Jane hosted a reception for Mrs. Hearst in their home.

After Senator Hearst's death in 1891, Phoebe devoted more of her time to philanthropy. As she wrote in a 1918 letter to Mary Jane Grier, she believed that "money should be used for the good of mankind; Homestake's gold should give benefit to those who mined it, as well as those who owned it." Equally strong was her belief in the fair treatment of labor and the need to place someone at the helm of Homestake's operations who shared her ideas on industrial relations. For this position, she chose Edward H. Clark,

---

15.   From a letter written to William M. Grier, Jr. by Evangeline Victoria ("Muddie") Grier Nelsen in the 1970s.

16.   In 1897, Phoebe Hearst became the first female regent of the University of California at Berkeley. There, she sponsored an international architecture competition to design buildings for the campus, donating $200,000 herself. The result was the creation of a group of classical, white granite buildings with red tile roofs and green copper flashing.

a cousin's son, and personally supervised his preparations to assume control of Homestake Mining Company.

Clark became a director of Homestake in 1894. For the next three years, he was vice president, and from 1914 to 1944, president. He directed the operation from the firm's New York office in the Sherry Netherland Hotel, where T.J. and his family stayed when in town on Homestake business.

FIRE, LABOR CRISES

In the first decade of the new century, Grier's administration confronted many serious problems, stemming primarily from the demands of unionized labor and compounded by a fire that broke out on March 25, 1907. The underground inferno was fueled, ironically, by the excellent ventilation system installed to improve working conditions.

Grier was advised by experts that the only possible course of action was to let the fire burn itself out. He rejected this view and, instead, had a creek diverted into the mine by constructing a flume down one hill and up another. The mine was then flooded for forty days and, as a result, a possible explosion was averted. Madge Ferrie recalled that "the town of Lead sat on the mine, so it was a very worrisome time." Draining the shafts of water later on was a monumental task.

After the western Federation of Miners attempted in 1909 to force all Homestake crews to join their union, Grier responded by publicly announcing that the company, in future, would hire only non-union men. Repeated negotiations between the warring factions failed, as union representatives added demands for higher wages and shorter hours to their agenda.

A lockout ensued in November, and the small community of Lead endured bitter hostilities and a bruised economy. Disgruntled union men attempted to destroy company property, and the area became something of an armed camp, with more than 100 guards and detectives patrolling the mine's perimeters.

Meanwhile, Homestake began recruiting non-union labor from other states. By mid-January, the mine reopened with crews consisting of out-of-staters and those Lead miners who were either non-union or disenchanted former union workers. Within two months, all facets of the operation were running again—with an entirely non-unionized workforce.

To avoid recurring labor unrest, and with the full support of humanitarian Phoebe Hearst, Grier granted many significant benefits to his crews in the years following the 1909–1910 disputes. A pioneering health and accident insurance program—the Homestake Employee's Aid Fund—was established in the summer of 1910, generating sick benefits to ailing miners and death benefits to their survivors.

PUBLIC FIGURE

As the years passed, T.J. was increasingly in the public eye. He became widely recognized for his expertise in efficient mining operations, as well as his skill and judgment in labor relations. In August 1914, he was called to testify at length before the United States Commission on Industrial Relations. The Commission's questions centered upon the age, salaries, working conditions, and type and amount of work expected of the miners. Other questions dealt with the ownership and control of Homestake.[17]   The transcript of his testimony was over 100 pages long. T.J.'s responses prompted a comment from the commission that "they had never found any corporation so equitably managed or so perfectly systematized as the Homestake" under what they termed "Mr. Grier's benevolent despotism."[18]

Despite the power and influence of his position, Grier was a modest and caring man. He also possessed a wry sense of humor, which is evident in the following excerpts from his speech on "The Importance of the Public Forest Lands to Mining" (delivered to the American Forestry Association Congress in Washington, D.C.):

> I wish, at this time, to thank our President for inviting me here as a delegate, because I have profited by listening to the speeches that have been made. I have also been, to some extent, amused, because I think I have discovered between the lines of the papers that have been read and between the lines of the speeches that have been made a confession of guilt and have heard the sighing of the contrite hearts that are now before me. Some place in holy writ 'tis written "The sighing of a contrite heart, O God, Thou wilt not despise." At some other place in the good book it is also written that "a wrong confessed or acknowledged is half repaired," so that gentlemen you may take heart because you have only to repair the other half of the wrong, and if you will set about industriously repairing the forest that you have so devastated I think that you may yet be saved and, in support of that belief, let me quote to you the 27th verse of the 18th chapter of Ezekiel, "When the wicked man turneth away from the wickedness that he hath committed and doeth that which is lawful and right he shall save his soul alive."

---

17.   *U.S. Commission on Industrial Relations: Proceedings of Public Hearings Held at Lead, South Dakota, August 3-4, 1914* (Kansas City, Missouri: Shorthand Reporting Company, 1914).

18.   *South Dakota: De Luxe Supplement to the History of Dakota Territory and South Dakota: Its History and Its People* (Chicago: S.J. Clarke Publishing Company, 1915), p. 29.

. . . I do not know how many trees there were upon the earth's surface when Adam appeared upon the scene, but it seems that when Eve came to him there was, at least, one tree, because she soon found it, and from one of its branches plucked tempting fruit with which she so tickled Adam's palate that I think his heirs and successors will hereafter always love, protect and perpetuate trees. [19]

Something of his business philosophy and personal morality is revealed in his commencement address to the 1907 graduates at the South Dakota State School of Mines:

Do not forget either that, in addition to your liberal and technical knowledge, you must be otherwise worthy. Your business methods must be such as will inspire confidence. Your word must be as good as your bond. You must always do that which is right and love that which is just and true. If you do make a mistake in your work, don't try to cover it up by some sort of deceit. Rather confess it and do what you can to repair it. Two wrongs don't make a right. A wrong confessed is half repaired, the other half will be forgiven, you will be assisted in righting it, and confidence in you will not be forfeited. . . . We learn from each other daily. None so humble but can teach us something. No matter how much you may know in either a technical or practical way, or in both ways, you cannot accomplish much in developing the great natural resources of the country, or of the district in which you find yourself, by your own individual effort. You must have the co-operation, help and assistance of someone, perhaps of a large number of persons. In order to be assured of, or to merit this co-operation, help and assistance, which goes so far towards insuring success in your undertakings, you must be civil, kind, considerate and mindful of the comfort, happiness and welfare of your co-laborers; you must confide in them; you must make each and every one feel that some measure of the success attained is due to his personal efforts and that not all of it is due to your efforts. You must respect if you would be respected. Be sure too that you are right in small things and you are pretty sure of being right in those matters that are of greater import. Do not think or say it's only a small matter and amounts to nothing. It's the small things that make the greater ones. "Little drops of water and little grains of sand make the mighty ocean and the beautiful land." Cents makes dimes and dimes make dollars. Come honestly by your cents and dimes and the dollars that you acquire will all be white and clean, your heirs will not be ashamed of the heritage you leave them.

    If you go from here to a great industry, with many departments needing many classes of energy, it will not hurt you to begin service in a lower seat, to start at the bottom round of the ladder, to find yourself below the horizon as it were, because when you rise, as you will if there is no cloud or flaw in your ability and willingness to do right, your light will so shine that your good works

---

19. From the text of a speech presented by T.J. Grier on January 6, 1905 to the American Forestry Association Congress in Washington, D.C.

will be seen and the speedy advancement that will surely follow will have all the more glory in it. I think it is better to start in that way. While rising from the horizon to the high noonday-point you learn what it means by having done it yourself, you are afterwards the better able to direct the operations of subordinates all along an ascending line or scale, and to say what is right and proper at each notch or step of the scale.[20]

CONSERVATIONIST

T.J.'s expertise and acclaim were not, however, confined to mining and labor relations. He was also recognized for his lifelong interest in and concern for conservation. In his speech on "The Importance of the Public Forest Land to Mining," T.J. expressed an opinion commonly held today, but truly in its infancy in the early 1900s:

> Prodigal in the use of our woods, and forgetful of the damage to our mountain streams and springs resulting from that prodigality, perhaps, we have too long neglected tree culture across the length and breadth of our fair land. Or, does our rapid progress in the development of its manifold resources, which call for most generous quantities of forest products, induce us to imagine that such is the case?. . . A visit to the spots within our forest areas once covered with forest giants but now baldheaded, and to the places where springs of clear water once were, will bear me out in the belief. If then, that is our condition, we must be up and doing. We must meet the demands of such rapid progress, or a halt must be called in the progress. I do not believe that the American people are built upon lines that would make palatable the calling of a halt to their onward march, but that the necessity being made apparent to them, they will rise to the occasion as one man, and with all of the energy with which they are endowed, quickly set about correcting the sins of omission of which they have heretofore been guilty.[21]

In the remainder of his speech, Grier elaborated on those aspects of the government's forest reserves policy that he felt were unfair to the mining industry. This address reflected a balance that had been struck in Grier's mind between fulfilling the genuine needs of the mining industry and protecting and preserving nature.

T.J.'s beliefs sprang in part from his long association and friendship

---

20.   From the text of an address given by T.J. Grier on June 3, 1907 to the South Dakota State School of Mines.

21.   From the text of Grier's January 6, 1905 speech to the American Forestry Association.

with Gifford Pinchot, who headed the U.S. Forestry Service from 1898 to 1913. Pinchot, America's first professional forester, was an important intellectual whose conservation policy was based in a belief in "the greatest good for the greatest number for the longest time." As Theodore Roosevelt's chief forester, Pinchot imprinted his conservation ethic on government land policy and helped to establish many of the principles of land management still in use.

As further evidence of Grier's public recognition, he was asked in August of 1909 to deliver a speech before the South Dakota Pharmaceutical Association Convention in Lead. His introductory remarks hint of his keen sense of humor:

> About three weeks ago, I received a program of the proceedings to be held at the 24th annual convention of the South Dakota Pharmaceutical Association to be held on August 18th to 21st inclusive, at the City of Lead, and was surprised to learn from it that, on the first day of the convention, there was to be an address or a paper devoted to a brief history of the Homestake Mining Plant by its superintendent. A day or two later, there came a letter from the secretary of the association, who is also a compounder of programs, asking me to have filled at once the prescription that he had had printed in the program and to take the medicine as directed. I am not permitted, even after shaking the bottle well, to take a teaspoonful every four hours until relieved, but I have to swallow the whole darn thing at one dose. I think when your secretary diagnosed my case and undertook prescribing for it, that he was bent on doing me mischief.[22]

LATER YEARS

The years of heavy responsibility took their toll on T.J.'s health. As Madge recalled:

> I will never forget the strain that the U.S. Industrial Commission hearings put on T.J.'s heart. He was questioned for ten days, and how at the end, the Commission's president summed him up as a "benevolent despot." They discovered what a big hearted man he was and how much he and the Homestake had done for all the people in the town.[23]

Grier's health problems had arisen several years earlier. In 1912, on her

22. From the text of a speech presented by T.J. Grier on August 18, 1909 to the South Dakota Pharmaceutical Association.

23. From a letter written to William M. Grier, Jr. by Margaret Ferrie Christie.

way home to Lead from Columbia University in New York City, Madge spent a night in the Presbyterian Hospital in Chicago where her father was recovering from a heart attack. For several months, she also looked after her half brothers and sister while T.J. was recuperating at Chateau Frontenac, in Quebec, and in California. Mary Jane went with him to both of these convalescence retreats, and Dr. Freeman, a surgeon from Lead's Homestake Hospital, accompanied them to the Chateau Frontenac.

In the summer of 1912, Mary Jane received the following note from the mayor of Lead:

> Your card received with much pleasure. It was like yourself to remember others even in times of anxiety and care. We are so glad to hear of Mr. Grier's continued improvement and have a firm belief that Divine Providence will send him back here to us where his influence for good counts for so much. You must be prepared for a great welcome when you return, and it will be from us "just common folks." I think it will be the best day Lead has ever seen.[24]

One of Grier's most lasting contributions to his community was the Homestake Opera House and Recreation Building, a facility he conceived as a gift from Homestake to the people of Lead. As Grier had hoped, the center quickly became the focus of the recreational, social, and cultural activities of the community.

Grier announced the project to the public on November 13, 1911. The $250,000 complex was to be built on Main Street, between the Hearst Free Kindergarten, located in the basement of Christ Episcopal Church, and the Halloran Block to the east. Selected to draw the plans was the architectural firm of Shattuck & Hussey in Chicago. T.J. revised the firm's preliminary design in early 1912, making it a "T"-shaped building that better fit the site and took less land from the kindergarten. Construction began in July 1912.

When completed two years later, the complex included an opera house, library, bowling alley, swimming pool, social rooms, and facilities for billiards and pool, all free to the public, except for performances at the opera house.

---

24. From a letter written by Lead mayor H.L. Howard to Mrs. T.J. Grier at Chateau Frontenac, Quebec, Canada on July 15, 1912.

OPERA HOUSE DEDICATION

The opera house, later called "The Jewel of the Black Hills," was adorned with a graceful pair of sculptured angels holding up a central gilt medallion positioned directly above the stage; another series of medallions extended along the length of the ornamented, gilded fascia. Just below the ceiling and encircling the theater were panels of beautiful western nature paintings that included elk and buffalo standing on forested hills or beside picturesque streams. The seating capacity of 1,016 included eight boxes of 100 chairs, with 350 seats in the balcony and 566 on the main floor.

The dedication and opening night was held on Monday, August 31, 1914. Following a matinee performance for the citizens of Lead not employed by the company and for miners working the night shift, the Sheehan-English Opera Company performed great scenes from *Il Travatore*, *Bohemian Girl*, and *Martha* to a full house. Though it was pouring rain outside, ticketholders to the evening performance came undeterred and were fashionably dressed for the occasion. The price of admission ranged from 25¢ to $1.

Before the opening curtain rose, T.J. Grier, on behalf of the Homestake Mining Company, dedicated this splendid building to the employees of Homestake and to the good people of Lead and the surrounding county. He credited Richard Blackstone for his role in bringing the building to life, expressed gratitude to the Sheehan-English Opera Company, and wished the audience an evening of the greatest enjoyment. Then the curtain arose on Scene I from *Il Travatore*. Grier's stepdaughter Madge Ferrie was in charge of the ushers; his daughter Muddie was an usher; and his sons Lisgar and Ormonde served as program boys for the afternoon and evening performances. The evening was a great success. The audience enthusiastically applauded with repeated encores and curtain calls. The true attraction, however, had been the dazzling new facility itself. The first patrons had found themselves, as would later generations, under the spell of the Opera House, awed by its beauty and elegance.

LAST FAREWELL

After the dedication, T.J., Mary Jane, and two of the children departed by train for Los Angeles, to purchase and furnish a home for their retirement. T.J. also decided that he should see a doctor about what he termed "indigestion and nervous condition." On September 22, after a full day in Los Angeles with family and friends (including Homestake president Edward Clark), T.J. began to feel dizzy and retired to his upstairs bedroom.

There, he died in his sleep that evening.

Thomas Johnston Grier's death was mourned not only by his family and the city of Lead but by mining circles in the U.S. and abroad. A few days after his death, T.J.'s body arrived at the Pluma station in Lead. Mrs. Grier and family were accompanied to their home by Dr. D.K. Dickinson, with the hearse following behind, as thousands of people lined the streets to watch.

The next morning the casket was taken to the lounge of the Recreation Building, where the body lay in state from 9:30 a.m. to 1:30 p.m., and the Homestake Orchestra played softly, to muffled drums, Grieg's "Funeral March."

Afterward, the body was taken by members of Grier's Masonic Lodge to nearby Christ Church for the Episcopal service, followed by an elaborate procession to West Lead Cemetery. The crowd was estimated at 14,000 people.

Thomas Johnston Grier was buried among the tall pines and conifers in the Masonic Cemetery overlooking Lead and his beloved Homestake Mining Company. Thirty-two years later, Mary Jane was buried next to him. In June 1972, the author and his bride-to-be Joan Grafmueller visited the graves of his great-uncle and aunt.

TRIBUTES
Builder

The *Lead Daily Call* of September 23, 1914 extolled T.J.'s many accomplishments as superintendent, the last, of course, being the handsome new complex he had presented to the city:

> The Recreation Building and Opera House were conceived by Mr. Grier and the plan for its completion is one thing that will stand as a monument to Mr. Grier, and a reminder of the thought and care which he gave to the interests of those who worked under him....Under his regime was built the great water system which supplies the company's works, the city of Lead, and other towns. The Spearfish hydroelectric plant was completed during his term of office, the great Ellison hoist, the viaduct connecting the mills with the railway system of the company, the Star and Amicus mills, adding to the capacity of the company's milling plants...and under him, the work of building the new B. and M. hoist, the power plant and boiler plant, which is now under way, was started....As manager for the Homestake Company, Mr. Grier superintended the efforts of twenty-five hundred people with a payroll of two hundred and twenty-five thousand dollars per month, the mines turning out over six million dollars in gold and owning over sixteen million dollars worth of property.[25]

25.   *Lead Daily Call*, 23 September 1914.

Progressive Industrial Policies

The essence of T.J. Grier's life's work can best be seen in remarks made by Professor Commons, of the United States Industrial Commission, after his investigation of the Homestake during the 1908 labor difficulties:

> You have here the most remarkable business organization that I have come across in the country. You have developed welfare features which are beyond anything that I know of, and they are given a liberal hand. You have a high scale of wages, reasonable hours—very fair hours. There has been evidently great progress made in taking care of the employes in the hospital service, and you have taken care of the cost of living, have kept it down below what employes in other communities have been forced to pay. You have practically been able by your great strength here as a huge corporation, dominating the whole community, to look out for the welfare of your employes, and to bring in an admirable class of citizens. It seems also that you are influential in politics, that you secure a good class of officials, and that you have secured the enforcement of law, the reduction of immorality. It seems also that you make an effort to build up the religious life of the community and that your policy is broad and liberal in all respects. I take it also that this policy depends solely upon your personality.[26]

High Character, Generosity

Another local paper lauded these qualities:

> It was not his great executive genius alone, his ability for the management of a great property involving countless details and unlimited capacity for work, that Mr. Grier in his superintendency of the Homestake Mine made Lead unique in the industrial world. It was by the high character of the man—the honor, courage, justice and generosity. It was not merely a working policy that gave to Homestake employes and to Lead people in general whatever of good it lay in his great power to bestow—it was the big, fatherly heart that made it possible for every man to look to Mr. Grier for justice and generous treatment and never to look in vain. In the management of Homestake affairs Mr. Grier was given all power. It rested with him to institute and carry out policies and plans for the control of an industry upon whose successful working Lead and her people depend absolutely while all the Hills is to a great degree dependent

---

26. *South Dakota Deluxe Supplement*, pp. 30-31.

upon it. How many men would have been able to lay aside every consideration of personal aggrandizement or personal ambition and think only of the interests of the employes of the company and the rights of the stockholders? There was no reason why Mr. Grier should not have been a heavy stockholder. No reason why he should not have been a millionaire many times over without in any way breaking the requirements of law and honesty. There was no reason, that is, except the fine sense of honor that prompted him, feeling that not being a stockholder would place him in better attitude toward the company and its operatives, to refuse to profit himself by the increase in values brought about largely through him. That unselfishness showed itself in many ways. Mr. Grier could have spared himself much of anxiety and of effort had he been less concerned for the welfare of others and more for his own. But in all things the well-being and happiness of those under him and the interests of the company whose property he controlled came before any personal consideration.[27]

T.J. Grier, in thirty years as superintendent, had succeeded in making Homestake the largest and most productive gold mine in North America. At his death, T.J. was credited with having set the company on the successful course it would follow for the next half century. Concomitant with the growth of the mining operations, the city of Lead had been growing vigorously, becoming the second largest city in South Dakota by the year 1912.[28]

During T.J.'s tenure, he had touched many lives. His concern for the miners' safety, as well as his interest in their ideas and opinions, made him particularly beloved.

Mary Jane was also much esteemed. When she departed from Lead after her husband's death, she received a letter from the Ladies Aid Society, expressing the ladies' desire "to send [you] a last word of greeting and farewell. They especially remember at this time your keen interest and generous aid in the work of their society and...express their deep appreciation for all that you did from time to time in the past. They, like all the people of the community, deeply regret your leaving here and indeed feel it to be a personal loss. They wish to bid you and your family Godspeed on your prospective journey."[29]

27. Ibid., pp. 31–32.

28. T.J. also served as president of the First National Bank of Lead, organized on September 23, 1891. For many years, he was also vice president of the First National Bank of Deadwood, South Dakota.

29. From a letter written by the Ladies Aid Society secretary Mrs. H. Nienhuis, on October 30, 1914.

MEMORIAL STATUE

As an expression of their deep affection for T.J., the miners and local residents raised funds to construct a bronze statue in his memory. Sculptor Allen Newman of New York was commissioned to complete the likeness which was dedicated in Lead on September 28, 1916 and placed next to the recreation building, against a background of the Black Hills. Of the event, the *Lead Daily Call* reported:

> The monument...will stand as evidence of the admiration of a community for one whose devotion to duty built up a great industry and fostered the prosperity and happiness of those who worked with him.[30]

Milt Grier (or "Will," as T.J. affectionately called his nephew, the son of his younger brother William John) traveled to Lead, where he and several thousand people gathered for the ceremony dedicating the statue. The choir of Christ Episcopal Church, the Lead High School glee club, and the Homestake band participated in the program. The main speaker, Homestake's new superintendent, Richard Blackstone, summarized T.J.'s achievements, noting that, although the latter were significant, he believed Grier's greatest accomplishments were the many things he had done to lessen suffering and to increase the recreational and educational opportunities for the local residents.

The *Daily Call* noted:

> ...the sculptor chose one of T.J.'s characteristic poses...standing, left hand thrust into the pocket of his inside coat, overcoat thrown back, and right hand grasping his lapel. He is wearing his customary soft, wide-brimmed hat, and his face reflects the earnestness that was the dominating mark of his character.[31]

---

30.   *Lead Daily Call*, 28 September 1918.

31.   Ibid.

PHOEBE HEARST'S LETTERS TO THE GRIERS

Hacienda del Pozo de Verona
Pleasanton, Calif.
7th November, 1901

My dear Mrs. Grier,

My son has been with us the last two weeks and during his stay I had so little time for correspondence, I now find myself in arrears to such an extent I scarcely know where to begin.

My thoughts have been with you many times and if the letters I wished to send had been written, you would have received a volume.

I was happy to have the photos of you and the dear children. They are all good, but do not do full justice especially the one of you. When the package was opened and the smiling faces greeted me, I longed to speak with you.

The tea cozies have given me great pleasure. They are beautiful and useful, as well as a constant reminder of your loving thought. I have been absent from home since Monday and do not know if your gift of gloves has arrived. As soon as the package reaches me I will write but cannot wait longer to express my thanks.

I hope all are well and you have protected your health by ceasing to nurse dear little baby. I wish you and Mr. Grier could come here for a visit and enjoy the operas. The season opens next Monday and we are anticipating a great musical treat. When do you and Mr. Grier expect to go to N.Y.? A fine list of operas will be given there during the winter and if you are there I wish you to be my guest several times. Mr. Clark will secure the tickets and I hope that he and Mrs. Clark can go with you and Mr. Grier.

My son wished me to tell Mr. Grier he appreciated his very kind telegram conveying the invitation to visit Lead. He intends to go there sometime in the summer, either next year or the one following. He liked the Hacienda so much, he wanted to stay for a long time. We went to see my mother who was extremely happy to see him. He spent several days in town. Went to Berkeley and many old friends came to see him.

The chrysanthemums at the Hacienda are more beautiful than any previous year. I wish I could send you large boxes every week. A man is there now taking photographs. He is slow but they will be finished some time and you shall have a set. With kindest regards to Mr. Grier and much love to you, I am most sincerely your friend,

Phoebe A. Hearst

* * *

Hacienda del Pozo de Verona
11th September, 1905

My dear Mrs. Grier,

I am starting this week for San Simeon to visit my ranch there and, a few days after my return, that is, toward the end of the month, I leave for Mexico to visit my Chihuahua property.

After closing up my house here, I will start east by way of the Black Hills. I will let Mr. Grier know the exact date on which I am to leave. I may not reach the Hills earlier than the twenty-fifth or twenty-sixth of October.

I shall be so glad to see you all again, and am sorry we can stay such a short time.

The young ladies who have been my guests will not be with me as they go east a little earlier so as to visit friends. I think I shall have only Mr. Clark with me, as my maid also may go east on another date.

With love to you and the children and kindest regards to Mr. Grier, I am yours very sincerely,

Phoebe A. Hearst

* * *

135 East 28th St., New York City
4th January, 1907

Dear Mrs. Grier,

Your beautiful gift came with your kind messages and I thank you most sincerely for both. The work on the handkerchief is extremely fine and exquisite. I shall think of you at all times though no reminder was needed to bring me loving thoughts of you. I am glad to know that your trip to England proved a benefit to all. I wish you could have remained longer and had some real rest. I should have felt most happy if you had all met us in Switzerland and spent the month of August. Mr. Grier and you would have enjoyed the magnificent scenery and delightful air. Such good times we could have had together. When you go over again I do hope you and Mr. Grier will travel about and stay long enough to see and enjoy much.

I hoped we might have the pleasure of seeing you here during my stay. Mr. Grier had lived through a trying time and we felt that he needed the change. We were all disappointed that you could not come.

I came over for the holidays to spend them with my son and family and to talk over several matters with Mr. Clark. As I am a good traveler I do not find the voyage fatiguing and have had great pleasure in my visit. My little grandson is a fine little fellow and we are great friends. I feel sorry to go away from him. I sail on Tuesday, January 8th and if the voyage is good I expect to be in Paris on the night of the 16th. The *Kaiser Wilhelm II* of the North German Lloyd line is a fine and fast steamer and I hope will make her usual time.

If my son goes abroad in May I will not come home until October or November and will probably give up my apartment in Paris. I have had a long rest from many cares and my health has improved. I feel that I should go to California and try to help in all ways that I can. I shall never again be able to undertake any large work as I have done my part already but my duty is to help those who are truly worthy and there are many small ways of helping. My kindergarten work must be built up again in S.F. [San Francisco]. A few classes have been reorganized and a small temporary building has been erected on the lot where the good building stood. It was at North Beach where many poor families lived. Now they are scattered and it may not be necessary to rebuild in same part of town. The Settlement building gymnasium and all equipment that was at South Park were burned. It was my gift and now I cannot make another gift of same accommodation and value. It may not be so greatly needed as the working men are the prosperous people these days. Still the influence of the Settlement work is good and reaches many. It is a great satisfaction to me that the Kindergarten work has been successful at Lead. I hope to go there again soon after going to California and to stay a few days longer. With all good wishes for a happy New Year for you and all who are dear to you. I am as ever yours affectionately,

Phoebe A. Hearst

* * *

Hacienda del Pozo de Verona
10th November, 1909

My dear Mrs. Grier,

I feel so anxious about you all at this time and am now writing to ask if you won't all come out here for Christmas. You might not be willing to leave Mr. Grier, but yet he might think it and think the best thing you can do is to come and let all of your dear ones come to the Hacienda.

You can say you all have an invitation to spend Christmas. In my mind you have had it for a whole year, so you can let it be known that it has been extended to you for some time if it seems best. Indeed, you have a general invitation to come here at any time.

I shall not leave the Hacienda this winter, and I believe my son and his family will spend Christmas in New York, so it will add to our joy at the Hacienda if you will come to us.

With kindest greetings I am

> Yours very sincerely,
> Phoebe A. Hearst

* * *

> Hacienda del Pozo de Verona
> 1st December, 1909

My dear Mrs. Grier,

I am so sorry that you feel you cannot come to me for Christmas. I am going to send you a special letter to urge you further at least to send the children, but now I am writing about something else. I want to say that I have Christmas packages ready for all the children excepting Lisgar and Ormonde and I do not know what they would like.

Would Ormonde like a big rocking horse that he could ride, and would Lisgar care for an automobile big enough for him to ride in or a large engine? Or could you tell me what would give them most pleasure. I do not know what toys they already have nor what they long for most. The box is all ready now for shipment excepting for Lisgar's and Ormonde's packages. Of course if they should come as I hope they may there is no hurry, but if not, it would be as well to ship the case before the usual holiday congestion of the express.

With kindest thoughts of you all, I am

> Yours very sincerely,
> Phoebe A. Hearst

* * *

> Hacienda del Pozo de Verona
> 16th February, 1914

Dear Mrs. Grier,

I am so glad to learn that you and Mr. Grier are coming to California before long and that you mean to take the trip to Honolulu, which is usually so pleasant at this time of the year. The number of good steamers in that service is limited, however, and I hope your arrangements can be made long enough in advance to secure passage on one of the best.

Of course I expect a visit from you both before you sail, with just as many of the children as you can bring. You know that you have a standing invitation, which includes the whole family and that I always look forward with pleasure to every opportunity of having you here.

I have not been well since the holidays and have suffered a good deal from nervous indigestion, probably the result of fatigue and many worries.

I shall expect to hear from you as soon as your plans are definitely settled, and hope you can set an early date for your visit.

With much love to you all, I am

Yours affectionately,
Phoebe A. Hearst

* * *

Wyntoon
McCloud, Calif.
9th August, 1916

My dear Mrs. Grier,

Your letter came this evening just when I had said I would write you. I am sorry to have Lisgar leave us but I understand that you need one of your boys with you. He will leave here on the evening of the 15th, reach San Francisco early in the morning of the 16th, leave that evening at 8 o'clock. Mr. Edward Clark and family are coming here on the 15th to stay about two weeks. You know he is like a son and I am always happy to have him in my home. I feel anxious when Helen is here. You know why.

I think Mrs. Clark, Helen and Edward Jr. will probably make few and short visits to my homes in future. They are socially affected and I am not fond of gay people and the Burlingame set. Mr. Clark came up here yesterday to see me about some important business. He returned to San Francisco that night. He is capable and his integrity is beyond question. It is a great comfort to have such a man manage my business.

I must send this off. It carries much love to you and your family.

Affectionately,
Phoebe A. Hearst

* * *

Hacienda del Pozo de Verona
19th October, 1918

My dear Mrs. Grier,

I was very glad to have your letter with these from Muddy enclosed and to hear she is so happy in her school. I hope she escapes the influenza and keeps well during the year. Thank you very much for sending me her letters and for the Kodak pictures of the family. They are all very good and I am very pleased to have them. I was also pleased to hear that Lisgar is happy in his school and doesn't forget to write regularly to his mother. I am sure you miss him and Muddy very much. This place does seem large and lonely without my dear boys and the babies but of course their parents can't let them stay with me all the time. George and William are in St. John's school at Manlius near Syracuse, New York and both seem to be very happy there. John is in a private school near home and quite content.

Miss Garden writes that the babies are well, but feel the restriction and confinement keenly after their liberty and freedom at The Hacienda. If the influenza epidemic subsides in time I hope to spend the holidays with my family in New York.

With greetings and best wishes to all of your family,

Affectionately yours,
Phoebe A. Hearst

85

Phoebe Hearst

George Hearst
(*Courtesy of the Black
Hills Mining Museum,
Lead, South Dakota*)

(Courtesy of the Bancroft Library, University of California at Berkeley)

Phoebe Hearst's
northern
California
homes: *at top*,
"The Hacienda"
in Pleasanton,
and *left*, "Wyntoon"
on the McCloud
River

(Courtesy of Victoria Grier Nelsen)

Office of the Homestake Mining Co.

Room 49 Nevada Block

San Francisco, Cal.

July 9th 1885

f the Homestake Mining Company her

ng of the Directors of said Com-

the same Room 49 Nevada Block

lifornia July 9th 1885 among other

following:-

s B. Haggin duly seconded Thomas J.

Grier, Dakota Territory was unanimously elected

Superintendent of the Homestake Mining Co.

Secretary Homestake Mining Co.

Portrait engraving of Thomas J. Grier, Sr., c. 1885. Homestake Mining
Company letter signed by Irwin C. Stump, secretary, naming
T.J. Grier superintendent
(Courtesy of Black Hills Mining Museum, Lead, South Dakota)

Left: T.J. Grier, Sr., 1898
Above: T.J. Grier's mother, Eliza
Anne Patterson Grier

T.J.'s home and office in Lead, South Dakota, before his
marriage to Mary Jane Palethorpe in 1886
(Courtesy of the Black Hills Mining Museum)

(Courtesy of the Black Hills Mining Museum)

The T. J. Grier residence, Lead, South Dakota.
The home, seen from the rear below,
overlooked the bustling activity
of Homestake Mining Company

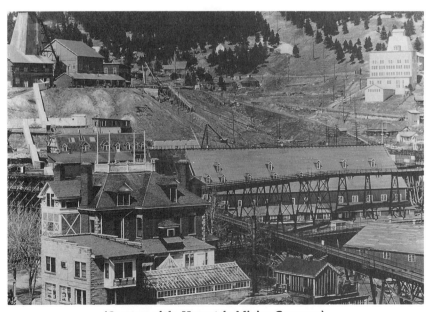

(Courtesy of the Homestake Mining Company)

Mary Jane Grier
(Mrs. Thomas J. Grier, Sr.)
c. 1901
*(Courtesy of Victoria
Grier Nelsen)*

Margaret Wright Palethorpe and James Palethorpe
(Courtesy of Victoria Grier Nelson)

T.J. and Mary Jane at "The Hacienda," Pleasanton, California, c. 1908

T.J., Jr., Ormonde, Henderson (the chauffeur), Lisgar,
Muddie, and T.J., in Spearfish Canyon, South Dakota,
c. 1909 *(Courtesy of Victoria Grier Nelsen)*

The T.J. Grier family, c. 1911: *from left,* back row—T.J., Jr., Evangeline Victoria, T.J., Margaret Ferrie, Mary Jane; front row—Ormonde Palethorpe, Lisgar Patterson *(Courtesy of Victoria Grier Nelsen)*

TOM GRIER, JR., TO SINK SHAFT

MINING OPERATIONS AT GRIER HOME PROMISE TO SOON BE UNDER WAY

Tom Grier, Jr., seems to be making preparations for sinking a shaft and running several drifts in the earth beneath. the home of his parents, on Grier hill.

He had erected a hoist, equipped it with a reel and a cage and it is in perfect working order.

The youthful builder of mining machinery, uses a cat in determining the capacity of the hoist and the feline seems to enjoy it.

At the bottom of the hoist, which occupies a corner in the yard, are railroad tracks, with dump cars all ready to receive the ore which will be raised in the hoist and so far as surface indications are concerned, the Homestake mine, jr., is about ready to prove its rich find.

But that is not all of this story.

The interior of the Grier home is said to be threatened with abandonment by the family, and all because the youthful promoter is making his own patters and preparing to manufacture his own mining machinery.

He has a pattern shop in the upper story of the home and when he it as work there, the noise of his operations is sufficient to draw from his partenal ancestors, remarks which are seldom heard in polite society.

And in the basement of the home, the young man has another department, the machine shop, power for which is supplied by an electrical motor. Between the pattern shop and the machine shop, on the middle floors of the home quiet abidith not.

Just when the family will move has not been determined.

Article on T.J.'s son published in the *Lead* (South Dakota) *Daily Call,* October 25, 1909

Charles W. Merrill, metallurgical engineer, T.J., Jr.,
and Thomas Johnston Grier, Sr., c. 1908
(Courtesy of Victoria Grier Nelsen)

T.J. Grier Sr.*(center, with black fedora and bow tie)* in Bucks, South Dakota, May 11,
1908

Main Street, Lead, South Dakota, c. 1912
(Black Hills Mining Museum collection)

96

Rare Homestake Mining Company stock certificate for 50 shares issued in 1878, the year in which T.J. Grier joined the firm (*Black Hills Mining Museum collection*)

T.J. Grier stands to the immediate right of President William Howard Taft during an underground tour of Homestake Mining operations on October 21, 1911
(*Courtesy of Mildred Fielder; photographed by Ross & Gee*)

The South Dakota Engineering Society

Office of Secretary-Treasurer

Mitchell, S. Dakota

Refer to File No. 610   September 27, 1911.

Mr. T. J. Grier,

Lead, S. Dak.

Dear Sir:-

     By request of the members and by unanimous vote of the
Board of Direction you have been elected as an Honorary Member of The
South Dakota Engineering Society. This is done in accordance with
Section I of Article III of our Constitution and imposes on you no
obligation whatever. We hope that this election will be satisfac-
tory to you and that the Society may have the benefit of your in-
fluence in the state. Below we quote the article in reference to
Honorary Members.

     "Honorary Members shall be proposed by a least ten mem-
bers and shall be elected only by a unanimous vote of the Board of
Direction. A PastPresident, or a member of the Board of Direction
porposed for Honorary Membership, shall not be required to vote
either for or against his own admission."

                Very truly yours,

Dict. RGC-LRS   Sec'y.

Letter electing T.J. Grier an honorary member of the South Dakota Engineering
Society, Mitchell, South Dakota, September 27, 1911
(Black Hills Mining Museum collection)

The unveiling of T.J. Grier's memorial statue, Lead, South Dakota, September 28, 1916 *(Black Hills Mining Museum collection)*

100

The statue of T.J. Grier, June 1972
(*Photographed by William M. Grier, Jr.*)

Mary Jane (nee Palethorpe) Ferrie Grier
(Mrs. Thomas Johnston Grier)
c. 1890s

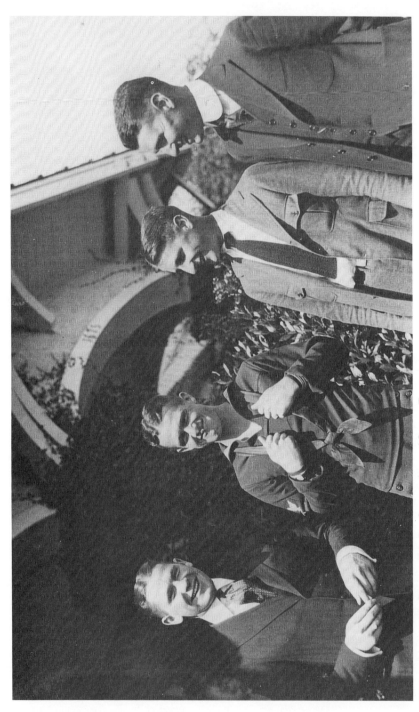

T.J.'s sons, c. 1918: Lisgar, T.J. Jr., Ormonde, and James Ferrie

8

T.J.'S FAMILY

THOMAS JOHNSTON GRIER, JR.
1897–1929

A Tragically Short Life

Thomas Johnston Grier, Jr., the oldest child of T.J. and Mary Jane Grier, was born on May 9, 1897 in Lead, South Dakota. Like his brothers Lisgar and Ormonde and sister Evangeline Victoria, he enjoyed a privileged childhood in Lead, where his father, as superintendent of the Homestake Mining Company, was a leader in the community.

T.J., Jr. attended public school in Lead. On June 25, 1917, at age twenty, he joined the Navy Reserve Fleet, serving as Gunner's Mate First Class at Mare Island in San Francisco Bay until discharged in 1919. In January 1918, he enrolled at the University of California at Berkeley, completing one semester in the College of Arts and Sciences.

He worked for several investment firms in Los Angeles before his marriage to Sally Havens on June 20, 1920. Sally was the daughter of Mr. and Mrs. Wickham Havens, of Piedmont, California. (See Part Three: 9)

Their wedding, attended by several hundred people, took place in Sally's grandparents' home, "Wildwood Gardens," in Piedmont. Built by the bride's grandfather Frank C. Havens as a tribute to his second wife, Lila Rand, their opulent home was designed by Bernard Maybeck and modeled after a maharajah's palace. It was begun in 1906 and completed the following year. Maybeck was to gain renown as the architect of the Palace of Fine Arts at the Panama-Pacific International Exposition.

After their honeymoon, the couple lived in Los Angeles. T.J. later became president of Citizens Guaranty Loan & Investment Company (at 1028 South Broadway), which he founded in January 1925. In 1926, he and his partner sold the firm. In writing to his mother Mary Jane, who was in Mombasa, Kenya visiting his half sister Madge Ferrie Christie, T.J. enclosed a check with this note:

August 18, 1925

Dearest Mother,

Just a little profit from the first six months' business; don't spend it all in one place. And don't worry about the three Grier brothers, as we are going to be all you want. So have a good time. Love, Tom and Lisgar

The couple's first and only child, Thomas Johnston Grier 3d ("Tommy"), was born on August 20, 1926 in Los Angeles. Shortly thereafter, the Griers returned to San Francisco, living in a Spanish-style, two-story stucco home in the Sea Cliff district, at 29th Avenue and Lake Street (2801 Lake Street). T.J., Jr. became an officer with Fireman's Fund Insurance Company at 401 California Street and a member of the Bohemian Club. Promoted to assistant treasurer on September 10, 1926, he was responsible for the firm's investments.

Tragically, his promising life ended on Friday evening, July 20, 1929. He was driving a friend, Theron P. Stevick, in his Pierce Arrow to the Bohemian Club's summer encampment, trying to make that evening's opening ceremony which ironically was titled "Cremation of Care." Two miles north of San Rafael, the car overturned on a curve at the foot of Puerto Suello, instantly killing thirty-two-year-old T.J., Jr. His passenger, thrown from the car, escaped serious injury.[1]

After settling his estate, Sally and her son lived with her mother, Florence Havens, in Piedmont. In 1932, Sally married Timothy E. Colvin of Piedmont in Stanford University Memorial Chapel. His family owned an automobile dealership in Oakland. The couple first resided in Piedmont and later moved to Detroit. Their marriage, however, ended in divorce after a few years. Sally married twice again and, for a time, lived in Honolulu, Hawaii.

Thomas Johnston Grier 3d (1926–1982)

After his mother's marriage to Timothy Colvin, Tommy returned to live with his grandmother at "Wildwood" in Piedmont and remained with

---

1.   The Bohemian Club, formed in 1872 in San Francisco, began as a celebration of civilization and the arts. From 1890 on, however, the membership shifted from artists (Mark Twain was a member) to businessmen. The club's Bohemian Grove near Monte Rio, California, on 3,000 acres along the Russian River, has two outdoor theatres, a dining circle seating 1,100, and a trap-shooting range.

her until her death in 1937. Then he was cared for by his uncle and aunt, Walker and Virginia (nee Martin) Havens, with whom he lived and who became his legal guardians. Young Tommy attended the Frank C. Havens School, which was named after his mother's grandfather, and Piedmont High School.

In summer of 1943, they moved to West Los Angeles, where Tommy enrolled in University High School. The family later moved to Flintridge, California.

Tommy was a compact man—5' 6 1/2" tall and 140 lbs.—with brown eyes and hair and a ruddy complexion. During the Second World War, he served in the U.S. Navy from August 18, 1944 to May 23, 1946. After completing Landing Craft School in San Diego, he worked in amphibious operations and saw duty in the Pacific for a year aboard the U.S.S. *Auburn* from 1945–1946. From May 31 to June 21, 1945, he participated in the occupation of Okinawa Gunto-Ryukyu Islands, and in July of 1945, he completed the radar operations course at Camp Catlin.

After his discharge on May 15, 1946, Tommy obtained his high school diploma and entered the insurance business in Los Angeles.

He married four times, to Sue Jackson, Nancy Bauer, Helen Johnson, and Teresa Keyser. With his second wife, he had two children, Stephen and Cynthia, who were later adopted by their mother's second husband, Jack Hopper.

Tommy died at age fifty-seven, on July 9, 1982 at the UCLA medical center. He was buried at sea.

EVANGELINE VICTORIA GRIER
1899–1988
Muddie

The only daughter born to Thomas Johnston, Sr. and Mary Jane Grier, Evangeline Victoria ("Muddie") was born on August 18, 1899 in Lead, South Dakota and baptized in the town's Episcopal church.[2] Her early schooling was in Lead, and later she attended the All Saints School in Sioux Falls, South Dakota.

---

2.   Muddie's first name was derived from Henry Wadsworth Longfellow's classic poem, *Evangeline*, set near Wolfville, Nova Scotia.

After her father's death on September 22, 1914, she moved with her family to their Los Angeles home, at 1675 Buckingham Road, which her father had bought shortly before his death. She finished high school at the Harvard School in Los Angeles and then, in 1918, attended Mount Vernon Junior College in Washington, D.C. Between 1918 and 1919, Muddie studied at the University of Southern California, becoming president of her junior class.

On December 7, 1921, Muddie married William Phineas Banning in her mother's home on Buckingham Road.[3] (See Part Three: 9) William, born in Los Angeles on May 2, 1899, had served in the U.S. Navy between October 1918 and September 1921. He became an investment broker, beginning as a bond salesman and progressing to partnerships in Graves & Banning; Bogardus, Frost & Banning; and finally Shearson-Hammill (now Shearson-American Express). The Bannings lived at 1016 West 31st Street in Los Angeles. A daughter, Evangeline Victoria ("Paddy"), was born to the couple on September 11, 1922, and they had a son, William Phineas, Jr., in 1929. Muddie and William were divorced in Los Angeles on March 3, 1935.

During these years, Muddie had been active in the community, belonging to the Junior League, serving on the board of "Pro Musica," working on case histories at the clinic of Children's Hospital, and organizing and promoting a lecture series.

Muddie's second marriage was to Edwin Ingwald Nelsen, of Chicago. Edwin worked in Los Angeles for the Ornamental Iron Works Company. Their daughter, Ede Mary Kristine Nelsen, was born in 1938; son Thomas Johnstone ("T.J.") Nelsen, in 1939. From the late thirties to the early fifties, the Nelsen family lived at 10600 McNerney Street, in Southgate, California. Muddie worked in the fifties as an assistant supervisor of maids at the La Playa Hotel in Carmel, California.

In 1956, the Nelsens moved to Green Street in San Francisco and, in the sixties, to Sausalito where Ede Kris and Tom completed their schooling. At the time of Edwin's death in 1984, the couple was living in Corte Madera, California. When Muddie died four years later, she was sharing the Sausalito home of her daughter Ede Kris.

Evangeline Victoria Banning (1922–1974)

Muddie's first child, Paddy, attended Pomona College. There, she

---

3.   The Grier-Banning wedding was highlighted in the society column in the *Los Angeles Times* of 7 December 1921.

majored in philosophy and Oriental studies and was crowned "Queen of the May." She later was a student at Stanford University Business School. Paddy's objective had been to work with an oil company in China, but her aspirations were cut short by World War II and the Chinese Revolution. Paddy married Richard Swick Harding on September 11, 1947, in Phoenix, Arizona.[4] A Texan, Richard was born on May 27, 1923, in San Antonio. He attended Washington and Lee University and Pomona College before becoming a combat engineer in the Army and serving in the European Theater. Following the war, he resumed his studies at the University of Texas. Paddy and Richard had four children: Robert Brent, born August 6, 1949; Victoria Grier, April 1, 1951; Richard Swick, Jr., July 31, 1952; and Karen Louise, June 11, 1954. In the last part of her life, Paddy, always active in the Episcopal church, was a minister. At the time of her death from cancer in 1974, she was living in East Bay near Berkeley, California.

William P. Banning, Jr. (1929–)

William Phineas Banning, Jr. graduated from the American Institute for Foreign Trade (now the American Graduate School for International Trade) in Phoenix, Arizona. With his first wife, Suzanne Boushey, Bill spent most of his business life selling pharmaceutical products in Latin America. She bore him five children: Pamela, born August 11, 1951; William Theodore, April 30, 1953; William Phineas 3d, February 22, 1957; and twins Sallie and William Gregory, May 6, 1966. Bill was divorced from Suzanne in the early 1980s and shortly thereafter married Marian Lowry, who had three children by a previous marriage: twins Matthew and David Winter (b. 1969) and Luke Winter (b. 1962).

In her first marriage, to Jorge Cabrera, Pamela had one son, George; she subsequently married William Taylor, then Jay Aronow. William Theodore Banning married Margaret Riester; their daughter Sarah Elizabeth was born in 1982. William Phineas Banning 3d has a child, Christopher Ryan (b. 1982), by his first wife, Cinthia Lee Wood, and he and his second wife, Karen Dillenburg, are the parents of William Phineas Banning 4th, born in 1988. Sallie Banning is unmarried; her twin brother William Gregory and his wife Jolynn Kerr have a daughter, Brittany Jo, born in 1986.

---

4.   "Descendant of Pioneer Family and Fiance Fly to Phoenix for Evening Ceremony" was the headline in the society column in the *Los Angeles Times* on 12 September 1947.

Ede Kris Nelsen (1938–)
Thomas Johnstone Nelsen (1939–)

Ede Mary Kristine Nelsen, now divorced from Peter Alvarado, has two children: Carmen Kristine Alvarado, born in 1958, and Peter Edwin Alvarado, born in 1959. She is the manager of the Pacific Telephone Yellow Pages, a position which takes her on special assignments to various cities in California.

Thomas Johnstone ("T.J.") Nelsen married Paula Kay McKenzie (1949–) and lives in Sausalito, California. An independent businessman who enjoys boating, T.J. has one son, Samuel Johnstone Nelsen, born in 1988.

LISGAR P. GRIER

1901–1941

Bachelor

Born on January 20, 1901 in Lead, South Dakota, Lisgar Patterson Grier was the third child of Thomas Johnston and Mary Jane Grier. Named after the Scottish Lord Lisgar, a friend of his father, he completed school through the eighth grade in Lead, then finished his studies at Harvard School in Los Angeles, where the Grier family had moved in 1914.

Lisgar was called "Nickel Boy" by his father, for young Grier showed an interest in having ready cash on hand at all times. Lisgar's sister Victoria ("Muddie") remembers her short, freckled brother with slightly red hair as being "swell," always well dressed, gregarious, and charming.

Although Lisgar remained a bachelor, he had a long affair with Phyllis Barnes (Mrs. Jack Barnes), with whom he had a daughter. Shirley, who was aware of her real father's identity, was adopted by Jack Barnes.

Like many others, Lisgar's life was affected by the Depression. He worked as a stockbroker and lived with his mother Mary Jane, at 6601 Maryland Drive in Los Angeles, until he died of alcoholism on January 20, 1941, just three days before his fortieth birthday. Lisgar was buried in the Rosedale Mausoleum in Los Angeles.

ORMONDE P. GRIER
1903–1964
Musician

The fourth child of Thomas Johnston and Mary Jane Grier, Ormonde Palethorpe was born in Lead, South Dakota on May 13, 1903. According to his sister Muddie, his given name came from that of an Irish racehorse; his father soon nicknamed him the "Prodigal Son." Ormonde was eleven years old when the Grier family moved from the small mining town of Lead to Los Angeles, California.

Strong-willed, quiet, and with a hooked nose (broken in football), he graduated from Harvard School in Los Angeles.

Following high school, Ormonde earned a living primarily as a musician. Although he could not read music, he was a gifted vocalist with perfect pitch who played the piano, violin, saxophone, and several other instruments.

From his late teens to his early thirties, Ormonde played with the "all college" Lake Arrowhead Orchestra that, in Los Angeles, was known as the Packard Six Aggregation. The other five players in the group included Don Parker, on piano; Mel Lemon, banjo; Shirley Monatt and Bud King, saxophones; and Stuart Peters, drums. The group appeared around Los Angeles, playing in movie theatres and once a month performing a program of dance melodies on the *Los Angeles Examiner*'s radio station, KFI. On summer evenings, the Lake Arrowhead Orchestra appeared in the pavilion of the village of Lake Arrowhead. They also performed in England and Europe. Some of the popular tunes that the musicians played and recorded were "I Can't Realize," "Hotsy Totsy," "Dreaming," and "Thelma."

During the Depression, Ormonde worked in a gas station, the only job available to him at the time. Then, the tall, rugged, and big-hearted young man fell in love with a wealthy divorcee named Muriel ("Patty") Patrick, who had two children from her marriage to Stanley Taylor—a son named Benjamin Franklin ("Bud"), born January 9, 1926, and a daughter named Joan, born July 31, 1927. As Muddie later recalled, Patty one day said to Ormonde, "Let's go to Daddy and tell him we want to get married and we can't, unless he promises to continue my allowance." Apparently, Ormonde won her father's approval, for the couple was soon married, and after the death of her father, Ormonde assisted in managing his wife's investments.

Ormonde adopted Bud and Joan, and son Peter was born on June 18, 1933. Tragically, Peter contracted viral pneumonia and died at age seventeen, and Patty, after a long bout with cancer, died in the 1950s.

Ormonde remarried, and, with his second wife Betty, he made several trips abroad. From the mid-1930s until his death, Ormonde was a partner and manager in Jans Quality Piston Company, a piston manufacturer in Los Angeles. He died of a heart attack on July 10, 1964 and was buried in the Westwood Memorial Park in Westwood, California.

Benjamin Grier (1926–)

Benjamin ("Bud") Franklin Taylor Grier and his wife Marilyn Steward live at 133 South June Street in Los Angeles. They have three daughters: Sarah, Catherine, and Cynthia.

Sarah married Abraham M. B. de Koning and has two children, Philippe (b. December 7, 1988) and Emily Martine (b. July 5, 1990). Cynthia (b. July 3, 1951) married Pat Capper Haden, a University of Southern California graduate and former quarterback of the Los Angeles Rams. They have four children: Natalie Kathleen (b. 1978), Ryan Steward (b. 1981), Katherine Driscoll (b. 1980), and Benjamin Taylor (b. 1983). Catherine, married to Stephen Warner Olsen, has two daughters—Kristen Katherine (b. 1984) and Brittney Cynthia (b. 1986).

Joan Grier Bird (1927–)

Joan Taylor Grier married twice. With her first husband, David Woodard Simpson, who died in 1971, she had two children—David (b. 1950) and Patricia Leigh (b. 1952). Patricia is married to Donald Scott McCormick and the mother of Matthew Joseph (b. 1979), Nicholas Simpson (b. 1979), and Christopher Paul (b. 1980). Today, Joan lives in Sunriver, Oregon with her second husband, Lawrence Lancashire Bird.

Thomas Johnston Grier, Jr., 1928

112

Sally Havens Grier, 1920

Sally Havens and her attendants at her wedding to
Thomas Johnston Grier, Jr., June 20, 1920
(*Courtesy of the California State Library*)

Evangeline Victoria (Grier) Nelson and daughter Evangeline Victoria ("Paddy") Banning, c. 1944
(*Courtesy of Victoria Grier Nelson*)

Thomas Johnston Grier 3d and Susan Jackson Grier, his first wife, c. 1948
(Courtesy of Victoria Grier Nelsen)

Victoria ("Muddie") Grier, c. 1901
(Courtesy of Victoria Grier Nelsen)

Ormonde Palethorpe Grier, c. 1906
(Courtesy of Victoria Grier Nelsen)

Victoria ("Muddie") Grier, c. 1912
(Courtesy of Victoria Grier Nelsen)

William P. Banning, Jr. at Culver Military
School, c. 1943
(Courtesy of Victoria Grier Nelsen)

Evangeline Victoria ("Paddy")
Banning, c. 1945
(Courtesy of Victoria Grier Nelsen)

Ede Mary Kristine Nelsen, c. 1956
(Courtesy of Victoria Grier Nelsen)

Private Thomas Johnstone ("T.J.")
Nelsen, U.S. Army, Green Berets,
Fort Bragg, Bennington, Georgia,
late 1950s
(Courtesy of Victoria Grier Nelsen)

Lisgar Patterson Grier, c. 1938
(Courtesy of Victoria Grier Nelsen)

T.J., Jr. and wife Sally with son Thomas Johnston Grier 3d, 1926

Frank Colton Havens (1848–1918), grandfather of
Sally Havens (Mrs. Thomas J. Grier, Jr.)

9

ALLIED FAMILIES
Ferrie/Christie, Havens, Banning, Hopper

MARGARET FERRIE
1891–1975

Margaret Eliza ("Madge") Ferrie was born in Glasgow, Scotland in 1891 to William and Mary Jane Palethorpe Ferrie.[1] After settling in Lead, South Dakota and becoming the town librarian, Madge's mother Mary Jane divorced Ferrie, a mining engineer. On August 8, 1896, she married Thomas Johnston Grier, superintendent of Lead's Homestake Mining Company. Madge and her brother James William Ferrie remained with their maternal Palethorpe grandparents in Glasgow, Scotland.

In 1908, sixteen-year-old Madge and her brother emigrated to the United States to join their mother and stepfather in Lead.

Although the environment of the bustling mining town differed greatly from that of their native Scotland, both Ferrie children responded well to life in Lead. Every July 4th, Madge, atop the sheriff's big black horse, led the Independence Day parade, dressed in white and carrying a silk American flag.

After graduating from Lead High School in 1910, Madge studied for three years at Columbia University in New York City, where she received her teacher's diploma.

When her stepfather died in 1914, Madge lived with her mother, brother, and four Grier siblings in their Los Angeles home. During this period, the Griers were guests of Phoebe Hearst (widow of U.S. Senator George Hearst) at her California homes "Hacienda del Pozo de Verona" in Pleasanton and "Wyntoon," her gothic-styled residence in McCloud near Mount Shasta.

During World War I, Madge was briefly engaged to Donald Hamilton McLaughlin, a geologist who later became president and chairman of the

---

1. The name "Eliza" was that of Margaret's great-grandmother Ferrie.

Homestake Mining Company.[2] However, when Madge finally married, it was to a fellow Scot, James Christie, with whom she had grown up in Glasgow.

Although they had not seen each other in some fifteen years, Madge and James occasionally corresponded when she lived in the American West and he, an attorney, moved to East Africa. Then, in 1924, James traveled to Los Angeles to see if Margaret were, in fact, "the ideal he had held in his heart." Apparently she, indeed, was, for they were married on October 7 of that year in her mother's Los Angeles home, at 1675 Buckingham Road. For their honeymoon, the Christies traveled to Washington, D.C. and New York, then sailed for Europe. There, they visited Scotland and Paris before journeying to their new home in Kenya (then known as British East Africa), where James served as the Queen's Counsel in Mombasa.[3]

The Christies had two children: Rachel Margaret Jane ("Jean") and James Carron ("Hamish"). Jean married Ian Mills and had three children—a daughter, Fiona, and two sons, John and Malcolm. The couple owned and ran Ibsley Manor Farm in Ibsley, Hants, England. Following Ian's death, Jean married Patrick John Gillies. Hamish and his wife Isobel, residents of Edinburgh, Scotland, had two children, James Grier and Janet.

James and Madge spent the rest of their lives in Kenya, except for a one-year period during World War II when, while visiting friends, she was stranded in Edinburgh. James died in the late 1960s; Madge died of a heart attack in Mombasa on August 2, 1975 and was buried there.

JAMES FERRIE
Orthodontist

James William Ferrie, the first child of Mary Jane Palethorpe and William Ferrie, was born in Glasgow, Scotland and lived there until a high school student. He then emigrated to the United States in 1908. There, he joined his mother and stepfather T.J. Grier in Lead, South Dakota. James became an orthodontist in San Jose, California. He and his wife had three daughters.

---

2.   Raised in Berkeley and an alumnus of the University of California, Donald H. McLaughlin earned both an M.A. and a Ph.D. from Harvard. He served as a professor in the Engineering School and the department of geology at Harvard from 1925 to 1941 and as a faculty member and dean of the College of Mining and College of Engineering at the University of California. His mother had been a friend of the Griers and of Phoebe Hearst.

3.   One of James Christie's ancestors owned Carron Iron Works in Scotland.

FRANK C. HAVENS
1848–1918
Transportation, Water, and Land Developer—Art Collector

T.J. Grier, Jr.'s wife Sally was the granddaughter of Frank Colton Havens, a prominent figure in the history of Oakland and Piedmont, California.

Frank Havens, born in Sag Harbor, New York on November 21, 1848, was the son of Wickham Sayre Havens and Sarah Darling. His early years reflected the seafaring pursuits of his father, a sea captain, and of most of his male ancestors. At age sixteen, Frank left home to become a cabin boy on a vessel sailing around Cape Horn to California. Following two years in Honolulu, Frank sailed to China, visiting Shanghai and other coastal port cities, where he worked on river boats which carried passengers and cargo into the interior of the country.

When he turned twenty-one, Frank crossed the Pacific again. Afterward, he settled in San Francisco and became, in succession, a banker, a member of the San Francisco Stock Exchange, a founder of three investment associations, and a real estate developer. It was in the latter field that young Havens made his fortune.

In partnership with F.M. Smith of Borax fame, Havens bought and developed thousands of acres in and adjacent to Oakland, California. The project was facilitated by his construction of an interurban transportation system, the Key Route, which came to include both the Claremont Hotel in Berkeley and the Key Route Inn in Oakland. Through his People's Water Company, Havens also developed Oakland's water system. By the early 1900s, he owned land and utilities worth $72 million.

Frank Havens was married twice. In 1873, he married Sadie Bell of Virginia City, Nevada. She died thirteen years later at the age of thirty-three, leaving Frank with four children: Wickham, Harold, and twin brothers Seyd and Paul. In 1893, Frank married Lila Mandana Rand, for whom he built "Wildwood Gardens," an East Indian mansion in Piedmont. This was especially fitting for Lila, a devotee of yoga who not only followed the precepts of leading Indian gurus but welcomed them to her lavish home.

The exquisite estate was modeled after a maharajah's palace that Frank Havens had seen on his Far Eastern travels. True to the style of the mountain palaces, the house was built on five levels, terraced down from the crest of the hill. Visitors entered by the upper floor, which had a Chinese temple hall in golden teakwood. Ming rugs, more than 300 years old, covered the floors. Reception rooms and tea rooms, decorated in the Chinese and Japanese manner with straw-matted floors and walls of sliding doors, surrounded the temple hall.

The Buddhist room was finished in gold leaf and lacquer and furnished with a Buddha made in the late 1600s, while the East Indian drawing room measured fifty-five feet by thirty-five feet and featured an arched fireplace.

The house was replete with teakwood and intricately carved panels that took East Indian and Japanese artisans years to complete. Many of the rooms were put up in sections and held together with wooden pegs.

While the house was the work of several architects and interior decorators, Bernard Maybeck was the principal, supervising professional. (Maybeck had gained renown as the architect of San Francisco's Palace of Fine Arts at the Panama-Pacific International Exposition of 1915.) "Wildwood" was completed about 1917, shortly before Frank Havens's death the following year.

In addition to his interest in the development of the Oakland and Piedmont areas, Frank was also devoted to books, poetry, and art. Indeed, he amassed a fine art collection for which he built a museum in Oakland.

Havens died at "Wildwood" on February 9, 1918 after breaking his hip in a fall at the front gate of the estate. Shortly thereafter, the City of Piedmont named its elementary school in his honor —the Frank C. Havens School.[4] Lila Havens lived on in "Wildwood" for many years and died on June 20, 1937.

Wickham Havens, one of Frank's sons and father-in-law of Thomas Johnston Grier, Jr., became a prominent real estate broker in Oakland, as did his brother Harold, in Berkeley. Another brother, Seyd Havens, lived in New York City for a time, then returned to California, where he operated a small food business. Married several times, Seyd and his last wife had four children: Florence, Wickham, Seyd, and Judy. His twin Paul lived in Oakland with his wife and son Roland. Roland Havens, his wife Adele, and their two sons live in Oakland.

PHINEAS BANNING
1830–1885
"Transportation King"

Evangeline Victoria ("Muddie") Grier's first husband, William Phineas

4.   Two Griers attended the Frank C. Havens School: Thomas Johnston Grier, Jr. (1926-1982) and William Milton Grier, Jr. (1928-).

Banning, was the youngest son of Joseph Brent Banning and a grandson of Phineas Banning, an astute businessman and developer in Wilmington, California, a suburb of Los Angeles.

Phineas Banning, born in 1830, was a young man of meager resources when he arrived in California in the 1850s. In time, however, he became a successful commodity broker, dealing in grain, flour, and lumber. Recognizing the increasing demand for commodities and the difficulties of off-loading ships at Wilmington's port, Phineas developed Wilmington harbor, as well as other businesses there. After building a rail system which connected the harbor with the Los Angeles market, he became known as the "Transportation King." Phineas Banning's first wife was Rebecca Sanford, born in 1837. They had eight children: Fanny A. (1854–1857); John Griffen (1856–1859); William (1856–1946); Joseph Brent (1861–1920); a fourth son whose name is unknown (1863–1863); Bessie (1865–1866); Hancock (1866–1925); and Vincent Edgar Griffith (1868–1868). In 1864, Phineas built a handsome two-story frame house in Wilmington for his wife and children, on an estate that also included three large barns.[5]

Following Rebecca's death in 1868, Phineas married May Hollister and had three children: Mary Hollister (1871–1953), Ellen (1874–1875), and Lucy Tichenor (1876–1927).

Phineas served in the California State Legislature and in the California National Guard, becoming a general—a title he assumed permanently. He died in 1885.

WILLIAM BANNING
1856–1946

Rancher, Stagecoach Collector

William Banning, the third child of Phineas and Rebecca, owned land near Walnut, California on which he had a large ranch; nearby, he had a second ranch on rented land. He had a marvelous collection of stage-coaches there, including a Concord coach made in Concord, New Hampshire. He was an expert stagecoach driver who could handle six horses with

---

5.   Completely restored and now a museum, the Banning residence in Wilmington, California is a Historical Landmark which, since the 1920s, has been owned by the City of Los Angeles. A restored barn on the property houses a collection of coaching vehicles.

William Phineas Banning, Jr. was an advisor on the restoration and oversaw the installation of an antique ornamental fence, which was made in New Orleans in the late 1800s.

absolute dexterity.

Known as Captain Banning, William commanded several ships that sailed around California, particularly on the Wilmington-Avalon route. He was a lifelong bachelor.

CYNTHIA AND STEPHEN GRIER HOPPER

Cynthia and Stephen Grier were Thomas Johnston Grier 3d's children, born to him and his second wife Nancy Bauer. When Nancy remarried, the children were adopted by her second husband, Jack Hopper.

Cynthia married Douglas Whitaker and has two sons, Michael Jack and Daniel Douglas. The Whitakers live at 909 North Benley Street, in Santa Ana, California.

Stephen Grier Hopper married Cheryl Douglas; they have two daughters, Teryl Jacqueline and Kaylie Dorothy, and live at 234 Delgado Road, San Clemente, California.

Frank C. Havens's home, "Wildwood," in Piedmont, California, modeled after an East Indian maharajah's palace on five levels, supervised by renowned architect Bernard Maybeck, and completed in 1917

Margaret E. ("Madge") Ferrie and Donald
Hamilton McLaughlin in northern California,
c. 1918 *(Courtesy of Victoria Grier Nelsen)*

Madge Ferrie at Pheobe Hearst's ranch "Hacienda" in
Pleasanton, California, c. 1916
(Courtesy of Victoria Grier Nelsen)

Hamish and Isobel Christie with Bill Grier, Vancouver, B.C., June 1978

Jean and Ian Mills at Madge Christie's home in Mombasa, July 1973

James and Margaret Christie in Mombasa, Kenya
(Courtesy of Victoria Grier Nelsen)

PART FOUR

WILLIAM JOHN GRIER
BRANCH

THE GRIER FAMILY

Genealogical Tree of William Milton Grier, Sr.

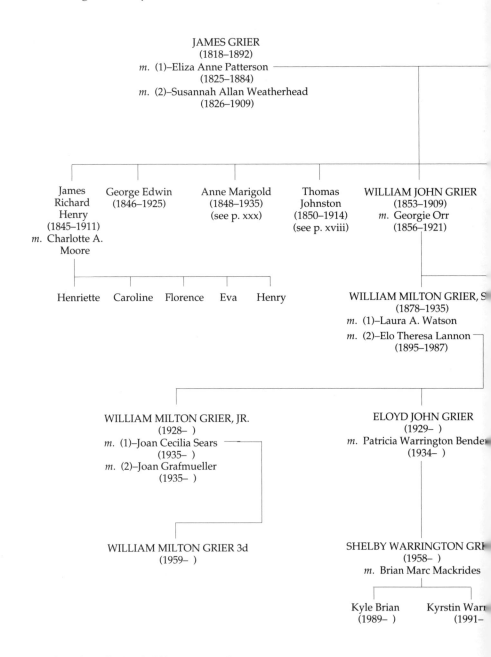

JAMES GRIER
(1818–1892)
m. (1)–Eliza Anne Patterson
(1825–1884)
m. (2)–Susannah Allan Weatherhead
(1826–1909)

| James Richard Henry (1845–1911) *m.* Charlotte A. Moore | George Edwin (1846–1925) | Anne Marigold (1848–1935) (see p. xxx) | Thomas Johnston (1850–1914) (see p. xviii) | WILLIAM JOHN GRIER (1853–1909) *m.* Georgie Orr (1856–1921) |

Henriette   Caroline   Florence   Eva   Henry

WILLIAM MILTON GRIER, S
(1878–1935)
m. (1)–Laura A. Watson
m. (2)–Elo Theresa Lannon
(1895–1987)

WILLIAM MILTON GRIER, JR.
(1928–)
m. (1)–Joan Cecilia Sears
(1935–)
m. (2)–Joan Grafmueller
(1935–)

ELOYD JOHN GRIER
(1929–)
m. Patricia Warrington Bende
(1934–)

WILLIAM MILTON GRIER 3d
(1959–)

SHELBY WARRINGTON GRI
(1958–)
m. Brian Marc Mackrides

Kyle Brian
(1989–)

Kyrstin Warr
(1991–

* *Name changed to Marigold in next generation.*
** *Daughter died in infancy.*

135

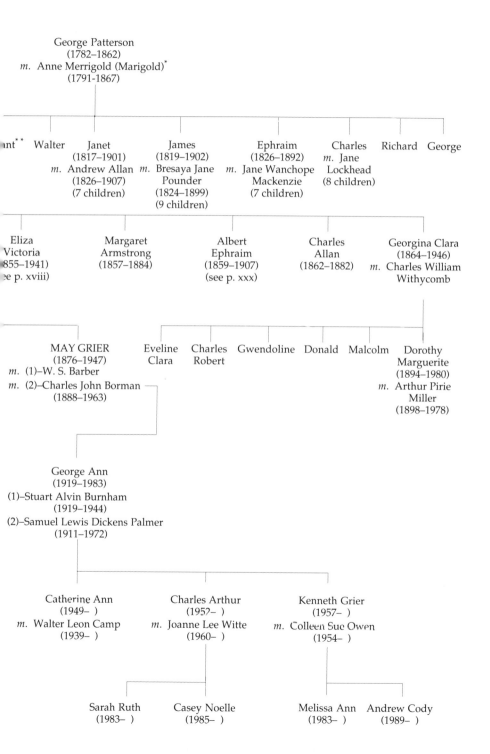

THE LANNON FAMILY

Genealogical Tree of Elo Lannon Grier's Paternal Branch

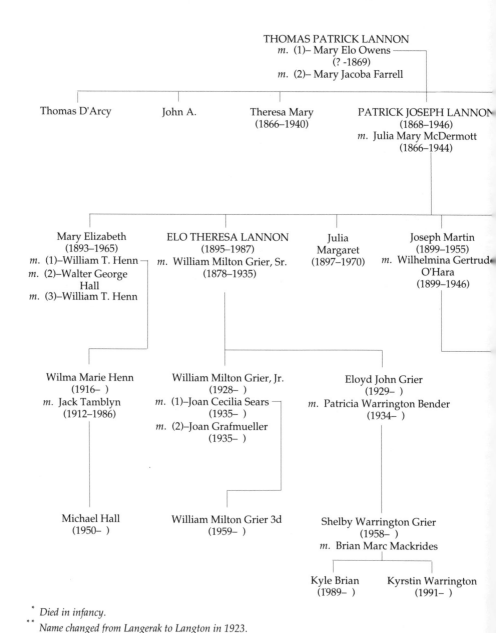

THOMAS PATRICK LANNON
m. (1)– Mary Elo Owens
(? -1869)
m. (2)– Mary Jacoba Farrell

Thomas D'Arcy   John A.   Theresa Mary
(1866–1940)

PATRICK JOSEPH LANNON
(1868–1946)
m. Julia Mary McDermott
(1866–1944)

Mary Elizabeth
(1893–1965)
m. (1)–William T. Henn
m. (2)–Walter George
Hall
m. (3)–William T. Henn

ELO THERESA LANNON
(1895–1987)
m. William Milton Grier, Sr.
(1878–1935)

Julia
Margaret
(1897–1970)

Joseph Martin
(1899–1955)
m. Wilhelmina Gertrude
O'Hara
(1899–1946)

Wilma Marie Henn
(1916–)
m. Jack Tamblyn
(1912–1986)

William Milton Grier, Jr.
(1928–)
m. (1)–Joan Cecilia Sears
(1935–)
m. (2)–Joan Grafmueller
(1935–)

Eloyd John Grier
(1929–)
m. Patricia Warrington Bender
(1934–)

Michael Hall
(1950–)

William Milton Grier 3d
(1959–)

Shelby Warrington Grier
(1958–)
m. Brian Marc Mackrides

Kyle Brian
(1989–)

Kyrstin Warrington
(1991–)

* *Died in infancy.*
** *Name changed from Langerak to Langton in 1923.*

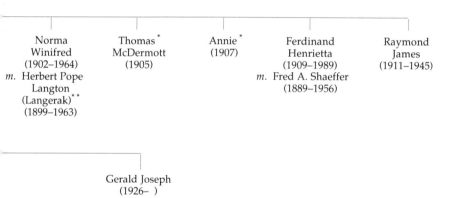

Matilda Ellen
(1869–1955)

Norma
Winifred
(1902–1964)
m. Herbert Pope
Langton
(Langerak)**
(1899–1963)

Thomas*
McDermott
(1905)

Annie*
(1907)

Ferdinand
Henrietta
(1909–1989)
m. Fred A. Shaeffer
(1889–1956)

Raymond
James
(1911–1945)

Gerald Joseph
(1926–)

THE MCDERMOTT FAMILY
Genealogical Tree of Elo Lannon Grier's Maternal Branch

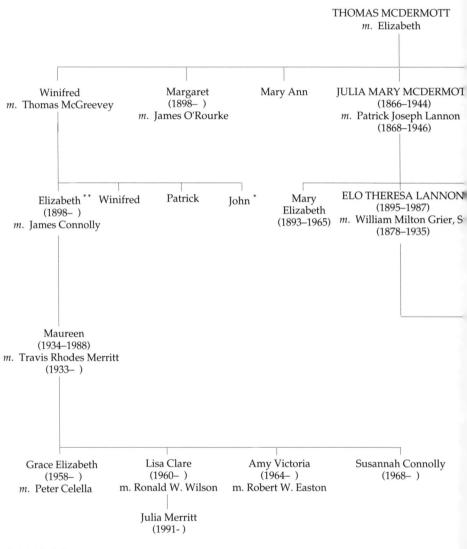

THOMAS MCDERMOTT
m. Elizabeth

Winifred	Margaret	Mary Ann	JULIA MARY MCDERMOT
m. Thomas McGreevey	(1898–)		(1866–1944)
	m. James O'Rourke		*m.* Patrick Joseph Lannon
			(1868–1946)

Elizabeth ** Winifred   Patrick   John *   Mary Elizabeth (1893–1965)   ELO THERESA LANNON (1895–1987)
(1898–)
m. James Connolly   *m.* William Milton Grier, S (1878–1935)

Maureen
(1934–1988)
m. Travis Rhodes Merritt
(1933–)

Grace Elizabeth	Lisa Clare	Amy Victoria	Susannah Connolly
(1958–)	(1960–)	(1964–)	(1968–)
m. Peter Celella	m. Ronald W. Wilson	m. Robert W. Easton	

Julia Merritt
(1991-)

* *Died in infancy.*
** *Raised by her mother's sister and brother-in-law,*
  Margaret McDermott and James O'Rourke, in Providence, Rhode Island.

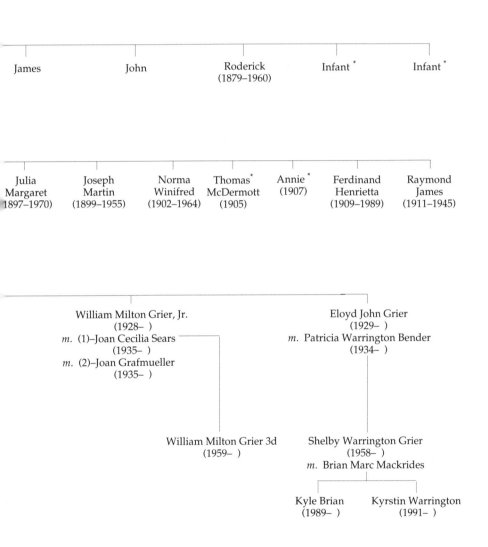

James   John   Roderick   Infant *   Infant *
(1879–1960)

Julia   Joseph   Norma   Thomas*   Annie *   Ferdinand   Raymond
Margaret   Martin   Winifred   McDermott   (1907)   Henrietta   James
1897–1970)   (1899–1955)   (1902–1964)   (1905)   (1909–1989)   (1911–1945)

William Milton Grier, Jr.   Eloyd John Grier
(1928–)   (1929–)
m. (1)–Joan Cecilia Sears   m. Patricia Warrington Bender
(1935–)   (1934–)
m. (2)–Joan Grafmueller
(1935–)

William Milton Grier 3d   Shelby Warrington Grier
(1959–)   (1958–)
m. Brian Marc Mackrides

Kyle Brian   Kyrstin Warrington
(1989–)   (1991–)

Cliff House, San Francisco, c. 1898
(Courtesy of the California Historical Society Library)

CHRONOLOGY OF WILLIAM JOHN GRIER

1853	Born in Iroquois, Upper Canada on June 19
1858–1870	Attends Iroquois public schools; works in father's post office
1870	Graduates from Iroquois High School; moves to Montreal to work as telegrapher for Montreal Telegraph Company
1872	Emigrates to the American West; works as telegrapher with Western Union in Denver, Colorado and Corinne and Salt Lake City, Utah
1875	Marries Georgie Orr in Salt Lake City
1876	Daughter, May, born in Salt Lake City
1878	Moves to San Francisco; continues with Western Union; son, William Milton, born in San Francisco on September 24
1880	Moves to Napa, California for eight months; returns to San Francisco as supervisor of telegraphers with Central Pacific Railroad
1888	Joins Palermo Land and Water Company (PL&W) as bookkeeper and land manager; moves to Palermo, California
1891	Becomes superintendent of George Hearst's citrus ranch in Palermo, while continuing with PL&W
1909	Retires and moves to Oakland, California; dies there on June 25

William John Grier (1853–1909)

10

WILLIAM JOHN GRIER
1853–1909
Land Manager

The life and career of William John ("W.J.") Grier reflected the increasing mobility of the people of his era. Seeking greater opportunities than were available in his native Canada, he emigrated to the American West in early 1872, settling first in Colorado, then moving to Utah and finally to California. Beginning as a telegrapher, he later worked in land management, development, and sales and supervised George Hearst's 225-acre fruit ranch in Palermo, California.

EARLY YEARS

Born in Iroquois, Ontario on June 19, 1853, William John was 5'8" tall, lean, fair, and blue-eyed. After graduating at age seventeen from Iroquois High School, he joined his older brother, Thomas Johnston ("T.J."), in Montreal where they worked as telegraphers for the Montreal Telegraph Company. Two years later, they emigrated to the United States via Detroit, carrying with them the Montreal experience and the skills honed under James Grier, their postmaster father, in Iroquois.

In Denver, Colorado, William John and T.J. worked briefly as telegraphers in the downtown Western Union office before they moved to the company's branch in Corinne, Utah. There, they were near their sister Annie Grier Fell and brother-in-law Gilbert, who lived in Ogden. In 1874, the brothers transferred to the Western Union office in Salt Lake City, a town of 26,000, where T.J. became manager.

MARRIAGE

In 1875, William John married Georgie Orr in Salt Lake City; T.J. was his best man. Georgie, born in Kansas City, Missouri on August 5, 1856, was the daughter of Joseph Milton Orr and Martha H. Whitney, who had migrated to Utah in the early 1870s.[1]

The Griers' first child, May, was born in Salt Lake City in 1876. It was the nation's centennial year when the United States had a population of forty million and just thirty-eight stars flew on its flag.

Two years later, the brothers parted. T.J. headed east to the Black Hills of the Dakota Territory, joining Homestake Mining Company as a book-keeper and telegrapher in Lead. William John moved west: He, Georgie, daughter May, and in-laws Joseph and Martha Orr traveled by train from Salt Lake City, arriving in Oakland, California in the spring of 1878. Sea gulls wheeled about the deck as they boarded the ferry for the short trip across San Francisco Bay, where three-masted schooners dotted the harbor.

SAN FRANCISCO

In San Francisco, the family lived at 417 Mason Street and William John continued with Western Union Telegraph Company. It was there that son William Milton was born on September 24, 1878. Two years later, William John was reassigned by his firm, and the young family lived in Napa, California for a few months in 1880. Returning to San Francisco, he became supervisor of telegraphers with Central Pacific Railroad, at Third and Townsend Streets.

The contrast between life in Salt Lake City and that in San Francisco during this period could not have been greater. First built on the gold of the Sierra Nevada, then the silver and gold of the Comstock Lode, San Francisco attracted people from around the world after the Gold Rush of 1849. According to one journalist, the city was "spiced with the seductive scent of sin," [2] hardly a characteristic of the Mormon capital of Utah. In Bret Harte's words, San Francisco was "a city indifferent to fate, where anything is tolerated but meanness." [3]

San Francisco was the financial capital of the West at the time of Grier's arrival. A small Mexican village in the late 1840s, it had become, by the

---

1.   Joseph Milton Orr was born in Ohio in 1829; Martha Whitney, in Illinois in 1837. Georgie's paternal grandfather was from Kentucky, while her paternal grandmother was from New York. Her maternal grandfather was born in Vermont, and her grandmother, in Kentucky.

2.   *Los Angeles Times*, 13 February 1883.

3.   Quoted in *Los Angeles Times*, 13 February 1883.

1870s, one of the major cities in the United States. Unlike the typical frontier town, which developed gradually from an agricultural base, San Francisco was almost immediately a center of commerce, transportation, communication, and finance that grew with lightning speed.

William John and his family entertained visiting relatives and friends at the Palace Hotel, which had opened in 1875. The hotel's carriage entrance, the Grand Court, was paved with marble and encircled by layer upon layer of balconies rising from a garden of lemon, orange, and lime trees; light poured in through the opaque-glass rotunda.[4] William John's brother T.J. stayed here when in town on Homestake Mining business.

The Griers worshipped at Trinity Church, the oldest Episcopal church on the Pacific Coast, which was located at Post and Powell Streets, and at Grace Church, at California and Stockton Streets.

PALERMO LAND AND WATER COMPANY

Early in 1888, after William John had worked for seven years with Central Pacific Railroad Company, he resigned as supervisor of telegraphers and accepted a bookkeeping and land management position with the Palermo Land and Water Company (PL&W). The family then relocated to Palermo, some 160 miles northeast of San Francisco in the foothills of the Sierra Nevada in Butte County.

First surveyed in 1865, Palermo had long been an agricultural area, where cattle raising was the principal industry and farmers experimented in growing cotton. In 1870, sheepherding was introduced and became the dominant activity until the fall of 1887 when the PL&W was formed. By 1892, cattle, sheep, and grain production had declined dramatically, while 1,600 acres had been planted with oranges, olives, figs, prunes, pears, peaches, apricots, and grapes.

The large northern California citrus fairs of that day were concentrated in the Palermo area. The 1877 fair, for example, was held in Oroville, the old gold mining town five miles north of Palermo, the county seat of Butte County. When it became clear that oranges and olives could be successfully grown in northern California, this land, which was cheaper than that in southern California, was in great demand. As a resort and agricultural community, Palermo had three factors in its favor: mild winter temperatures, excellent rail connections (Northern Railroad line stop), and abun-

---

4.   The first electric light in San Francisco was placed in the courtyard of the Palace Hotel in 1878, the year of William Milton Grier's birth.

dant water.

The PL&W was formed by the firm of Perkins and Wise, owners of the Palermo Ditch and 5,000 Palermo acres. The company quickly drew up a detailed map of the area, dividing land into house lots and orchards. Streets and avenues were planned, and land was set aside for a school, park, hotel, railroad depot, and businesses. The Palermo Citrus Colony was incorporated on January 7, 1888, billing itself as the "Riverside of the North." Lots of five and ten acres were offered for sale, houses were built, and trees were planted.

In its first year, Palermo grew by leaps and bounds. In addition to its commercial attraction, the town was also becoming a health and pleasure resort for tourists. In twelve months, twenty-three buildings were completed, one of which was the school attended by May and Milt Grier.

In 1888, a San Francisco realty firm, McAfee Brothers, began promoting the community via a special first-class excursion train which made a round-trip between San Francisco and Palermo for a cost of three dollars. William John and his family were among some 700 passengers on the inaugural ride on May 30.

In an article published in the October 17, 1890 edition of Palermo's frontier newspaper, the *Progress*, Frank Rutherford described the town's dramatic changes:

> Could one of our citizens of Palermo have stood in this place forty-one years ago, he would have seen in the north the same mountain ranges, in the south and west the same open plains, with the blue Coast Range and the rugged Buttes in the background....He would have seen a band of startled antelope galloping across the prairie or have been greeted by the howl of a coyote, announcing the friendly shades of evening had once more arrived and his predatory raid on his long-eared neighbor was ready to begin, or perhaps he might have seen a red man with his long pole threshing, from the oaks, acorns which he hulled, dried, and placed away for winter store, while his dusky squaw swept the grass with her willow basket, greeting with a glad heart, what is today painful to the ear of the farmer and fruit grower, the snap of the grass-hoppers wing....[By mid-year of 1888] all at once a transformation began and surveyors with their assistants began to wander about and drive down little white stakes seemingly without order....The winter and spring of 1889 developed livelier times than this district ever saw, and clearing, grading avenues, building fences and ditches furnished occupation for upwards of 300 men. Improvements of a permanent character grew rapidly and constantly and many small dwellings were scattered over the colony in all directions.[5]

---

5.   Frank Rutherford, "Palermo Chronicles," from the *Palermo Progress*, 17 October 1890, reprinted in *Diggin's*, Butte County Historical Society, Inc., Oroville, California, Vol. 18, No. 3, Fall Edition, 1974, pp. 4-8.

Palermo land sold rapidly at $75 and $100 per acre, attracting many wealthy investors. Among them was William John's brother T.J., then superintendent of the Homestake Mining Company in Lead, South Dakota. He purchased a little more than twenty acres on March 22, 1888[6] and built a magnificent home on his ten lots. George Hearst, U.S. senator from California and one of the three owners of the Homestake Mining Company, acquired 700 acres.

When William John and his family moved to Palermo in the summer of 1888, evidence of a boom was everywhere. The Villa Hotel had been completed and was open for business; the PL&W had built a large barn, stables, and several other dwellings; and T.J. Grier's residence, then the most costly structure in town, was finished.

Although only in his first year in Palermo, William John had primary responsibilities as bookkeeper; he also administered the sale of the PL&W's fruit crops. Soon, he acquired and planted land of his own, and his holdings were increased on May 1, 1891 when T.J. sold him twenty acres for $1.

LATER YEARS

After George Hearst's death on February 28, 1891, William John became superintendent of the Hearst estate's 225-acre citrus ranch in Palermo. In 1909, when smoke inhalation from a fire affected his lungs and health, he retired, and he and Georgie moved to 1414 21st Avenue in Oakland, California, near her younger sister, Mattie Orr Barber and husband Robert, who lived at Eighth and Warren Streets. William John died in Oakland of a heart attack on June 25, 1909. His ashes were placed in the Oakland Columbarium.

Georgie lived in their home until she died on October 23, 1921 of uremia following an operation for uterine cancer at Providence Hospital in Oakland. Her ashes were placed beside those of her husband.

6.   The acreage was in Palermo's subdivision one, block seventy-six, consisting of ten lots: 1,000 feet on Lloyd's Avenue and 1,040 feet on Messina Avenue.

Above left: Georgie Orr in
Salt Lake City, 1875

Above right: Martha H. Whitney,
(Mrs. Joseph Milton Orr), c. 1872

Left: Georgie Orr Grier
(Mrs. William John Grier)
in San Francisco, c. 1880s

Palace Hotel, San Francisco, c. 1900
(Courtesy of the California Historical Society Library)

The interior court of the Palace Hotel, c. 1880s
(Courtesy of the California Historical Society Library)

Palermo, California
Church, 1904, *left*,
and *below*, Palermo
Colony, c. 1888
(John H. Nopel Collection)

W.M. ("Milt") and May Grier in an amateur theatrical
production, 1890s

153

In Palermo, California—*right:* William John
Grier, c. 1900; *below:* George and Phoebe
Hearst's home, 1897 (*John H. Nopel Collection*);
bottom: William John and Georgie Grier
outside their home, c. 1900

154

William John and Georgie, and W. M. ("Milt") Grier at their home in Palermo, California, c. 1898 (Milt is in his California U.S. Volunteers blue uniform).

Georgie Grier with her daughter May Grier Borman and granddaughter
George Ann in Oakland, California, c. 1920

CHRONOLOGY OF MAY GRIER BORMAN

1876	Born in Salt Lake City
1878	Moves to San Francisco; brother, William M. Grier, born on September 24
1880	Lives in Napa, California for eight months
1881	Returns to San Francisco; attends Lincoln School
1888	Moves to Palermo, California
1893	Graduates from Oroville Union High School
1900	Returns to San Francisco; works in retailing and markets own artwork
early 1900s	Marries William S. Barber; first child is born, but dies in infancy; husband dies; works for George W. Caswell Company in San Francisco; forms Thayer and Barber
1915	Visits Panama-Pacific International Exhibition
1917	Marries Charles J. Borman; moves to Detroit
1919	Daughter, George Ann, born in Detroit on January 24
1920	Moves to Oakland, California
1921	Mother, Georgie Orr Grier, dies on October 23; moves to San Francisco
1921–1947	Lives in San Francisco as homemaker; member of San Francisco Garden Club
1947	Dies in San Francisco on March 21

May Grier Borman, c. 1940

11

MAY GRIER BORMAN
1876–1947

Artist, Businesswoman

The first child of William John and Georgie Orr Grier, May Grier was born in Salt Lake City, Utah in 1876, the nation's centennial. Two years later, the young family moved to San Francisco, where her father was a telegrapher at Western Union's office on Montgomery Street. Except for a few months in Napa, California (1880), the Griers lived in San Francisco for nearly ten years. May's younger brother, William Milton ("Milt"), was born there on September 24, 1878.

SAN FRANCISCO YEARS

In the 1880s, when William John worked as a supervisor of telegraphers for the Central Pacific Railroad Company, young May and Milt attended the Lincoln School on Fifth Street and worshipped with their parents at both Trinity Church and Grace Church.

During these years, May, always atuned to nature and art, was stimulated by the beauty of San Francisco. She enjoyed climbing the city's steep hills with her parents, especially Telegraph, Russian, or Nob Hills. There, she could see that San Francisco was almost an island, surrounded by the Pacific Ocean on the west, San Francisco Bay on the east, and the Golden Gate Straits on the north.

For May and Milt, San Francisco was like a telescope to the entire world. Atop Telegraph Hill, they could watch schooners sailing away to distant places and many-masted clipper ships arriving with cargo from the East Coast or the Orient.

The city was especially picturesque during those Victorian years. Gas lights, lit each night by lamplighters, gave suffused illumination at dusk along the many undulating hills, and fog rolling in from the Bay added to San Francisco's many moods. In this colorful environment, May's talent for landscape and still-life painting and illustration was further nurtured by both her mother and grandmother, Martha Whitney Orr.

She had begun drawing and painting, gardening and sewing at an early age and continued these interests when her family moved to Palermo, California in 1888, after her father joined the Palermo Land and Water Company (PL&W) as a bookkeeper and land manager. May attended Palermo's public schools and received her diploma from Oroville Union High School in 1893, at seventeen.

She and her brother were devoted to each other all their lives. As her maternal grandparents, the Joseph Milton Orrs, lived near the Griers' homes in Salt Lake City, San Francisco, and Napa, May in effect grew up with her aunt Mattie, her mother's younger sister, who was two years May's junior. They attended the same schools in San Francisco and Palermo and remained close throughout adulthood.

As a young woman, May was slim, blond, blue-eyed, and of medium build. She was artistic and adventuresome, with a self-effacing humor and great charm, as well as outgoing, resourceful, affectionate, and resilient.

When in her twenties, May returned to San Francisco and worked as a china decorator for the George W. Caswell Company, continued to paint still-lifes and landscapes, and frequented the city's art galleries and museums. She also married William S. Barber, whom she had met through her aunt Mattie.[1] Tragically, the couple's only child died in infancy, and soon after, Barber himself died, leaving her a young widow.

Then, returning to business, she and Flora Thayer formed Thayer and Barber, a beauty salon on Kearny Street near the city's financial district and Union Square,[2] which they successfully operated for several years.

In 1915, May often visited San Francisco's world's fair, the Panama-Pacific International Exposition, whose exhibits, art, architecture, and gardens fascinated her. She and her family—mother Georgie, brother Milt, sister-in-law Laura, aunt Mattie, aunt and uncle Anne and Gilbert Fell—celebrated a festive July Fourth there. They were enchanted with architect Bernard Maybeck's Palace of Fine Arts; the Jeweled City, a walled enclave of palaces with an arcaded and colonnaded courtyard; and the Tower of Jewels, a structure with 100,000 free-swinging lights.

---

1. Mattie, first married to Robert J. Barber (the brother of May's husband), was also widowed early. With her second husband, Edward Culberson, she had two children, Edward and Gladys.

2. Some of May's earlier San Francisco residences were: 427 Mississippi, in 1907; 306 Munich Street, in 1908; 391 Valencia Street, in 1909; and 905 I Street, in 1910. Flora Thayer lived in San Francisco at 1172 Ellis Street and, later, at 1403 Octavia Street.

MARRIAGE AND FAMILY

During World War I, May married Charles John ("C.J.") Borman, twelve years her junior, whom she met at a dance in San Francisco.[3] For a few years, they lived at 361 1/2 Hamilton Avenue in Detroit, Michigan, where Charles worked as an automotive trimmer. The couple's only child, a daughter named George Ann, was born there in Good Samaritan Hospital on January 24, 1919.

In 1920, the Bormans moved to Oakland, California, living near May's mother Georgie until her death on October 23, 1921. They then moved to San Francisco, where Charlie became a successful independent businessman through his firm Borman and Company.[4] Charlie, who had a lifelong interest in automotive design, eagerly followed the new model and engineering changes in trade journals and through his friends in the dealerships near his shop. His firm designed and built "autobeds," reupholstered automobiles, and recovered convertibles. The autobed concept—Charlie's own—provided a double-bed extension from the rear seat into the trunk of a four-door sedan. Another innovation was a convenient dressing area addition—a folding, hinged wooden frame with canvas that formed a tent between the opened front and rear passenger doors.

Charlie also designed and built Art Deco club chairs and sofas. For his daughter George Ann and nephews Bill and Eloyd Grier he built child-sized upholstered armchairs which they used through their early years.

HOME NEAR THE PACIFIC

In 1922, the Bormans bought a two-story, white-stucco house in San Francisco. A garage-basement occupied the street level; the living area on the second floor was reached by an exterior brick staircase. Located at 818 41st Avenue, between Fulton and Cabrillo Streets, the house was a block from Golden Gate Park and eight downhill blocks from the Pacific Ocean.

It was furnished in contemporary and period pieces. The living room, with a three-windowed bay, fireplace, and bookshelves, had a large French

---

3.   Charles Borman was born in Seymour, Indiana in 1888, the son of Henry ("Harry") William and Louise Raehm Borman. He had younger twin brothers, Earl and Elmer.

Earl and his wife lived in Los Angeles; Elmer lived in Cincinnati, Ohio. Earl died in 1976 at age eighty-five, outliving his wife by three years and his twin by thirty-eight years.

4.   Charles Borman's business partnerships in San Francisco included: Borman & Dahneke (Harry L.), 1656 Pine Street (1920s–1930s); Borman & Decker (Elmer), 1355 Bush Street (1931–1933); and Borman & Company, 1355 Bush Street (1934–1950s).

tapestry hung on one wall. The dining room had a Chinese rug and English furniture (wedding gifts from May's brother Milt). Their bedroom had a white-stained oak Victorian set (inherited from her parents, William John and Georgie Grier). Next to the kitchen and breakfast room was a sunroom that faced east and overlooked the flower garden.

An interior staircase led to the garden which was rectangular-shaped and enclosed by a weathered wooden fence. It had narrow pink cement walks, two goldfish ponds (built by Charlie), a rough-hewn cedar log gazebo to the rear, a birdhouse atop a tall post in the center, and, under the cantilevered sunroom, a sitting area.

Sam and Amelia Leavitt and their daughter Janet were the Bormans' neighbors on the south. (Amelia and May, both ardent gardeners, often talked over the fence.) Other neighbors were Roy and Ruth Binns and their son Billy and daughter Gloria; Gerrit and Vera Harder and their son Duane; the Hoovers; Mrs. Anna J. Jorgens, an interior designer whose studio was in her basement; and Howard and Ethel Hickey.[5]

Whiskers, the Bormans' affectionate, liver-colored Irish fox terrier, enlivened their home and camping trips.

FAMILY LIFE

Following their marriage, May withdrew from outside employment and became a full-time homemaker. She was also a dedicated member and officer of the San Francisco Garden Club, participating in its activities and shows.

After breakfast and tidying up, May, in fair weather, would don her green visor and tend her flower garden, or cut and arrange flowers for her home. Between chores, she listened to two morning radio serials—"Helen Trent" and "The Goldbergs." In mid-afternoon, she shopped at nearby greengrocers, bakeries, and meat and fish markets on Balboa Street. Several times a week she went downtown on business or to lunch with friends or her daughter. She kept both her family's and her husband's business books and managed their accounts at Bank of America's headquarters at 1 Powell Street and the branch on Balboa Street near her home.

After starting dinner and awaiting Charlie's return from work, May sometimes played solitaire, a game that totally held her attention, at the

---

5.   In the mid-1920s, May introduced her brother to Mrs. Jorgens, a neighbor at 884 41st Avenue, who decorated Milt's home in Piedmont, California, as well as his yacht, ELOGRIER.

dining room table, analyzing her cards and moves.

In the evening, they read the San Francisco *Call Bulletin* and publications on art, gardening, wildlife, and sports. Before dinner, Charlie worked the newspaper's crossword puzzle. They also played cards and listened to favorite radio programs—the Jack Benny, Bob Hope, Walter Winchell, and Fred Allen shows; "Amos and Andy"; "Abbott and Costello"; "Kay Kyser's Kollege of Musical Knowledge"; "Gangbusters"; "Lucky Strike Hit Parade"; "I Love a Mystery"; and Joe Louis's prize fights.

Charlie followed the baseball fortunes of the Detroit Tigers, Cincinnati Reds, and San Francisco Seals, and occasionally attended games. An avid fly-fisherman and camper, he found adventure and solace in being in the wilderness near lakes and streams. In the off-season, he honed his fly-casting skills at a club in Golden Gate Park, tied flies, and planned future trips. Although Charlie smoked a pack of cigarettes a day, both he and his wife enjoyed good health and led active lives. May, who never drove a car, liked to walk and ride streetcars, trains, and ferryboats.

Following her brother's 1927 marriage to Elo Lannon and the birth of his sons Bill and Eloyd, May, Charlie, and George Ann were frequent guests at the Grier home in Piedmont and aboard Milt's yacht, *ELOGRIER*, cruising along the coast, San Francisco Bay, and Sacramento River.   After Milt's death in 1935, May and Charlie included Elo and the boys in their holiday celebrations and cared for Bill and Eloyd in their home during school vacations.

May adored her nephews, as they did their beloved aunt. She warmly greeted them with embraces, hugs, and kisses. She delighted in taking them on picnics and outings about the city, opening its beauty and magic to them, as her mother and father had done for her and Milt in the 1880s. When traveling with them by ferryboat, May always had a bag of bread crumbs which she and the boys gleefully threw to the sea gulls.

The Bormans traveled widely by automobile in the U.S., visiting Charlie's family—cousin Helen and her husband Theodore Hansard in North Hollywood, where Helen was a set designer for Republic Studios; brother Earl in Los Angeles; brother Elmer, his wife Minnie, and sons Bobby and Harold in Cincinnati. In summer , they camped and fished in northern California and Yosemite National Park and drove to Detroit biannually to buy new-model cars.

May, suffering from arteriosclerosis, was under her doctor's care from 1945 until her death from a heart attack at her home on the evening of March 21, 1947. Following her funeral in San Francisco, she was cremated and her ashes were placed near those of her brother, father, and mother at the

Columbarium at 4401 Howe Street in Oakland.[6]

Afterward, Charlie's brother Elmer and his family moved to San Francisco, living with him and helping him in his business for a while before buying their own homes and continuing their careers. Charlie died in 1963; his ashes are also in the Columbarium in Oakland.

---

6.   May's physician was Dr. C.P. Thompson, at 2253 Clement Street in San Francisco.

May in Golden Gate Park,
San Francisco, c. 1916

May, George Ann, Charlie, and Grandmother Borman in the Upper Mariposa
Grove of Yosemite National Park, by the famous Wawona Tunnel Tree, 1927.
The tunnel was cut in 1881 as a tourist attraction and stood for 88 summers. The
tree itself was about 2,100 years old, 234 feet high, and 26 feet in diameter at the
base. It fell during the severe winter of 1968-1969.

May Grier Borman at Treasure Island (Golden Gate International Exposition), San Francisco, 1939—*at left*, with her aunt Mattie Orr Barber, and *below*, with her nephews, Eloyd and Bill

Left: Helen Borman (Mrs. Theodore Hansard, set designer for Republic Pictures) and Bill Grier, in the May Grier Borman home, San Francisco, c. 1942

Below: The Bormans' pet "Whiskers" on the deck of the *ELOGRIER* , c. 1929

CHRONOLOGY OF GEORGE ANN BORMAN PALMER

1919	Born in Detroit, Michigan on January 24
1921	Moves with family to San Francisco, California
1925–1931	Attends Lafayette Elementary School in San Francisco
1934	Graduates from Presidio Junior High School in San Francisco
1937	Graduates from Lux School in San Francisco
1937–1938	Attends San Francisco State College
1938	Works in an import office in San Francisco
1940	Joins D.C. Heath & Company, in San Francisco, as a secretary and bookkeeper
1942	Marries Stuart Alvin Burnham on April 11 in Reno, Nevada
1944	Husband dies in San Francisco
1946	Marries Samuel Lewis Dickens Palmer in Reno, Nevada; lives in San Francisco
1947	Moves to Hayward, California
late 1940s	Manages family business, "Palmer's" drug and variety store, with husband in Hayward, California
1949	Daughter, Catherine Ann, born on October 15 in Hayward
1952	Son, Charles Arthur, born on May 28 in Hayward
mid-1950s	Moves to Berkeley, California and opens second store with husband near University of California campus

1957	Son, Kenneth Grier, born on January 26 in Berkeley
mid-1960s	Moves with family to Alamo, California
1972	Husband dies in Alamo in September; moves to Danville, California
1977	Buys home in St. Helena, California; continues to manage "Palmer's"
1979	Sells business and travels abroad
1983	First grandchild, Melissa Ann Palmer, born on May 9; after five-year illness, George Ann dies in Napa, California on July 25

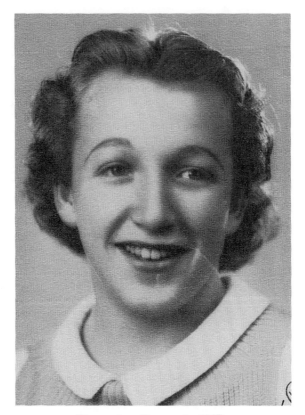

George Ann Borman in 1937

12

GEORGE ANN BORMAN PALMER
1919–1983

Pianist, Manager

George Ann, the only child of May Grier and her husband Charles J. Borman, was born on January 24, 1919 in the Good Samaritan Hospital in Detroit, Michigan. Like her mother, she was raised and educated in San Francisco. (See Part Four: 11)

After a brief stay in Oakland following the death of her maternal grandmother, Georgie Orr Grier, on October 23, 1921, George Ann and her family moved to a house at 818 41st Avenue in San Francisco, near Golden Gate Park and the Pacific Ocean. (This house would be the family home for over thirty years. After May suffered a fatal heart attack at home in 1947, Charles continued to live there until the 1950s.) Her room was furnished in white contemporary pieces accented by Oriental rugs; her walls were covered with mementos, photos, and a red-lettered sign reading "Hi Toots!" In the adjacent sunroom, she played the piano.

George Ann was shapely, lithe, fair, pretty, and of medium height with blue-gray eyes. Vivacious, bright, and humorous, she was a gifted musician and athlete. Growing into her teens a tomboy, she reveled in spirited roughhousing, fence-climbing, rollerskating, and outdoor sports.

SCHOOL YEARS, 1925–1937

A good student, she graduated from two public schools (Lafayette Elementary in 1931 and Presidio Junior High in 1934) and the private Lux School for girls in 1937, before completing a year at San Francisco State College (then located at 124 Buchanan Street) from 1937–1938.[1]

---

1. Lux School, founded in 1913, was privately endowed by Miranda Lux. Phoebe Hearst was an early Lux trustee. Located at 2450 17th Street in San Francisco, Lux was later consolidated with another institution, renamed Lick-Wilmerding High School, and privately endowed by James Lick and Jillis Wilmerding. It was located at 2250 17th Street. The school's three bene-

George Ann was a member of the Presidio Junior High School Glee Club and played the piano in the school orchestra and in its spring 1934 one-act operetta, "The Treasure Chest," and the play, "Mr. Dooley, Junior."

At home, George Ann played popular music on the piano. Her cousins Bill and Eloyd recall joyous singing sessions: Standing on each side of her and peering over her shoulders at the lyrics, they sang the songs of Berlin, Gershwin, Porter, Hart, and others. Though some melodies of that time were trite and trivial, many have proved durable, retaining their beauty, wit, and charm—"Beyond the Blue Horizon," "I'm Confessin' (That I Love You)," "Let's Fall in Love," "Lullaby of Broadway," "Pennies from Heaven," "Blue Hawaii," "Sweet Leilani," "My Heart Is Taking Lessons," "Easter Parade," and "White Christmas."

An all-around athlete, George Ann played on intramural basketball, volleyball, and baseball teams. She also starred on the championship kickball and volleyball teams and served on the Lux School Athletic Association Board of Control in 1935. She swam each Wednesday afternoon at the YWCA and participated in the 1937 mid-term carnival, with its relay, balloon, and pigeon races. She also organized and participated in the Lux Athletic Association's hiking party on June 20, 1936. For that occasion, the group boarded a bus at the Western Women's Club in San Francisco, then rode a ferryboat to Sausalito and proceeded to Muir Woods for a day of hiking and picnicking among the redwoods.

During these early years, she was nicknamed "Jo-Jo," according to the Presidio Junior High yearbook, *The Panther*, and her ambition was to become a librarian.

From her mother, she learned to be a gracious hostess, an adept seamstress and cook; from her father, she learned an appreciation of nature, the wilderness, and wildlife. After her Lux graduation, he let her drive his second car, which he acquired from an owner in financial distress—a sleek, dark green Pierce Arrow convertible sedan.

SCHOOL LEADER

Two of her closest school friends were Betty ("Bets") Calhoun and Virginia ("Ginger") Klute. George Ann and Ginger, who lived nearby at 682

---

factors wished to integrate book knowledge with what Lick called "the practical arts of life," to train young women in marketable skills, and to help them become "modern homemakers." George Ann also took college preparatory courses at Lick-Wilmerding on Tuesday and Thursday afternoons from 1934–1937.

39th Avenue, remained best friends through their years together at Lafayette, Presidio, and Lux Schools.

Another classmate was Judy Turner, better known in films by the name
she would adopt years later—Lana Turner. Judy attended Presidio Junior
High after being expelled from a nearby Catholic school, Visitacion.

George Ann attended Lux School from 1934 to 1937. Elected student
body president in the fall of 1936, she presided over the party in Merrill Hall
honoring George A. Merrill's seventieth birthday on September 9, 1936.
(Merrill had been the director of Lux, Wilmerding, and Lick Schools since
their inception.) Ginger succeeded George Ann as student body president
in the spring of 1937, while George Ann was elected secretary for the same
term. Another close friend, Carmen Aquado, was an artist on the staff of the
student yearbook, *L.W.L. Life.*

COLLEGE AND CAREER

After completing two semesters at San Francisco State College in 1937
and 1938, George Ann entered the business world. In her first position, she
helped manage a one-man import office near the San Francisco Civic
Center. In 1940, she accepted a secretarial and bookkeeping position with
the San Francisco office of D.C. Heath & Company, educational publishers,
at 182 Second Street (second floor). During the workweek, George Ann
would occasionally lunch with her mother and friends at downtown
restaurants.

In 1941, George Ann took a short leave of absence from her job to join
her parents on an automobile trip east. They stopped in Salt Lake City,
where her mother May had been born in 1876; toured Yellowstone National
Park in Wyoming and Rocky Mountain National Park in Colorado; and
visited Seymour, Indiana, where Charlie was born on January 28, 1888.
After buying a 1942 Dodge sedan in Detroit, the Bormans then visited
Charlie's brother Elmer, his wife Minnie, and their sons Harold and Bobby
in Cincinnati, Ohio.

FIRST MARRIAGE

Early in 1942, George Ann became engaged to Bruce Quartly, a young
Army Air Corps recruit from Rodeo, California, who left his Model A Ford,
"Leapin' Lena," with George Ann. One evening a week, she drove it across
the San Francisco-Oakland Bay Bridge to visit Bruce's widowed mother in
Rodeo, near Berkeley. Her young cousin, Bill Grier, sometimes joined her on

these trips.

Fate intervened, however, as George Ann fell in love with a sailor, Stuart Alvin Burnham, whom she married on April 11, 1942. The ceremony, held in Reno, Nevada, was witnessed by M. Dowd and Drasnap J. Lowe.

Stuart, born on February 25, 1919 in Blanding, Utah, was a Machinist's Mate, First Class in the Coast Guard. Stationed in San Francisco, they lived in an apartment at 1080 Bush Street. Their young marriage ended tragically on January 5, 1944, when Stuart died of spinal meningitis in Marine Hospital. He was buried in the Presidio National Cemetery. After settling Stuart's estate, George Ann continued her work at D.C. Heath & Company and moved back with her parents.

SECOND MARRIAGE

On December 27, 1946, George Ann married Samuel Lewis Dickens Palmer in the Episcopal church in Reno, Nevada. Sam, born on March 26, 1911 and raised in Knoxville, Tennessee, received his Bachelor of Science degree in accounting from the University of Tennessee at Knoxville in 1934 and the following year a Master of Arts in linguistics from Gallaudet Teacher's College in Washington, D.C., a federally chartered institution for the hearing impaired. Palmer taught deaf students in Honolulu from 1938 to 1945; at age twenty-seven, he became the principal and superintendent of the school—the youngest principal in Hawaii at that time.

FAMILY LIFE

From 1946 to 1947, George Ann and Sam lived in a San Francisco apartment at 801 Baker Street before moving to Hayward, California, where Sam had opened "Palmer's," a large drug and variety store on the main street. George Ann resigned from the publishing firm to help her husband manage the store. In the 1950s, the Palmers opened another store in Berkeley, at Shattuck and University Avenues, near the University of California campus.

Three children were born to the Palmers: Catherine Ann, on October 15, 1949, in Hayward; Charles Arthur, on May 28, 1952, also in Hayward; and Kenneth Grier, on January 26, 1957, in Berkeley, where the family had moved in the 1950s. In the mid-sixties, the Palmers moved to 6 Garden Estates Court in Alamo, California. The children graduated from San Ramon High School in Danville, in 1967, '70, and '75, respectively. During their vacations and weekends, they worked in the family's Berkeley store.

In September 1972, Sam died of a heart attack in his sleep at his home in Alamo, having returned from a family vacation the previous day.

Following Sam's death, George Ann bought a townhouse at 180 Lawnview Circle in Danville, California. In 1977, she purchased a home in the Napa Valley (at 12 San Lucas Court, St. Helena, California), which she shared with Paul Wilcox, a retired musician who had played with bands in San Francisco and the West in the forties, fifties, and sixties.

With views of the coastal mountains, George Ann's St. Helena home was bordered on one side by the winding Napa River and on the other by vineyards. Built in the 1960s, the subdivision had a clubhouse with library, game rooms, restaurant, swimming pool, and putting green; in another location, there were woodworking and arts and crafts studios. At a nearby golf and tennis club, she and Paul played its nine-hole course several times a week.

From St. Helena, George Ann continued to manage "Palmer's," driving the fifty-eight miles to Berkeley twice a week in her yellow Honda Civic. When the business was sold in 1979, she and Paul traveled to Scandinavia, England, and Scotland, where they played a week of golf at St. Andrew's. Thereafter, they rented condominiums and played golf in Kona, Hawaii during winter months.

After having battled breast cancer since a March 1977 mastectomy, George Ann died in the Napa Hospital on the day she was admitted, July 25, 1983. A member of the Neptune Society, she was cremated, and her ashes were scattered by plane over San Francisco Bay.

CHILDREN

Catherine Ann Palmer (1949–)

Cathy graduated in 1971 with a Bachelor of Arts in sociology from the College of Holy Names in Oakland. After teaching in Oakland parochial schools for several years, she moved in the early 1980s to Willits, California, where she married Walter Camp. Now divorced, Cathy earned a master's degree in education at Oregon State College and hopes to teach.

Charles Arthur Palmer (1952–)

Charles received his Bachelor of Arts in business administration from Chico State College in 1975. He married Joanne Lee Witte and has two daughters, Sarah Ruth (born August 24, 1983, in Oakland, California) and Casey Noelle (born December 20, 1985, in Willits).

Joanne—born in Kansas City on April 19, 1960—graduated from New Canaan (Connecticut) High School in 1977. In 1983, she earned a Bachelor of Arts in anthropology from San Francisco State University. Charles and Joanne were divorced in 1990.

Prior to settling in Willits, Charles had managed a camera store in the East Bay for seven years. (As a schoolboy, he had worked in the camera department of his family's drug and variety store in Berkeley.) In 1983, Charles acquired twenty-one acres of land in Willits, where he helped design and construct his family's home at 4809 Bear Canyon Road.

Kenneth Grier Palmer (1957–)

Kenneth, his wife Colleen Sue Owen ("Teddy"), daughter Melissa Ann (born May 9, 1983, in Oakland), and son Andrew Cody (born January 22, 1989) live at 951 Stow Lane, Lafayette, California. Kenneth is a contractor and owner of Ken Palmer General Contractor, Inc., in Oakland.

George Ann (Mrs. Sam Palmer) and daughter Cathy, c. 1950
(Courtesy of George Ann Palmer)

George Ann Palmer and her children in 1981:
Cathy, Kenneth, Charles
(Courtesy of George Ann Palmer)

George Ann Borman Palmer
(Courtesy of George Ann Palmer)

CHRONOLOGY OF WILLIAM M. GRIER, SR.

1878	Born in San Francisco, California on September 24
1883–1888	Attends Lincoln School in San Francisco
1888	Moves with family to Palermo, California
1895	Graduates from high school at age sixteen in June; joins Bills & Putnam's general merchandise store in Oroville, California
1896	Opens own general merchandise store in Palermo
1898	Sells business; enlists in First Regiment California U.S. Volunteers (Spanish-American War and Philippine Insurrection) on July 20; trains at the Presidio in San Francisco from July to October
1898–1899	Serves in Philippines from December 11 to July 23
1899	Visits Japan during summer; returns to San Francisco on August 24; mustered out of service on September 21; hired by Phoebe Hearst to work with Hearst Real Estate and Development Company in San Francisco, embarking on career in construction, in November
1901	Promoted to position with Hearst Oil Company
1902–1903	Tutored by University of California-Berkeley professor in metallurgy and mining engineering (arranged by Phoebe Hearst)
1903	Works for Phoebe Hearst at Homestake Mining Company in Lead, South Dakota; returns to California in December, supervising Hearst gold mining projects in Palermo
1904	Marries Laura A. Watson on June 20; joins Twohy Brothers Company in San Francisco in October

1904–1907	With Twohy Brothers, works on Southern Pacific Railroad's Bayshore Cutoff project in San Francisco
1906	San Francisco earthquake on April 18
1906–1909	Made partner in Twohy Brothers Company; supervises North Bank project in Washington State
1909	Father, William John Grier, dies in Oakland, California on June 25
1909–1919	Continues with Twohy Brothers, working on Deschutes project and various contracts in Montana, Washington State, Oregon, and western Canada
1914	Uncle, T.J. Grier, Sr., dies in Los Angeles, California on September 22; attends funeral and burial in Lead, South Dakota
1915	Visits Panama-Pacific International Exhibition in San Francisco; visits cousin, Denham Grier, in Treadwell, Alaska
1916	Attends unveiling of uncle T.J. Grier's statue in Lead, South Dakota
1919	Forms General Construction Company in Oregon on January 29; forms Boschke Miller Grier Company in Oregon in May
1921	Mother, Georgie Orr Grier, dies in Oakland on October 23; divorces Laura Watson Grier; purchases partners' interest in Boschke Miller Grier Company and relocates to San Francisco in December; acquires 40% interest in Erickson Petterson Company in San Francisco and changes its name to Erickson Petterson Grier Company
1923	Erickson Petterson Grier awarded contract for Southern Pacific Railroad's Blue Canyon-Emigrant Gap project in January

1925	Erickson Petterson Grier dissolved on November 2; forms Grier and Mead in San Francisco with partner Winfield Scott Mead (offices move to Oakland in 1927)
1926	Grier and Mead awarded contract for construction of Claremont water tunnel in Orinda and Oakland, California in July
1927	Marries Elo Theresa Lannon in Reno, Nevada on November 9; moves into Piedmont, California home on November 19
1928	Son, William Milton Grier, Jr., born in Oakland on September 23
1929	Son, Eloyd John Grier, born in San Francisco on July 4; private yacht, *ELOGRIER,* completed; stock market crashes on October 29
1930	Suffers first heart attack
1933	Suffers second heart attack
1934	Kidnapped in Sacramento, California; forms Grier and Fontaine, gold mining firm; moves family to Sacramento in fall; leases out Piedmont home
1935	Dies in Sacramento on December 8, after third heart attack, at age fifty-seven

William Milton Grier, Sr., 1927

13

WILLIAM MILTON GRIER, SR.
1878–1935

Builder in the West

William Milton Grier was the embodiment of the self-made man. With modest beginnings as the son of a San Francisco bookkeeper, he completed his high school education by sixteen and opened his first business just two years later. Gifted and industrious, he built a remarkable career over the next two decades and was, by the age of forty, one of the leading entrepreneurs in the West.

Born in the last quarter of the nineteenth century, Grier came of age during a period of vast expansionism in the West. Through his subsequent work in engineering and construction, he became a contributor to the growth of the American frontier—growth which brought him both professional acclaim and wealth.

The forces acting upon William Milton Grier's life were multiple: the urban—birth and early years in San Francisco; the bucolic—adolescence in a small northern California town in the Sierra foothills; the patriotic—service in the Spanish-American War; the altruistic—the beneficence of Phoebe Hearst; the eruptive—the 1906 San Francisco earthquake; and the expansive—the feverish growth of the western states, which opened opportunities and stirred prospective entrepreneurs to action.

His friends and competitors in the construction industry included Henry J. Kaiser and Warren A. Bechtel. Another friend, Amadeo P. Giannini, founder of the Bank of Italy (later known as Bank of America), financed many of Grier's railroad contracting, civil engineering, and construction projects.

Grier's professional life touched on gold mining, railroads, construction, real estate, and oil. It led him to the Pacific Northwest, the Rocky Mountain West, and western Canada; to Lead, South Dakota and Palermo, California; to Japan and the Philippines; and repeatedly it brought him back to his native city, San Francisco.

EARLY YEARS IN SAN FRANCISCO, 1878–1888

When William Milton Grier was born in San Francisco on September 24, 1878, his native town was a vibrant city of 230,000 people, with another 50,000 residents living in the towns around the Bay. Robert Louis Stevenson described its magnetic qualities in an 1882 article, "San Francisco—A Modern Cosmopolis":

> A great city covers the sand hills on the west, a growing town lies along the muddy shallows of the east; steamboats pass continually between them from before sunrise til the small hours of the morning; lines of great seagoing ships lie at anchor; colors fly upon the islands; and from all around the hum of corporate life, of beaten bells, and steam, and running carriages, goes cheerily abroad in the sunshine....The town is essentially not Anglo-Saxon; still more not American. The Yankee and the Englishman find themselves alike in a strange country.[1]

But some 100 years before Grier's birth, San Francisco was itself being born. Although Gaspar De Portola's expeditional forces had discovered San Francisco Bay in 1769, the city's official birthday was celebrated on June 29, 1776, the date of the first mass at Mission San Francisco de Asis (Mission Dolores), the sixth religious center in Father Junipero Serra's chain of Spanish missions. In 1821, the area was transferred from Spanish to Mexican possession.

In the mid-1830s, a sleepy village named Yerba Buena (after a sweet-smelling local herb) grew up around a cove where ships anchored. English-speaking Californians launched and won a short-lived revolt against Mexican rule—The Bear-Flag Rebellion—in June 1846. Several weeks later, the area was absorbed by the United States, and in the following year, the village of Yerba Buena was renamed San Francisco.

Shortly thereafter, in 1848, gold was discovered in the foothills of the Sierra Nevada, 150 miles to the east at Sutter's Mill in Coloma, California. As a result, the population of San Francisco soared from less than 1,000 in 1849 to over 50,000 by 1855. By the time of William Milton Grier's birth some twenty-three years later, the city's population had increased nearly five-fold.

---

1. Cited in Katharine D. Osbourne, *Robert Louis Stevenson in California* (Chicago: A.C. McClurg & Co., 1911), pp. 53-55.

With the unbridled growth came wild times, fast fortunes, and an explosively alive city. San Francisco in 1878 was a lawless, roaring, exciting town, a city of courage and luck. Violence was still a part of life there, and many men routinely carried guns.

Grier spent the first nine years of his life in this stimulating San Francisco environment.[2] At the time, the city consisted of long blocks of narrow, two-story houses, their bay windows protruding. (In this city of frequent fog and chill winds, bay windows in the front parlor and the master bedroom were a necessity.) The streets were paved with cobblestones or planking and edged by board sidewalks.

William Milton (called "Milt" or "Billy" by his family) and his sister May attended Lincoln Grammar School on Fifth Street just south of Market Street—a four-story brick structure where 1,386 pupils were enrolled; Milt completed the first five years of his schooling there.[3]

In fair weather on Sundays and holidays during the 1880s, the Griers and the Orrs (Georgie Grier's parents) often went on picnics and promenades to Golden Gate Park, to Pacific beaches, and to Cliff House, overlooking the ocean. For these trips, they boarded horse-drawn streetcars or horse-and-buggies on Market Street in downtown San Francisco.

William John and Georgie also took Milt and May on outings around the city by horse trolley or the newer cable car. Public transportation was expanding rapidly during the 1880s and featured horse-drawn streetcars running between the business center of the city and the outlying industrial and residential areas. Five years before Milt's birth, Andrew Hallidie's plan to bury a moving cable in a slot beneath the trolley tracks, to which the cars could be attached by a device called a "gripping clamp," had also been put into operation, and in October 1873, the first cable car began its climb up Clay Street. (Sixty-six years later, in 1939, when Milt's widow Elo and his two sons lived in a third-floor walk-up apartment on Clay off Hyde Street, the cable car continued to run past their building.)

Out in the city at dusk, Milt and May watched as the lamplighter came around with his torch, placed his ladder against lampposts on the street

2.   From 1878 to 1880, the Griers lived at 417 Mason Street; in 1880, they moved to 1719 Jessie Street, which runs between Market and Mission Streets. Milt's father was then transferred to Western Union's office in Napa, California. In 1881, however, he returned to San Francisco after joining the Central Pacific Railroad Company. From 1881 to 1884, the Griers lived at 22 1/2 Langton Street; from 1885 to 1888, at 11 Langton Street between 7th and 8th and Howard and Folsom Streets. (The two-story structure at 22 and 22 1/2 Langton still stands there today.)

3.   First named in honor of the martyred president, the school burned on Washington's birthday in 1871. Reconstructed that same year, it was totally destroyed in the fire of 1906. David Belasco, the theatrical producer, was a member of the first graduating class and organized the Lincoln School Alumni Association.

corners, then climbed up to ignite the gas jets whose flames glowed softly up and down the streets.

During the summers in San Francisco when Milt was eight and nine years old, his family and friends crossed San Francisco Bay to camp on the beach near beautiful Sausalito in Marin County. At such times, William John would commute to work on the ferry from Sausalito to San Francisco every morning and return to the little tent colony each night.

The Griers sometimes lunched in the Cliff House at Point Lobos Avenue and Great Highway. Through its glass walls, they could look beyond Seal Rocks for miles across the Pacific, and the setting on a cliff was a perfect departure point for strolls along the beach. (The Cliff House had been purchased by Adolph Sutro in 1879, but fifteen years later, on Christmas Day, it burned to the ground. A second Cliff House was erected in 1896; ten years later, during the earthquake of 1906, it was thrown from its foundation and fell into the ocean.)

PALERMO YEARS, 1888–1898

In 1888, William John Grier left his post at Central Pacific to accept a bookkeeping and land management position with Palermo Land and Water Company (PL&W). The young family then settled in Palermo, Butte County, California, located some 160 miles northeast of San Francisco in the foothills of the Sierra Nevada.

The Grier children first attended Palermo's one-story frame school and, later, its replacement, a two-story brick building with tower. Milt, who had worked as a clerk for PL&W while in high school, graduated from Oroville Union High in June 1895, at age sixteen.

After Milt's graduation, his parents urged him to study metallurgy and mining engineering at the University of California at Berkeley, but, eager to enter the business world, Milt instead took a job with Bills & Putnam's, wholesalers and retailers of hardware and general merchandise (steel, coal, barbwire, crockery, tin, glassware, paints, and oils). The firm, which was also an agent for John Deere plows and Deering mowers, was located on Montgomery Street in Oroville, on the south bank of the Feather River.

In 1896, he resigned due to ill health and spent the next three months convalescing and traveling in the West. He visited his uncle T.J. in Lead, South Dakota; his uncle Albert, an attorney, and his cousins Denham and Frances ("Franny") Grier in Denver; and his aunt Anne Grier Fell and her family in Odgen, Utah.

On his return, Milt was offered his former position at Bills & Putnam's for twice his previous salary, but, intent on establishing his own business, he declined. He then opened a general merchandise firm in Palermo, which he ran successfully for over a year and sold at a profit in 1898, after the outbreak of the Spanish-American War and the Philippine Insurrection. The war, stirring his patriotism, had proved even more enticing than entrepreneurship.

SPANISH-AMERICAN WAR
AND PHILIPPINE INSURRECTION, 1898–1899

Perhaps seeking new horizons, eighteen-year-old Milt Grier responded to President William McKinley's call for volunteers and enlisted as a private on July 20, 1898. With his parents' permission, he joined the California U.S. Volunteers—the "Boys in Blue"—and was attached to Battery A of the First Battalion Regiment of Heavy Artillery. He was given ninety days of training at the Presidio in San Francisco—and thirteen dollars per month.

Called a "splendid little war" by Theodore Roosevelt, then Secretary of the Navy, the Spanish-American War was short-lived (April 1898–August 1899) and resulted in only 379 combat deaths.

The conflict grew out of America's sympathy for the oppressed people of Cuba and the desire to expand U.S. power in the world. In the Treaty of Paris, signed on December 10, 1898, the United States won the spoils of victory, including sovereignty over the Philippine Islands. Ten million Filipinos, however, were unwilling to become part of a U.S. protectorate. The ensuing Philippine Insurrection forced the United States to call upon its armed forces to secure that which U.S. officials had intended to acquire by diplomacy.

The First Regiment of the U.S. Volunteers of California was one of the original National Guard regiments to heed McKinley's call for volunteers in this war that was meant to end the rule of Spain in North America. California was also the first state to fill its national quota, and its soldiers were the first to depart from American soil. When the *City of Peking* steamed through the Golden Gate on May 25, 1898, bearing the initial wave of Volunteers to embark for Manila, it was a history-making voyage.

If the United States were to win the Spanish-American War, the strength of Spain as a colonial power would be shattered forever, and the ultimate acquisition of desirable territory, affecting the commerce of the world, would be secured. The high stakes in this war stirred an immense amount of patriotism, and the embarkation of the First Regiment was treated with enormous fervor, surpassed only by the incredibly joyous celebrations at the Regiment's return more than a year later on August 23, 1899.

In almost Whitmanesque language, the Patriotic Publishing Company extolled the virtues of the troops and the war in December 1898:

> In the ranks of that body of men [the First Regiment] can be found, either through birth or parentage, a representative of every great nation on earth. From out of the great human crucible of early California, has come the most thoroughly cosmopolitan body of military men that ever marched under a single banner. Here is found the American, the Frenchman, the German, the Irishman, the Englishman, the Scotchman, the Welshman, the Austrian, the Italian, the Hungarian, the Russian, the Swede, the Norwegian, the Greek, and in fact a representative of every distinct type on earth. In the matter of religious opinions the diversity is as great as it is in the matter of ancestry. Jew and Gentile have been made one by the cohesive bonds of patriotism. All the branches of science and all of the various callings of a great commercial commonwealth were represented within its ranks. The doctor, the lawyer, the merchant, the mechanic, and the laborer became one homogeneous body for the sake of country. The college student and the city clerk shared the same bed and the same board without a feeling of sacrifice or sycophancy. The sons of the rich and the sons of the poor stood upon the same social plane that their fathers stood upon in the days of the Argonauts. They were fighting for a cause; that cause was dear to all. With them a war for humanity knew neither tongue nor creed....[4]

The sinking of the battleship *Maine* near Cuba led to the First Regiment's sailing to assist Admiral Dewey in Manila in the far-off Philippines. Shortly after, this regiment "was the first to offer a life sacrifice upon the alter [sic] of its country...in the person of brave Maurice Justh, Sergeant of Company A, who sleeps in a soldiers [sic] grave 6,500 miles from home and friends."[5]

The battle cry became the famous "Remember the Maine!" and perhaps stimulated the fervid patriotism that helped America come through the war a victor, having won from Spain the independence of Cuba and possession of Puerto Rico, Guam, and the Philippine Islands.

Private Grier's First Battalion Regiment of Heavy Artillery, California U.S. Volunteers consisted of Batteries A, B, C, and D. The government's original intention in calling the First Battalion into existence was to man the coast fortifications which protected California from attack by sea. However,

---

4. *California's Tribute to the Nation* (San Francisco: Patriotic Publishing Co., 1898), p. 1.

5. Ibid., p. 2.

due to the successes of the American fleet beyond the seas, the prospective siege by Spanish vessels never materialized.

The call, however, was for Volunteer artillerymen of above-average intelligence and education to man these guns. Two hundred soldiers were to be recruited for each of the four batteries. While many hundreds presented themselves in an endeavor to enlist and don the blue and brown, only 800 were sworn in, making the full strength of the battalion equivalent to two full battalions of infantry.

Private Grier and his fellow Volunteers in Battery A were first quartered at the run-down Fontana Warehouse, located at the end of Van Ness Avenue in San Francisco. The men slept on its hard floor, and the wind and fog rushed through its broken windows. After ten days, the structure was declared unsafe, and the Volunteers were sent to the Presidio for training.[6]

There were several sailings to the Philippines over the next few months. Private Grier and most of Battery A, under the command of First Lieutenant J.B. Morse and accompanied by Second Lieutenant John F. Lucey of Battery D, sailed from San Francisco on October 18, 1898 on the transport *Valencia*.

Batteries A and D were reunited in the Philippines on December 11, 1898 in the historic town of Cavite, the former site of the Spanish navy yard and the point at which the first American flag was unfurled in the Philippine Islands. At that time, Battery A consisted of three officers and 182 men; Battery D had four officers and 184 men.

At Admiral Dewey's request, the battalion was assigned as his special support to protect the navy yard and its environs. After its capture by American forces on May 1, it had been made the supply base for all the ships

---

6.   In June 1776, when Benjamin Franklin, John Adams, and Thomas Jefferson were discussing the Declaration of Independence in Philadelphia, a Spanish soldier named Juan Bautista de Anza planted a wooden cross on a hillside above San Francisco Bay and decreed that a presidio would be built on the site.

The purpose was to protect Spanish interests from the Russians and British. After 70 peaceful years, the American flag was raised over the fort in 1846, when a band of twelve soldiers sailed across the Golden Gate from Sausalito and raided the Presidio.

This oldest continuously operating post in America served as a refuge for 70,000 San Franciscans after the 1906 earthquake and was also the home of General "Black Jack" Pershing.

The Presidio encompasses 1,500 wooded acres, miles of shoreline, and lush grass. Private Grier and his fellow volunteers had their physical examinations and shots in the post's first hospital, built in 1863; in 1973, it was transformed into a museum.

of the Asiatic Squadron, and valuable property was stored in the arsenal. The surroundings at Cavite were extremely pleasant, with various *palacios* used as barracks by the different organizations located there.

Cavite was also the first headquarters of the Filipino insurrectionists. After the fall of Manila on August 13, the insurgent troops withdrew from the city of Cavite and took up a position at San Roque, a town of equal size (5,000 people) separated from Cavite only by a narrow artificial causeway 600 yards in length.

Under the command of General Estrella, governor of the province of Cavite, the insurgents began massing their forces at San Roque on February 1, 1899. One week later, Admiral Dewey came ashore from the *Olympia*, and, after consultations with the district commander, issued a demand for the insurgents to evacuate the town of San Roque. An ultimatum accompanied the demand: If the evacuation were not completed by nine o'clock the following morning, the town would be bombarded.

As the deadline approached, the insurgents requested further time, but Dewey refused. Shortly thereafter, flames burst out all over San Roque, and the town was soon ablaze.

The entire garrison of Cavite was promptly called to arms. In addition to Batteries A and D of the California Heavy Artillery (in charge of two sections of Gatling guns), two battalions of the Fifty-first Iowa Infantry, U.S. Volunteers, the Wyoming Light Battery, and the Nevada Cavalry were dispatched across the causeway.

Every passage through San Roque was in flames. To gain entrance to the town, Grier and the Volunteers had to flank it by moving along the seashore, at times wading waist-high in water. Grier and the men fought through the flames of the burning city in pursuit of the retreating enemy, dragging their heavy guns by hand and skirmishing at every opportunity.

Together with the cavalry troop and the infantry, Grier and his artillery battalion took the town of Caridad, several miles away, and passed Dalhican, beyond which lay the causeway leading to the mainland. (It was here that insurgents in former rebellions had massacred hundreds of Spaniards by luring them onto the narrow causeway, then mowing them down.) Grier went ahead with scouting parties to assure that the woods were free of insurgents. Details were sent to bury the dead, and battalion, infantry, and cavalry went into camp.

On February 15, Grier's battery was on the firing line. The Filipinos had advanced to within 300 yards when the battalion opened fire, and the insurgents beat a hasty retreat. Firing continued all night between the outposts, and numerous exchanges would take place in the following weeks. On March 2, Grier and three other Volunteers were sent to reconnoiter. Their party advanced to within fifty yards of the insurgents' lines before being discovered; when the enemy opened fire, Grier and the scouting party fell back, their retreat covered by a portion of the battalion outpost guard.

At ten o'clock in the morning of June 14, white flags were seen on the beach near Rosario and Salinas. The next day, Grier and eighty Volunteers from Batteries A and D, under command of Captain Dennis Geary, started for Novaleta at 7:00 a.m. and routed the insurgents in time to return to camp for supper. A day later, the battalion scouted the roads leading to San Francisco de Malabon, Cavite Viejo, Salinas, and Novaleta, and on June 17, the battalion left camp at 5:00 a.m., marching to Caridad. They received the surrender of the town of Rosario on June 19. Grier and the scouting parties then moved in the direction of San Francisco de Malabon and Cavite Viejo and engaged the enemy in crossfire.

For sixty-nine consecutive days, the First Battalion was under fire, guarding a critical point to the advance on the navy yard. Although Grier and his fellow Volunteers were "subjected to all the rigors of a campaign, depleted by sickness, and hounded and shot at by the natives in their immediate front, with orders that they must grin and bear it; with attacks on their outposts every night...the men of this organization kept at bay 6,000 insurgents."[7] Before defeating the insurrectionists, Private Grier and his California Volunteers endured four months of battle in the Philippine swamps and jungles.

TUMULT IN SAN FRANCISCO

With hostilities ended, the troops prepared to leave the Philippines, and on July 23, 1899, Private Grier and the California Volunteers embarked on the U.S. Army transport *Sherman* for their return to San Francisco. En route, the ship passed through the Inland Sea of Japan, where Grier and his shipmates went ashore to visit Nagasaki, Yokohama, and Tokyo. The *Sherman* then sailed for San Francisco, arriving off its coast on August 23, 1899 at 5:46 p.m. They were greeted by the rosy glare of bonfires burning along the city's hilltops.

As the *Sherman* waited four miles off shore near the Farallone Islands, San Francisco's Mayor James D. Phelan sent a message to Lieutenant Colonel Duboce aboard the S.S. *Sherman*:

Colonel Victor Duboce: Greetings to the First California. Come in tomorrow

---

7.   *A Brief Historical Sketch of the California Heavy Artillery, U.S.V., and the Operations of Batteries A and D in the Philippine Islands* (San Francisco: Patriotic Publishing Co., 1898), p. 101.

and we will welcome you as soldiers have never been greeted before.

On the morning of August 24, 1899, the scarred white hull of the *Sherman* was ushered into port by a flotilla of colorful boats. The noise was deafening. Every tug had a band, and rapid-fire guns on the *Sherman* returned their salutes. Over 100,000 San Franciscans turned out to view the incoming ship. On her starboard decks facing the city, 1,800 "Boys in Blue," the heroes from San Francisco, stood at the rails. When the *Sherman* docked at Folsom Street Wharf at noon on that bright summer day, Grier's joyous parents William John and Georgie, his sister May, and his aunt Mattie Orr were waiting to embrace him.

The reaction of San Franciscans and the press to the return of the troops aboard the *Sherman* was ecstatic. The *San Francisco Chronicle* wrote:

> An hour after yesterday's noon the Golden Gate swung wide open and revealed, standing just within its portals, San Francisco waiting, arms out-stretched, to greet her own—no longer a weary, anxious, heavy-hearted San Francisco, but a city feverish with gladness, trembling 'twixt joy, tears and loving laughter....All last night the tremulous echo of those cheers beat on the eardrums of troubled sleepers, while there remained on their eyeballs the picture of a fair white ship, all a-flutter with bunting, and on her decks and in her rigging a swarm of noble fellows, all soberly garbed in blue and yellow. There have been other transports, but none like this one; other soldiers have come home, but not such as these. Other regiments did fine things in the Philippines, but these are household heroes, the proof that San Francisco can breed blood of her blood and bone of her bone....Rockets rushed high up into the veil of thin fog and then drowsily popped and loosened all the beauties of variegated colors in fantastic sprays of slowly dropping fire....More awful than blazing hulk and belching red fire on the water and myriads of electric lights in artistic designs ashore were the wailing, quivering, tremulous, thundering voices of the sirens on the *Sherman*....The *Sherman*, from which all the glories of the night radiated, loomed up like a great house illuminated for a festivity....Perhaps the most remarkable sight along the front was Telegraph Hill, where human beings were packed together like bunched cattle at the close of a day's round-up and formed for the promontory a vast cap as complete and dense as the earth on which they stood....[8]

The next morning, the soldiers appeared newly outfitted in khaki uniforms, wide-brimmed campaign hats, and red four-in-hand ties. A continuous shout kept pace with the men as they marched from the wharf to the Ferry Building, accompanied by beating drums and songs, including

---

8. *San Francisco Chronicle*, 25 August 1899.

"When Johnny Comes Marching Home Again" and "Hail, the Conquering Hero Comes." In the Ferry Building's grand nave, Private Grier and the Volunteers were reunited with their loved ones and were later served breakfast in the east nave at tables covered with white cloths.

The men were greeted by James Phelan, the patrician mayor of San Francisco—an orator, art patron, and uncommon public servant who was much esteemed by the Grier family for his reforms and his vision of San Francisco as a city of art and progressive government...the Florence of the Pacific. Private Grier, along with many other Volunteers, met the mayor during breakfast, exchanging a few words with him as he introduced himself around the tables.

As members of the Relatives' Association, Grier's mother, sister, and aunt—each dressed in white with red-white-and-blue sashes—had helped arrange the welcoming breakfast with other mothers, wives, and sisters of the First California Volunteers. Instead of trying to conduct the breakfast personally, the relatives secured a good caterer. After months of a monotonous diet, Grier and the men were served a sumptuous menu:

Eastern Oysters

Relishes

Olives   Pickles   Tomatoes   Lettuce

Entree

Chicken Fricassee

Vegetables

Green Peas   Mashed Potatoes

Roast

Turkey en Gelee   Filet de Boeuf

Eastern Ham   Smoked Tongue

Dessert

Chocolate Cakes   Coconut Cakes

Jelly Cakes

Coffee   Fruit in Season   Cheese

Mineral Waters

A feast for anyone, it was especially so for Private Grier and the other Volunteers who had endured a very different kind of breakfast for months: beans and slabs of fat bacon and hardtack, washed down by bitter coffee.

During the meal, there were cheers for the mothers, sisters, wives, and sweethearts, and the great hall rang with hearty expressions of love and approval.

As Grier and the Volunteers rose to leave, a band played patriotic airs, from "The Stars and Stripes Forever" and "The Star-Spangled Banner" to "Marching Through Georgia" and "Dixie."

After breakfast, Grier and the Volunteers marched up Market Street, past jubilant throngs of people crowding the sidewalks and peering out of office and hotel windows. By then, the men wore laurel wreaths on their brown campaign hats, and their gun barrels were filled with flowers and flags. The parade turned north on Van Ness Avenue, then continued west on Lombard Street and on to the Presidio.

An article on the front page of the *San Francisco Chronicle* described the scene:

> As the men turned in at the Presidio gates the band was playing in a reminiscent sort of way, "We shall meet, but we shall miss him, There will be one vacant chair." Over the hill, the refrain went, "One vacant chair." To each hearer the vacant chair stood for a different name. Some thought of Justh and some of Dunmore, some of Richter, some of Dewar and Maher, and all the other brave fellows whose graves are down there.[9]

San Francisco's welcome had just begun. Private Grier and his fellow Volunteers marched once again, in a second parade on Saturday evening, August 26 that was watched by over 150,000 people. A newspaper reporter captured the evening's magic:

> It was...the most beautiful pageant the city ever saw....The illumination made the city more beautiful than fairyland...the lines of light zig-zagging across the street, here parallel, there oblique, with an irregularity that enchanted the eye....The tall, slender tower of the Ferry Building showed all its noble proportions....At the other end of the bridge of light...[the City Hall dome] gleamed and sparkled and twinkled....The late twilight had hardly died before the fireworks commenced. More beautiful rockets never soared aloft to a California sky. [10]

Still a minor at age twenty, Private Grier was mustered out on September 21, 1899, having served fourteen months and one day. His twenty-first birthday would be celebrated three days later with family and friends at home, in Palermo, California.

Young Grier had felt the fire of combat and the loss of friends; he had endured war and survived. Now, he was again eager to test his mettle in the world of business.

---

9. *San Francisco Chronicle*, 26 August 1899.

10. *San Francisco Chronicle*, 27 August 1899.

PHOEBE HEARST AND EARLY CAREER

After Grier's discharge and triumphant return from the Philippines, Phoebe Hearst hired him to work in San Francisco for the Hearst estate, which controlled business interests and philanthropies across the country—from saving George Washington's Mount Vernon home and building the Washington Cathedral in the East to supporting free kindergartens, libraries, and the University of California at Berkeley in the West.

Phoebe Apperson Hearst, widow of U.S. Senator George Hearst, directed these wide-ranging activities. Raised on a frontier Missouri farm, Phoebe began teaching in a village school at seventeen. Two years later, she married forty-one-year-old Hearst, who had left Missouri with a pan, pick, and shovel to seek his fortune in the California gold rush. He was a successful mine owner in the West and a prominent San Franciscan at the time of their marriage in Missouri in 1862. After their honeymoon, the couple returned to San Francisco in September, aboard a ship traveling via Panama.

After her husband's death in 1891, Mrs. Hearst was named the first female regent of the University of California at Berkeley. As a tribute to her late husband, she financed construction of the Hearst Memorial Mining Building to house the College of Mining. The words she chose to honor him, inscribed on a plaque placed there in 1902, read: "This building stands as a memorial to George Hearst, a plain honest man and good miner."

Over the years, Phoebe Hearst would become one of Berkeley's major benefactors. The International Competition, an architectural design for the university's site, was one of her projects. She also supported the Department of Anthropology, providing funds for archeological expeditions, research buildings, and equipment.[11]

In the 1880s, Phoebe Hearst became a close friend of William John and T.J. Grier (superintendent of the Hearst-owned Homestake Mining Company in Lead, South Dakota). Their families were often guests at her estates "Wyntoon," in northern California, and "Hacienda," in Pleasanton, east of San Francisco in the hills of southern Alameda County.[12]

---

11. Her son William Randolph Hearst gave the Hearst Gymnasium for Women to the university in her memory. Designed by Bernard Maybeck and Julia Morgan, the building was dedicated on April 8, 1927, with Mr. Hearst in attendance. He also gave Berkeley the Hearst Greek Theater, built in 1903.

12. "Hacienda" was completed in 1896 after a large addition designed by Julia Morgan was finished. Elaborate gardens surrounding the home were ablaze with color. Pergolas were overhung with wisteria, cloisters shaded with climbing roses and jasmine. The music room was crowded with art, statues, and rare tapestries. Mrs. Hearst died at "Hacienda" on April 13,

She also took a personal interest in Milt Grier, recognizing in him a young man of ability.[13] Through the years, she provided him with opportunities, first in her family's real estate development company and then with Hearst Oil. She also had him tutored by a professor from the University of California at Berkeley and later sent him to Lead, South Dakota to gain experience in the Homestake Mining Company.

In November 1899, young Grier began as a laborer with the Hearst Real Estate and Development Company, whose office was in the Mills Building, Room 926, at 220 Montgomery Street in San Francisco. The office was a short walk from his apartment at 526 Post Street, near Union Square and the St. Francis Hotel, where he would live until 1903. San Francisco's population by this point had boomed to 343,000.

Starting on Hearst's Potrero district project on the southwest hill of San Francisco, young Grier became a project foreman within six months. Later, he was promoted to supervisor of a 150-man crew, directing the construction of streets, sidewalks, utility lines, and twelve retail, residential, and office buildings.

In 1901, Mrs. Hearst promoted him to a position under her cousin's son Edward Clark, who managed Hearst Oil Company, also located in the Mills Building. While Grier was at Hearst Oil, she arranged for him to receive instruction in metallurgy and mining engineering two afternoons a week with a Berkeley professor. With this experience, Grier established a successful mine assaying laboratory while continuing with Hearst Oil.

For six months in 1903, Mrs. Hearst had Grier work and study at the Homestake Mining Company in Lead, South Dakota, where the superintendent was his uncle T.J. While en route by train, Grier stopped to visit his aunt Anne (Mrs. A. Gilbert Fell) and her four daughters and son in Ogden, Utah. (Anne's fifth daughter had died while visiting Milt's family in Palermo a few years earlier.) He also visited his uncle Albert E. Grier and cousins Franny (age ten) and Denham (age fourteen) during a stopover in Denver. (Albert, who was admitted to the Colorado Bar in 1888, was counsel for several Denver firms, including the early utility, predecessor of today's Public Service Company of Colorado.)

1919. William Milton Grier, then involved in civil and railroad construction in the Pacific Northwest, attended her funeral on April 16, 1919 at Grace Church (later Grace Cathedral) in San Francisco.

13. In 1886 at age eight, Milt had met the Hearsts' only child, twenty-three-year-old William Randolph, whose father soon after gave him the *San Francisco Examiner*, his first newspaper. Grier renewed his relationship with William Randolph while working with Hearst enterprises in San Francisco, from 1899 to 1904. Hearst married Millicent Willson of New York in 1903.

On reaching Lead, Grier settled in with his uncle T.J. and aunt Mary Jane. This was a challenging period for twenty-five-year-old Milt: In the next six months, he would work in all of Homestake's departments, toiling ten hours a day, six days a week as "the lowest paid man on the payroll," he wrote years later. His uncle saw to it that he learned all aspects of Homestake's operation which, under T.J.'s direction, was becoming the largest, deepest, and most productive gold mine in North America.

In the evenings, "Will" (as his uncle called him) studied or enjoyed the company of the Grier family, which included four young cousins: Thomas Johnston ("Tommy"), Jr. (1897–1929), Evangeline Victoria ("Muddie") (1899–1988), Lisgar (1901–1941), and Ormonde (1903–1964). T.J. frequently entertained Homestake officials and other guests from around the country, and their conversations were stimulating, as were the musical evenings organized by Mary Jane, an accomplished contralto and pianist who brought musicians from near and far to the superintendent's home.

Upon completing his unique apprenticeship at the Homestake Mining Company, Grier returned to San Francisco in December 1903. Phoebe Hearst then put his newly acquired skills to use in organizing and supervising gold prospecting activities on Hearst land in Palermo, California. Instead of utilizing the common prospecting method of drilling, Grier sank shafts to dredge for gold, a process which had been successful in the surrounding area. However, while some gold was recovered, the quantity was never economically significant, and the project was abandoned in the summer of 1904.

While working on the Hearst project, Grier married twenty-five-year-old Laura A. Watson, whom he had met in San Francisco after his return from the Philippines. The 4:40 p.m. ceremony took place on June 20, 1904 in the Superior Court of the County of Sacramento, with Judge Peter J. Shields presiding; Charles H. Holmes and Carolee W. Shields were witnesses.

TWOHY BROTHERS, 1904–1919
Bayshore Cutoff, North Bank Project

Grier's career continued to progress in the first decade of the new century. In October 1904, after five years of experience in real estate development, oil, mining, and supervisory posts, young Grier accepted an assistant foreman position in San Francisco with Twohy Brothers Company, an engineering and construction contractor with headquarters in Portland, Oregon.

At that time, Twohy Brothers had a contract with the Southern Pacific

Railroad Company to construct its Bayshore Cutoff in San Francisco—an assignment that would be the first of a series of major railroad and civil projects in the West in Grier's fifteen-year partnership with Judge John Twohy's firm.[14]

Begun in October of 1904, the Bayshore Cutoff involved laying 9.81 miles of double railroad track from the terminal station in San Francisco to San Bruno, California; constructing five tunnels totaling 9,938 feet in length; and building a 4,110-foot trestle over the Islais Creek Basin.[15] When completed in 1907, project costs would exceed $9 million.

On April 18, 1906, however, the Bayshore Cutoff was damaged by San Francisco's earthquake and fire. The earthquake struck at 5:12 a.m., and for sixty-five seconds, the city was pulled in all directions, leaving a mass of rubble and a raging fire. More than 100,000 residents were left homeless, and food, medical, and other supplies were rushed to the city from across the country.

The *Western Railroader* describes the devastating quake:

> From everywhere rose a terrifying rumble. Steeples wobbled in all directions at once. Chimneys crashed; walls toppled....Although Southern Pacific was hard hit, calm leadership by Vice-President and General Manager Edgar E. Calvin prevented panic among the railroaders. He re-organized railroad operations to meet the emergency. Office headquarters were temporarily established at Oakland and Alameda Piers and the Ferry Building. Later the Southern Pacific rebuilt the interior of the Flood Building and used it as its headquarters. On Valencia Street hill the rails lay twisted by the quake. Many small fires soon united into one huge conflagration in the neighborhood of Third and Market. The battle against the fire seemed hopeless. By noon of the first day it had consumed nearly a square mile of the city — and it was to burn for two more days....Through the night, 3,000 miles to the East, President E.H. Harriman of

---

14.   Judge John Twohy (1854–1927) was born in Copper Harbor, Michigan. After graduating from business school in Detroit, he was admitted to the bar and elected prosecuting attorney of Keweenaw County, Michigan. He practiced law and served as judge of the municipal court in St. Paul, Minnesota from 1890 to 1896. Two years later, he moved to Spokane, joining his brothers James C. and D.W. Twohy in their railroad and civil contracting firm, Twohy Brothers. Following the deaths of his brothers in 1908 and 1909, the firm was incorporated as the Twohy Brothers Company and run by Judge Twohy until his death in 1927. His four sons—John, James, Philip, and Robert—were also associated with this company.

   Twohy Brothers constructed portions of the Northern Pacific, Union Pacific, and Southern Pacific railroads and built ships for Great Northern Shipbuilding Company and the U.S. government during World War I.

15.   Four of the tunnels were of bore construction; the fifth was built up with bricks, its top covered with earth.

the Southern Pacific was racing westward by special train, smashing all speed records across the continent, to direct the railroad's rescue work personally. On the second day, famine threatened the city, and still the flames raged on....Within twelve hours after the earthquake the Southern Pacific and Union Pacific, under the direction of President Harriman, were turned over to the work of relief. Everything else was sidetracked. The record of the runs of relief trains will show all transcontinental freight train records shattered....Up to the night of May 3rd the Southern Pacific handled free into San Francisco 1,409 cars of freight totaling about 35,000 tons for the benefit of the sufferers. Besides this, Southern Pacific hauled over 224,000 passengers out of the city free of charge, and contributed $200,000 to other relief. [16]

As efforts to rebuild the city began, Grier's construction crew from Twohy Brothers laid track on city streets so that flat cars could haul away the rubble. Later, Grier supervised repairs on the Bayshore Cutoff, which included replacing twisted track and reconstructing the twin brick bores in Tunnel Two that had completely collapsed. Despite the delays caused by the earthquake, the Cutoff project was completed on December 8, 1907.

Ironically, the historic quake was directly preceded by a momentous cultural event in San Francisco. On the night of April 17, 1906, Enrico Caruso opened the Metropolitan Opera's run of *Carmen*, singing the role of Don Jose to rave reviews. For many, the event gave the night before the earthquake an aura of feverish excitement; as the critic in the *San Francisco Call* wrote, "The thrill, the throb, the quiver...was in the air."[17]

Caruso was staying at San Francisco's Palace Hotel. Situated on Market Street, the Palace was more elegant than anything of its time. As described by Oscar Lewis and Carroll Hall in *Bonanza Inn*, it featured "three large courts [supplying] light and air to the interior rooms [as well as] a circular driveway opening on the street, thus arriving guests would be driven [by horse and carriage] inside the building and deposited on a marble-paved floor in the midst of a forest of potted trees and plants. Extending upward on all four sides was...a series of seven galleries and, surmounting it all, a great domed roof of opaque glass."[18] Another unusual visual effect was the "vertical banks of bay windows [which] completely covered the great facades, giving an effect that natives proudly described as 'typically San

16.   Fred A. Stindt, "Peninsular Service: The Story of the Southern Pacific Commuter Trains," *Western Railroader*, 20 (1957): 17-19.

17.   *San Francisco Call*, 18 April 1906.

18.   Oscar Lewis and Carroll D. Hall, *Bonanza Inn, America's First Luxury Hotel* (New York: Alfred A. Knopf, 1939), pp. 19-20.

Franciscan'. For these angular projections, designed to catch a maximum of sunshine in a fog-ridden climate, had long been an almost universal feature of the local domestic architecture."[19] Within a few years of its completion, this enormous chamber was famous around the globe.

"The Palace ran not only to size but to massiveness. Its outer walls, of brick, averaged two feet in thickness....Five hydraulic elevators provided access to the acres of upstairs rooms....The upper floors contained 755 rooms, with accommodations for 1,200 guests....Most of them were twenty feet square....Ceilings were uniformly fifteen feet high....So great was the amount of marble used that contracts had to be made with fifteen different firms for 804 mantels, 900 wash-stands, 40,000 square feet of pavement. Finishing woods came from many parts of the world: mahogany, East India teak, primavera from Mexico, rosewood, ebony. Much of it was elaborately carved, all was highly polished....The exterior [was] a dazzling white, with gold trim, sparingly used. Some observers were reminded of a gigantic wedding-cake."[20]

While Caruso and many other notables were able to escape from the Palace during the earthquake, thus avoiding injury, the grandiose hotel itself was less fortunate. It was engulfed by the flames racing up Market Street and was destroyed with a more dramatic climax than any opera in which the great Caruso had starred. The famous tenor never returned to perform in San Francisco again.

The hotel had been a favorite and familiar place of entertainment for the Grier family. Milt was born near the hotel just two years after its construction, and when his father was a supervisor of telegraphers for the Central Pacific Railroad Company, his office was just a few blocks away from the landmark hotel. For many years, it was the center of family gatherings, for both Canadian and American Griers, including a few Christmas Day dinners in the hotel's festively garlanded dining room.

For Grier, the Bayshore Cutoff initiated the longest employment tenure of his career, and during this time, Judge John Twohy, a lawyer and entrepreneur, became an important friend and mentor.

In the fall of 1906, before the Bayshore Cutoff was completed, Grier was made a partner in Twohy Brothers Company and invited by Judge Twohy to supervise track construction on the Great Northern Railroad Company's new line on the North Bank of the Columbia River in Washington State.

---

19.   Ibid., p. 20.

20.   Ibid., pp. 20-27.

During the early period in Washington and Oregon, Milt and his wife Laura settled in The Dalles, a town just northeast of Portland along the south bank of the Columbia River. Later, they lived in Portland,[21] where Twohy Brothers had its main office in the Wells Fargo Building at southwest 6th and Oak Streets.[22]

The North Bank project at that time represented the largest and most complex of the contracts ever undertaken by Twohy Brothers. It involved laying double-track and constructing tunnels and bridges for one of the great railroad builders of the time, James J. Hill.

Hill had determined that the natural downslope of the Columbia River offered a logical railway route to the Pacific Coast. A substantial legal battle ensued over the plan, as Edward H. Harriman, who controlled the Southern Pacific Railroad Company and the route along the south bank of the Columbia River, sought to block the new railway.

In secrecy, Hill, his Northern Pacific Railroad Company, and officials of the Great Northern Railroad Company combined forces in 1905 to build the North Bank railroad. The Portland and Seattle Railway Company was then organized to build a line in Washington State from Pasco down the Columbia River's north bank to Vancouver, crossing the Columbia and Willamette Rivers to Portland, Oregon. In two-and-one-half years, 7,000 men laid 230 miles of track and built thirteen tunnels. The original estimate for the project was $8 million; at completion, however, costs for the North Bank had swelled to nearly $45 million.

When the North Bank's double-track construction was finished, a golden spike ceremony was celebrated on March 11, 1908 at Sheridan's Point on the Columbia River.[23] Local and national officials, including Judge Twohy, Grier, and their wives, attended, and a ten-car train—the first to cross the new tracks—brought some 500 Vancouver and Portland residents to the junction of the rails. Its engine was bedecked with flags and bunting and a banner proclaiming "Hurrah for the North Bank." Government

---

21.   From 1916 to 1918, the Griers lived at 268 14th Street; from 1919 to 1921, at 166 Saint Clair Street. During this period, they enjoyed yachting on the Willamette and Columbia Rivers with Judge Twohy and his family.

22.   When the Northwestern Bank Building at 6th and Alder Streets in Portland, Oregon was completed in 1913, Twohy moved his offices there. Grier and his companies also had offices there until December 1921, when he moved them to San Francisco.

23.   Sheridan's Point was the site of a military block house used as a refuge by forty-seven white settlers when they were attacked by more than 200 Klickitat and Yakima Indians in 1856. Lieutenant Philip Sheridan, who would later gain fame as a Union general in the Civil War, rescued the small band of settlers after several days of heated battle with the marauding Indians.

officials, who had gathered to mark the historic occasion, envisioned a great future for the region which would be served by the new railway, and Charles H. Carey, Portland counsel for the Hill lines, predicted that "down this road will come the great commerce to the Pacific Coast....Great cities will be built here and the population will be increased until it will be as dense as that along the Atlantic Coast."[24]

After the speeches concluded, Richard B. Miller, chief engineer on the North Bank project, drove in the golden spike.[25] Twohy Brothers laid the remaining stretch of track from Pasco to Spokane under Grier's supervision, completing the project in 1909.

On June 25, 1909, Grier's father William John died of a heart attack in his home at 1414 21st Avenue, Oakland, California. Grier attended his father's service at Albert Brown Company, a funeral home located at 584 13th Street, and was present at the interment of his ashes in the Columbarium at 4401 Howe Street in Oakland. Milt's mother Georgie Orr Grier, his sister Mrs. May Grier Barber, and Georgie's younger sister Mrs. Mattie Orr Barber also attended both services.

Grier continued on Twohy Brothers' next contract, the Deschutes project (1910–1911), laying track for James Hill in central Oregon's Deschutes River Canyon, as both Hill and Edward Harriman continued to carve railway out of rock, but on opposite sides of the river.

The bitter rivalry between Hill and Harriman was reflected in an almost constant state of warfare between each man's construction crews in the Deschutes Canyon.

> As early as the summer of 1909, when the only work being done was by engineering and survey gangs, one of the...surveyors recorded in his diary that they were lobbing bullets at each other across the river. "Fortunately," he wrote, "no one seems to be much of a shot." Later, when the construction crews were working right across from each other, things got rougher. After the evening meal it was quite common for a bunch to row across the river and take on anyone they could find from the other team for a session of thumping and knuckle-dusting. Nothing was barred, and the scraps got pretty rough with pick handles and rocks being used to balance the odds. Almost every train back to the Columbia on both lines carried one or more battered construction hands, bound for the hospital in The Dalles.[26]

------

24.   *Dope Bucket: The Spokane, Portland and Seattle's Golden Jubilee Issue*, March 1958.

25.   Chief Engineer R.B. Miller later became Grier's partner in Boschke Miller Grier Company (1919–1921) and in the Miller Grier Company (1921–1922).

26.   *Dope Bucket: The Spokane, Portland and Seattle's Gold Spike Issue*, 1961.

Most of the crews working on the Deschutes project were from the Portland and Spokane areas. Because of the rugged terrain along the Columbia's banks and the fact that there was a steady demand for laborers in other, less hostile settings, good men were hard to come by and even harder to keep. They were, however, attracted by the project's pay scale: roughly 20¢ to 30¢ per hour for common laborers, 35¢ to 40¢ per hour for concrete workers and carpenters, 50¢ per hour for steel workers, and up to $7 per day for well drillers and teamsters. Lodging in primitive camps was furnished without charge, while meals were offered at 25¢ or 30¢ each.

The railroad construction in the Deschutes Canyon was one of the last major projects to use black powder extensively, supplementing the manual labor of crews equipped with picks, hand drills, shovels, and wheelbarrows. In short order, however, the crews found another use for the black powder: industrial sabotage. Men from each side were sent to the clifftops to spy on the crews working across the river and locate the enemy's dynamite storage sites. Later, under the cover of night, five or six men would cross the river silently, climb the far banks, and detonate the opposition's black powder stock pile. As a result, both Hill and Harriman's projects experienced repeated delays due to lack of explosives, until a "cease-fire" was signed on May 17, 1910.

From 1913 to 1915, Twohy Brothers projects took Grier to Montana, where he stayed in the Bright Hotel in Lewistown; to Idaho; to Washington State; and to western Canada. In 1916, Grier worked on a 500-foot dam; the following year, he supervised the Prineville station project in Oregon. Tent camps were built at each of these sites to house the thousands of workers needed to complete the projects, but Grier's accommodations were considerably less Spartan: on-site, he had a private railroad car, complete with bedroom, bath, kitchen, dining area, office, and lounge.

In late September of 1914, Grier attended the funeral of his uncle Thomas Johnston Grier, superintendent of Homestake Mining Company, in Lead, South Dakota. T.J. had died on September 22, while vacationing in his Los Angeles home. Just three weeks earlier, he had left Lead after dedicating the Homestake Opera House and Recreation Building and addressing the opera's opening night audience, on August 31.

During their years with Twohy Brothers in Oregon and the Pacific Northwest, Milt and Laura visited San Francisco, where they saw his mother Georgie, his sister May, and his aunt Mattie. The 1906 quake had provided San Francisco with a chance to rebuild. Soon after, a "City Beautiful" plan was drawn up by Chicago's famed city planner, Daniel Burnham. A splendid new city hall was raised to celebrate the comeback. And in 1915, San Francisco dazzled the world with its Panama-Pacific International Exposition (PPIE), the fair of neoclassical wonder built on marshy landfill, which later became the Marina district. (A dozen years later, Milt moored his yacht *ELOGRIER* at the marina, at the St. Francis Yacht Club.)

In 1915, Grier, Laura, May, and Georgie enjoyed two visits to the PPIE, which opened on February 20, 1915 as Mayor Rolph led a parade of 150,000 people down Van Ness Avenue to its site by the Bay. The Griers were enchanted by the fair's romantic skyline of domes and towers, arcaded and colonnaded courtyards, its walled thematic palaces and gardens. Many critics still consider the PPIE the last, and possibly the most beautiful, of the great American world's fairs, which began with Chicago's phenomenal "Great White City" in 1893. Inspired by the precepts of the Ecole des Beaux-Arts in Paris and by European examples, ideal classical cities appeared in Buffalo in 1901, in St. Louis in 1904, and, finally, in San Francisco in 1915. The PPIE—considered the best planned, the most cohesive, and, by most accounts, the loveliest—was completed less than a decade after the city's ruin by earthquake and fire.

The Griers toured the fair's 635 acres, extending from Fort Mason to the Presidio. They admired Bernard Maybeck's Palace of Fine Arts, a stucco-faced lath and plaster pavilion which was mirrored by the waters of a lagoon. This semicircular building, with its fronting peristyle of terra-cotta Corinthian columns and its ornamental domed rotunda, was the fair's art museum and remains in San Francisco today. Although the PPIE site became today's Marina district, the Palace itself was saved and completely rebuilt of cast concrete in the 1960s. In Maybeck's booklet, *Palace of Fine Arts and Lagoon*, he wrote, "I find that the keynote of a Palace of Fine Arts should be that of sadness, modified by the feeling that beauty has a soothing influence."[27]

Coincidentally, some seventeen years earlier, Grier, as a private in the California Volunteers during the Spanish-American War and Philippine Insurrection, had been trained on that part of the Presidio where the Palace was later erected.

---

27. Bernard R. Maybeck, *Palace of Fine Arts and Lagoon* (San Francisco: Paul Elder and Co., 1915), pp. 9-11.

Grier met architects Bernard Maybeck and Julia Morgan while working for Hearst Oil and Hearst Real Estate and Development in San Francisco (1899–1904) and became a lifelong admirer of their work.

Maybeck had designed Phoebe Hearst's medieval castle, "Wyntoon," in northern California; the Hearst Gymnasium for Women at the University of California at Berkeley; and Frank C. Havens's home, "Wildwood," in Piedmont. Between 1897 and 1899, Maybeck oversaw Mrs. Hearst's International Competition, an architectural plan for the University of California at Berkeley.

T.J. GRIER'S STATUE UNVEILED, 1916

In September 1916, Milt returned to Lead, South Dakota to attend the dedication ceremonies for a monument in his uncle T.J.'s honor. Over 2,000 local miners, businessmen, and residents had contributed to a fund to construct this lasting memorial immediately after T.J.'s death in 1914. When completed two years later, the bronze and granite monument rose over seventeen feet in height and was placed near the Homestake Recreation Building that T.J. had had built for the people of his town shortly before his death.

ERICKSON PETTERSON GRIER COMPANY, 1919–1925
Blue Canyon-Emigrant Gap Project

William Milton Grier remained in the Pacific Northwest for fifteen years, thirteen of these with Twohy Brothers, where he had risen from construction supervisor to general manager and full partner.

In the course of these years, Grier's achievements had earned him both professional acclaim and wealth. He had built dams, tunnels, bridges, viaducts, and thousands of miles of track for the leading railroads and municipal governments in the Pacific Northwest, the Rocky Mountain West, and western Canada. In addition to his major contracts with James J. Hill's Northern Pacific, he had completed construction projects with seven other railroad companies: Oregon & Washington Railway & Navigation; Union Pacific; Southern Pacific; Great Northern; Spokane, Portland & Seattle; Milwaukee & Burlington; and Canadian Northern.

By the age of forty, Grier was ready to direct his own firm. On January 29, 1919, he formed and incorporated the General Construction Company and, four months later, the Boschke Miller Grier Company, both with offices in the Northwestern Bank Building in Portland, Oregon. His partners were George W. Boschke and Richard B. Miller, who had been chief engineer on the North Bank project with Twohy Brothers.

On October 23, 1921, Milt's mother Georgie Orr Grier died of uremia following an operation for uterine cancer at Providence Hospital in Oak-

Julia Morgan, a student of Maybeck's at Berkeley, completed her studies at the Ecole des Beaux-Arts in Paris, the first woman ever accepted there. Morgan practiced in San Francisco for fifty years, designing some 800 buildings. For twenty years, she was a designer and consultant to William Randolph Hearst on his San Simeon estate.

land, California. Milt, his sister May Grier Borman and her second husband Charlie, and his aunt Mrs. Mattie Orr Barber attended the funeral at Albert Brown Company, 584 13th Street and were present as her ashes were placed beside those of her husband William John at the Oakland Columbarium in Oakland, California.

Two months later, in December 1921, Grier purchased his partners' interests in the Boschke Miller Grier Company and moved its headquarters to San Francisco; the offices were located in the Monadnock Building at 681 Market Street, next to the Palace Hotel.

At this time, he also acquired a forty percent interest in the old San Francisco engineering and contracting firm of Erickson Petterson Company, which was already headquartered in the Monadnock Building. Changing its name to Erickson Petterson Grier Company, he ran the firm from December of 1921 until the fall of 1925.

In January of 1923, Erickson Petterson Grier was awarded the $614,000 contract for Southern Pacific Railroad Company's Blue Canyon-Emigrant Gap project, designed to improve railway passage through the famous Emigrant Gap in the Sierra Nevada, near Donner Pass—a rugged and precipitous location, nearly 7,000 feet in elevation, which offered a spectacular panorama of mountains and canyons.

Several hundred men were employed by Grier's company for this project, which began in March 1923. Using huge steam shovels and other equipment, they widened an existing tunnel and laid 5.2 miles of double-track over the original lines laid in the late 1860s by Central Pacific Railroad.[28] (The original tracks had formed the western arm of the first transcontinental railroad, which was completed at Promontory, Utah in 1869. Central Pacific's pioneer locomotive, the Collis P. Huntington— named after one of railroading's Big Four who built the Central Pacific— passed through Emigrant Gap en route from San Francisco to Ogden, Utah that same year.) The majority of the construction materials used on this project were brought in by rail, as was the food provided to the crews in on-site kitchens and dining areas.

With the help of one construction manager, a lead foreman, and several assistants, Grier directed and supervised the work's progress from his office in a private railroad car. Complete with kitchen, living, and dining facilities, this Pullman car was Grier's "home," as well, until construction was

---

28.   Today these tracks are still used as part of the Southern Pacific Railroad's route over the Sierra Nevada through Blue Canyon, Emigrant Gap, and the Donner Summit to Nevada and Utah. Emigrant Gap is 166 miles from San Francisco.

completed in September 1923.

During a typical week, Grier would spend one or two days in his San Francisco office. He would travel by Southern Pacific passenger train from the work site, often stopping in Sacramento before proceeding to the Oakland Mole depot and catching the ferryboat to San Francisco. From the Ferry Building, his office was then a short walk up Market Street. He also conferred regularly with Southern Pacific's officials in both their Sacramento and San Francisco offices.[29]

GRIER AND MEAD, 1925–1931

Claremont Tunnel Project

In mid-1925, the three directors of Erickson Petterson Grier Company—Gust Petterson, H. White, and William Milton Grier—decided to dissolve the firm, effective November 2, 1925. (Erickson had recently died, and Petterson wished to retire.) With its dissolution, Grier next organized a new company under his control.

That fall, he formed a partnership with Winfield Scott Mead, an experienced construction and railroad contractor who had completed projects in Oklahoma, Texas, California, and Mexico.[30] The offices of this new firm—Grier and Mead—were first located in San Francisco at 593 Market Street, Room 241, a block east of the Monadnock Building. In 1927, they were moved to the Ray Building in Oakland, at 1924 Broadway, Rooms 303 and 317, where the company remained until 1931. The building was acquired by Henry J. Kaiser for his construction company on November 20, 1944.

In July of 1926, Grier and Mead secured a contract with the East Bay Municipal Utility District for the construction of the inter-county (Alameda

---

29. More than fifty years after Grier completed this project, his eldest son, Bill, and wife Joan traveled from Denver by train over Donner Pass, Emigrant Gap, and Blue Canyon while en route to visit his mother and Lannon relatives in Sacramento.

30. Grier's partner Winfield Scott Mead, a Kentucky native, was an active contractor in Kern County, California before opening a San Francisco office when they formed Grier and Mead. His work on grading the Kern River canyon–Walker's Pass road, for example, was hailed as an engineering feat and involved removing 40,000 tons of rock from a cliffside location.

Mead and his wife Annette B. had two sons—Winfield Scott, Jr., who died in the 1940s, and John Stanley, now an attorney with Mead, Bradley and Kennan in San Francisco. From the late 1920s through the 1940s, the Meads lived at 110 Mesa Avenue, one block east of the Griers' home at 107 Highland Avenue in Piedmont, California.

and Contra Costa counties) Claremont water tunnel. Beginning in Orinda at a height of 340 feet above sea level, the transmountain tunnel gradually sloped to a 328-foot level at Rockridge district in Oakland, conveying 200 million gallons of water daily.

The Claremont project was one of three tunnels constructed between Oakland and the San Joaquin River to bring water from the Mokelumne River, in northern California's Calaveras County, into the East Bay district. It was the longest underground link in the Mokelumne project, which diverted the river's water from San Pablo Creek in Orinda, Contra Costa County, up to the Rockridge district in Oakland, Alameda County, and thus directly into the distribution area for the city of Oakland.

The East Bay Municipal Utility District, which granted the contract to Grier and Mead, was organized in 1923, the year the O'Shaughnessy Dam on the Tuolomne River in Yosemite National Park was completed to impound water for San Francisco. In addition to the Claremont tunnel, the utility district constructed both the Walnut Creek tunnel, a half-mile bore, and the Lafayette tunnel, which ran just over three miles in length.

The Claremont project had originally been awarded to the firm of MacDonald & Kahn, which had submitted the lowest bid—$1,068,140. After beginning work, however, they discovered that they had miscalculated their bid and asked to be relieved, whereupon the contract was awarded to Grier and Mead, the next lowest bidder at $1,374,374. Grier's firm was chosen over twelve other companies, including W.A. Bechtel Company, Twohy Brothers, and Utah Construction Company.

Grier and Mead directed construction of the Claremont tunnel from two field offices, one at the north entrance in Orinda and the other at the south entrance on Chabot Road in the Oakland hills.

In the course of completing the project, Grier and his colleagues overcame a number of major engineering obstacles. The rugged terrain of the coastal hills prevented them from using vertical shafts for excavating, which was the conventional (and far simpler) technique. Instead, the 3.6-mile inter-county bore had to be constructed by working inward from its two ends, and all materials were hauled through its nine-foot, horseshoe-shaped entrances.

Because of the unusual construction techniques, special measures were needed to insure adequate ventilation while work progressed. Three huge blowers were installed at each end of the bore to deliver fresh air to the workers. Giant compressors were also set up at Orinda and Rockridge district in Oakland, furnishing 2,000 cubic feet of compressed air to operate the drills with which the men were forging their way through the earth.

The crews also had to contend with coal, gas, and oil deposits, various fossilized formations, and large quantities of water which accumulated within the tunnel.

Grier and Mead's crews worked round-the-clock in three eight-hour shifts, first removing 100,000 cubic feet of dirt to hollow out the bore, then constructing the tunnel itself. The entire project would require more than 22,000 cubic yards of concrete.

Tragedy struck the Claremont project on Thanksgiving night, November 25, 1926, shortly after Grier and Mead Company had hosted a holiday meal. Flood waters, attributed to several days of heavy rains, broke the coffer dam on San Pablo Creek at Orinda, inundating a four-foot connecting conduit that ran into the Claremont tunnel. Eleven of Grier's men had just descended a seventy-five-foot shaft, some 800 feet from the mouth of the tunnel at Orinda, when a six-foot wall of water plunged down and filled the tunnel. The swirling waters caused a cave-in, trapping the eleven men. Only one survived.

The horrified town of Orinda kept vigil for two days while rescue workers tried to recover the bodies. Dr. George C. Pardee, president of the Board of Governors of the East Bay Municipal Utility District, paid tribute to the ten workmen who had lost their lives:

> The march of progress claims many lives. The men who thus died
> were the unsung heroes of this nation. We grieve for them; we
> honor them. May their souls find eternal peace in the great
> beyond.[31]

The broken coffer dam was located on the portion of the project under contract to Smith Brothers, Inc. An investigation of the tragedy assigned liability for the disaster to Smith Brothers, and the firm of Grier and Mead was absolved of any responsibility.

When the Claremont tunnel was completed, water flowed through pipes and conduits from the Lancha Plana reservoir on the Mokelumne River to the Claremont reservoir ninety miles away, coming to the surface at only one point for aeration purposes. At the Oakland end, a concrete building was erected above the buried standpipe to function as a control house and laboratory. Three fifty-four-inch steel pipes and giant gate valves controlled the flow of water at both Orinda and Rockridge; at the latter point, the water emptied into the "balancing" Claremont reservoir. The water flowed from the Mokelumne pipes into the Claremont tunnel at Orinda, near the site of the Orinda Country Club, and through the chlorina-

---

31. *Oakland Post Enquirer,* 26 November 1926.

tion plant and cistern. It then ran into mains for general distribution from that point, passing directly from the western end of the Lafayette tunnel into the mains that conveyed it to the faucets of Oakland and East Bay residents.

The tunnel was hailed as an engineering feat when it was completed in 1929. Extending in a straight line, it cut through hills which, at their highest, were 1,650 feet above sea level. Under the Claremont hills from Orinda toward Oakland, it was constructed on a twenty-five-degree slope.

The project's actual cost was $1,712,535, exceeding the original bid by $338,161. The overrun was calculated at cost plus fifteen percent, a portion of which included extra work required to rectify the November 1926 flood damage.

During the course of construction, Grier and Mead made some interesting archeological discoveries, as well. Their crews unearthed the fossilized shinbone of an *Eohippus*, a miniature prehistoric horse, as well as bones of a sabre-toothed tiger, which are normally found only in tropical climates.

Both Erickson Petterson Grier Company and Grier and Mead had completed large and technically demanding projects during the 1920s. These successes had, in turn, established Milt Grier's reputation for mastery in engineering and construction.

MARRIAGE TO ELO LANNON, FAMILY LIFE

In 1921, Grier's marriage to Laura Watson ended in divorce; they had had no children.[32] Two years later, while in the offices of Southern Pacific Railroad to discuss the Blue Canyon-Emigrant Gap project, he met an attractive young secretary named Elo Theresa Lannon. After a four-year courtship, Milt and Elo were married on November 9, 1927 in a civil ceremony in Reno, Nevada. George Bartlett, a Nevada district judge, officiated, and Harlan L. Heward and Bessie Ellsworth witnessed the ceremony. The couple then honeymooned at the newly opened Ahwahnee Hotel in Yosemite National Park.[33]

---

32. From 1922 to 1924, Milt Grier lived in San Francisco at 645 Leavenworth Street; from 1925 to 1927, at 2337 Chestnut Street. During this period, Laura A. Grier lived near Golden Gate Park, at 301 Carl Street.

33. Ahwahnee is an Indian name meaning "deep, grassy valley." The hotel's architect was Gilbert Stanley Underwood, a Harvard graduate who also designed two other high-country hotels: Timberline Lodge at Mount Hood, Oregon and Sun Valley Lodge in Idaho. Two art historians designed the interiors—Dr. Phyllis Ackerman and Dr. Arthur Upham Pope, husband and wife, who had a special interest in Native American design.

Seventeen years younger than her husband, Elo was born on September 26, 1895 in Sacramento, California, the second of Patrick Joseph and Julia McDermott Lannon's children. She was baptized on October 27, 1895 in the Cathedral of the Blessed Sacrament at 11th and K Streets in Sacramento.

Her parents were of Irish descent, both born in Strokestown, Roscommon, Ireland. They emigrated to the United States in the 1880s and were married in Sacramento on October 3, 1892, in the church where Elo would be baptized three years later.

Elo was educated in Sacramento's public and parochial schools, graduating from the John Marshall School, Mary Jane Watson Junior High School, and Saint Joseph Academy before entering the business world.

In mid-December 1926, Elo took a six-week winter vacation in the East. She went by train to New York City to visit her uncle John A. Lannon and his wife Sarah (nee Walsh) and to Providence, Rhode Island to visit her aunt Margaret McDermott O'Rourke (her mother's sister), Margaret's husband James, and Elo's cousin Elizabeth McGreevey. After celebrating the holidays with her relatives, she boarded the Southern Pacific Steamship Lines' *Creole* in New York City for its January 15 cruise to New Orleans, where she enjoyed several days of sightseeing before returning to San Francisco by train.

During the spring of 1927, Grier took his bride-to-be and her younger sisters—Ferdinand ("Ferdy") and Julia—to the Del Coronado Hotel in Coronado, California for a week of swimming, sailing, and sightseeing in San Diego and Tijuana.

For his first home with Elo, Grier bought a ten-room, English-style house in fashionable Piedmont, California.[34] Located at 107 Highland Avenue, the two-story, grey-stuccoed and timbered home had leaded windows, two dining rooms, a wine cellar, and a roof garden over the garage. While Elo helped select furnishings at antique shops and W&J Sloane in San Francisco, Anna Jorgens, a designer and neighbor of May Grier Borman, created its interior plan. Elo eventually had a cook and maid, a nanny and gardener to help her there.[35]

---

34. In 1820, the Piedmont, Oakland, Berkeley, Alameda, and San Leandro areas were part of a Spanish land grant called Rancho Antonio, which was given to Don Luis Peralta, a Spanish soldier. Peralta, never living on the Rancho, eventually divided it among his four sons. The first known settler in the Piedmont area, Walter Blair, came to San Francisco from Vermont. In 1852, he camped at what is now the corner of Blair and Highland Avenue, a block from William Milton Grier's home at 107 Highland Avenue.

35. After an attempted robbery at the Grier home in 1930, Milt installed a security alarm system between his home and his neighbors, the Joseph C. Merrick family, who lived on the corner of Park Way and Highland Avenue and often watched after young Bill and Eloyd.

Two sons were born to the Griers: William Milton, Jr., on September 23, 1928 in the Fabiola Hospital in Oakland, and Eloyd John, on July 4, 1929 in the St. Francis Hospital in San Francisco. They were baptized on March 22, 1930 at Trinity Episcopal Cathedral in Phoenix, Arizona, where the family rented a winter home. Edwin S. Lane, Dean, performed the baptism; witnesses included Grier's sister May and brother-in-law Charles J. Borman.

YACHT *ELOGRIER*

In 1927, Grier retained Nunes Brothers Shipyard in Sausalito to design and construct a diesel-powered yacht to sleep ten passengers. Named for his wife, the *ELOGRIER* was completed in 1929. It was finished in Philippine mahogany and Chinese teak and was powered by a seventy-five-horsepower, six-cylinder diesel engine. Fifty feet long by eleven feet wide, the yacht featured a raised deck and trunk cabin and had a cruising range of 1,000 miles; its official number was 229179. Anna Jorgens also oversaw the yacht's furnishings, including glass- and dishware, draperies and fabric coverings.

Garland Rotch, a San Francisco ship's captain who had sailed widely in the South Pacific islands and the Orient, was employed by Grier to operate the yacht and oversee its maintenance. The *ELOGRIER* was moored in San Francisco's marina at St. Francis Yacht Club, where the adjoining berth slip was occupied by Templeton Crocker's yacht *Zaca*.[36] Grier was a member of the St. Francis Yacht Club from 1927 to 1935.

The family cruised in San Francisco and San Pablo Bays, on the Sacramento River, and along the Pacific Coast to Monterey, where they slept aboard the yacht or at the Del Monte Hotel.[37] They also cruised to San Diego

---

36. A philanthropist and heir to his father Charles Crocker's Central Pacific Railroad fortune, Templeton Crocker attended Yale and supported the California Academy of Sciences, the oldest scientific institution in the West. Crocker's yacht *Zaca* (the Samoan term for peace) was used on the Academy's expeditions in Alaska, Panama, Asia, Africa, Australia, New Zealand, South America, and many of the Pacific islands.

The yacht was also used by actor Errol Flynn during the 1940s to entertain young starlets. Following one such excursion, Flynn was accused of statutory rape, leading to a sensational court trial in 1942 and '43 which made front-page headlines across America. Flynn was finally acquitted on all charges.

37. Pebble Beach, 125 miles south of San Francisco, was once a picnic ground for guests at Charles Crocker's Del Monte Hotel in Monterey. Crocker was one of the "Big Four" of the

and Coronado, where they were guests at the Del Coronado Hotel.

May and Charles Borman and their daughter George Ann were frequent passengers. Some ten years older than her cousins Bill and Eloyd, George Ann often watched after them during these family excursions.

In 1927, Grier bought new dining and living room furniture for Elo's parents' turn-of-the-century Victorian home at 5314 J Street in Sacramento. In the same year, he hired his young brother-in-law, Raymond James Lannon, to build a wine and beer cellar in the Griers' Piedmont home, where beer was brewed in large crocks and bottled, capped, and stored. He also financed sister-in-law Ferd Lannon's education at San Jose State College and hired her to care for his infant sons.

The Griers often entertained in their home and at the St. Francis Yacht Club in San Francisco. When Grier and Mead had offices in the Ray Building in Oakland, Milt often hosted lunches at the Leamington Hotel on 19th and Franklin Streets and at Hotel Oakland on 13th and Harrison, as well as at the Palace Hotel in San Francisco.

On July 20, 1929, Milt was saddened by the tragic death of his young cousin, Thomas Johnston ("Tommy") Grier, Jr. (1897–1929). He and a friend, Theron P. Stevick, were driving in the early evening in Tommy's Pierce Arrow near San Rafael, California, en route to the Bohemian Club summer encampment and its "Hi Jinks"—the annual play performed in the club's outdoor theatre at Bohemian Grove in northern California. The car overturned on a curve, instantly killing the thirty-two-year-old Grier. (His passenger was thrown from the car and escaped serious injury.)

Tommy and his wife Sally Havens had lived in Los Angeles following their Piedmont wedding in 1920. While there, he had been president of Citizens Guaranty Loan & Investment Company, a firm he founded in 1925. After the birth of his son Thomas Johnston Grier 3d in Los Angeles on August 20, 1926' the Griers returned to San Francisco, where Tommy became an officer with Fireman's Fund Insurance Company at 401 California Street. At the time of his death, Tommy was assistant treasurer, and his family lived in San Francisco's Sea Cliff district at 2801 Lake Street. Milt, his wife Elo, and sister May attended the funeral in San Francisco.

During the holiday season, the Griers and May Borman enjoyed taking young Bill and Eloyd to see the Santa Clauses and toylands at San Francisco department stores: The White House; City of Paris, with its dazzling Christmas tree rising above balconies to a glass dome and its Louis XVI window frames of white enamel and carved, gilded wood; and The Empo-

---

Central Pacific Railroad; his development firm, Pacific Improvement Company, later became Del Monte Properties.

rium, with an immense glass-domed rotunda, ringed by a pillared gallery, rising through four stories to the roof garden. Amongst the glittering toys, the boys eagerly pointed out electric trains, bright red tricycles, fire trucks, and automobiles.

Between 1928 and 1933, the Griers celebrated Christmas and New Year's in their Piedmont home, which was decorated with holly, evergreens, and a ceiling-tall tree. Presents were opened on Christmas Eve; afterward, before retiring, the children hung stockings on the mantle over the fireplace, then fetched and emptied them early Christmas morning. Later in the day, family and guests had a festive dinner, and the Griers hosted a reception on Christmas night. After the holidays, from 1930 to 1933, the Griers spent winters in rented homes in the Camelback Road area of Phoenix, Arizona.

TRAITS

Milt Grier, who possessed a keen intelligence and a captivating charm, inspired devotion and loyalty. He was 5' 8" tall and fair, with blue-gray eyes. In middle age, his brown hair receded and thinned, and he became stocky. He wore tailor-made, single-breasted suits, favored French and Italian food and wine, and smoked cigarettes, cigars, and pipes. (Some of his pipes were bought while he was in the Philippines and Japan during 1898-1899, including an elegant mahogany humidor.)

When living at a construction site, he often took along books of Emerson, Keats, Sir Walter Scott, and Dickens, and when time permitted, he enjoyed walking in the country, savoring and observing nature's beauty and wildlife.

Grier was a Republican, a conservative who believed in private enterprise and individual initiative. He admired Herbert Hoover's mining engineering achievements, his humanitarian work in Europe during World War I and turn-of-the-century relief work in China during the Boxer Rebellion, and his efforts to promote the Panama-Pacific International Exposition from 1912 to 1914.

Grier was a Mason for nearly thirty years. On March 4, 1907, he had joined Wasco Lodge Number 15, Columbia Commandery Number 13 in The Dalles, Oregon; on May 27, 1907, he became a Master Mason; on December 1, 1911, he received the Order of the Red Cross; and on February 9, 1912, he was made a Knight of the Malta and Knight Templar. While working in Montana from 1913 to 1915, he was an active member of the Algeria Temple in Helena. Grier retained his membership in the Masons until his death in December 1935.

In his leisure hours, Grier enjoyed woodworking at his bench in the garage of his Piedmont home—a skill passed down to him from his grandfather James, a carriage-maker—producing toy locomotives, railroad cars, and ships for his sons with saws, planes, chisels, and other tools. He also played cribbage, whist, poker, gin rummy, and dominoes. (Another purchase in Japan was a set of ivory dominoes in a rectangular oak box with sliding lid which he took with him when living at construction sites.)

A keen judge of character and ability, Grier selected able partners and associates in his companies, men of talent and integrity. He gave them broad responsibilities and compensated them well. Although bold and aggressive in directing his enterprises, Grier was unfailingly considerate and courteous in his personal relationships.

FRIENDS AND COMPETITORS
Giannini, Kaiser, Bechtel

Milt Grier modestly attributed his success to luck and help from family and friends—his parents and his uncle T.J., Phoebe Hearst, and Judge John Twohy. Yet, although doubtlessly helped by them, his ascendancy was, above all, the product of his own genius and industry.

Grier was a lifelong friend of Amadeo Peter ("A.P.") Giannini, who, in 1904, founded the Bank of Italy (renamed Bank of America in 1930) at the corner of Washington Street and Columbus Avenue in San Francisco.[38] The two men had met during the bank's first year, while Grier was working as manager with Twohy Brothers, contractor on the Southern Pacific Railroad Company's Bayshore Cutoff project. They soon developed a close business relationship, and in future years, as a client of Giannini's bank, Grier would build tunnels, bridges, water systems, and dams and lay many miles of railroad track.

Giannini admired Grier's achievements and entrepreneurial abilities; Grier esteemed Giannini's original banking practices that helped the common man—practices that laid the foundation for his bank's future growth and success. Giannini, in fact, proudly dubbed his Bank of Italy "the Little Fellow's Bank." Laborers, small businessmen, anybody with a little vision and a lot of determination could walk into Giannini's bank and walk out with a loan.

---

38. A.P. Giannini, eight years Grier's senior, was born on May 6, 1870 in San Jose, California. A consummate businessman, A.P. had a philosophy concerning the accumulation of wealth: "I don't want to be rich....No man actually owns a fortune; it owns him." At his death in 1949, he left an estate of $489, 278, a relatively modest amount for a person in his position.

Grier also applauded Giannini's daring immediately after San Francisco's disastrous earthquake in April 1906, even though many of Giannini's fellow bankers considered him a radical and would have nothing to do with him. While the majority of the city's bankers wrung their hands and declared they could not reopen until November, Giannini astounded everyone by announcing that the Bank of Italy would be ready for business the next day. Moreover, he set up a "bank" at a desk in a waterfront shack, where he loaned money liberally to area workers and quickly saw his faith rewarded. Soon after, he extended a loan to Grier, representing Twohy Brothers, to repair the damages on the Bayshore Cutoff project caused by the quake. Giannini's timely actions helped transform the city's pessimism into optimism.

Eschewing the trappings of corporate power and wanting to be in contact with his customers, Giannini did not have a private office at the bank's main branch at 1 Powell Street in San Francisco. Rather, he worked at his desk in the midst of the main floor, where he could readily greet and assist his customers. When Grier entered the Bank of Italy, Giannini would rise and walk over to welcome him with a warm embrace, affectionately calling him "Giamo." After Grier relocated his company to San Francisco at the end of 1921, he, Giannini, and others often lunched together at the Palace and downtown restaurants.

In 1922, '25, and '28, Giannini asked Grier to become a director of the Bank of Italy, but, already burdened with responsibilities, Grier respectfully declined each offer. Later, Grier also became a business friend of A.P.'s son Mario, a law graduate who was named president of the Bank of America in 1936.

Grier was also a long-time friend of Henry J. Kaiser and Warren A. Bechtel.[39] Like Grier, these construction entrepreneurs had begun working at an early age, gradually making their way up through the ranks and founding their companies after gaining field experience with other firms.

Kaiser, the son of German immigrants, left school at thirteen to enter the

---

39. Henry J. Kaiser (1882–1967) was born in Sprout Brook, New York and left home in the eighth grade to help support his family. His son Edgar (1908-1981) became president of Kaiser Industries Corporation in 1956.

Warren A. Bechtel (1872–1931) was born in Freeport, Illinois. His firm was originally headquartered in Oakland, California, but later relocated to San Francisco. In 1926, W.A. Bechtel Company lost the bid on the Claremont tunnel project to Grier and Mead.

Grier also knew the sons of these company founders—Stephen, Kenneth, and Warren, Jr. Bechtel and Henry, Jr. and Edgar Kaiser.

business world. He began with a $1.50-a-week job in upstate New York; within ten years, he was the owner of a photographic firm with stores in New York, Florida, and the Bahamas.

In 1906, however, he decided to head to the fast-growing western states, where he secured a job with a hardware company in Spokane, Washington. Six years later, he began work in the construction industry, joining a Pacific Northwest firm as a salesman and manager.

At the age of thirty-two— in the year 1914—he founded the Henry J. Kaiser Company, Ltd. in Vancouver. By the time his firm relocated to its permanent headquarters in Oakland, California in 1921, Kaiser had completed millions of dollars worth of construction projects across California and the northwest—highways, dams, and sand and gravel plants.

In 1927, Kaiser was awarded a $20 million contract to build over 200 miles of roads and 500 bridges in Cuba. His company was also a member of the Six Companies, Inc., a consortium of builders who completed the Hoover Dam in the 1930s. Other projects in that period included the Shasta, Grand Coulee, and Bonneville dams and the San Francisco Bay Bridge piers.

Like Kaiser and Grier, Warren Bechtel—known to friends as "Dad" — was a self-starter from humble beginnings. An Illinois native, he was a muleskinner in his early years and had an unprofitable tenure in the cattle business before entering the heavy construction industry. By coincidence, he founded his own firm—W.A. Bechtel—in the same year that Kaiser had launched his business, 1914.

Over the next half-century, Bechtel's company, incorporated in 1925 in Oakland, would expand dramatically, building bridges, rail lines, dams, and natural gas lines. It, too, was part of the consortium that built the Hoover Dam.

Although Grier, Kaiser, and Bechtel were often competitors bidding on the same project, neither their friendship nor their mutual respect was affected by the outcome. During this period, they often talked by telephone and sometimes lunched together to discuss the exigencies of construction and future projects.

Since then, the companies formed by Kaiser and Bechtel in Oakland and San Francisco have grown into international firms—Kaiser Industries and Bechtel Group, Inc. The founding fathers' sons and grandsons have succeeded them and today continue to direct these enterprises.

Unlike Kaiser's and Bechtel's children who were grown and experienced in the business, Grier's sons Bill and Eloyd—only seven and six years old when he died—were, of course, too young to succeed their father, and thus his enterprise ended with his death in 1935.

'29 CRASH

Milt Grier's professional life and prosperity in the first third of the century reflected the nation's unprecedented growth. The United States was then producing twenty-five percent of the world's goods and services, and in this climate, all but the least efficient firms grew rich, especially those in manufacturing, construction, and real estate.

Accompanying this growth and prosperity was a strong spirit of optimism, leading many people to invest their money in the corporations that were making America great. Sound investment decisions, however, soon gave way to rash speculation. Between 1923 and 1929, speculative fever gripped the market, driving stock prices higher and higher. The vastly inflated prices of corporate equities soon bore little resemblance to actual corporate asset value and profitability.

Free of debt and enjoying a high income during the 1920s, Grier, too, invested in the stock market. Among the stocks soaring in price at this time were Giannini's Bank of Italy and Transamerica Corporation,[40] of which Grier accumulated 20,000 shares. Other holdings included U.S. Steel, Standard Oil of New Jersey, Petroleum Corporation of America, North American Oil Company, Inter Coast Trading Company, City Service Company, and various railroads.

When the bull market crashed on October 29, 1929—"Black Tuesday"— it brought ruin to many. For Grier, who was at the peak of his career as his Claremont tunnel project neared completion, the Crash seriously reduced his wealth and impaired his participation in future ventures, including the Hoover Dam (1931–1936), the San Francisco-Oakland Bay Bridge (1933–1936), and the Golden Gate Bridge, which was started on January 14, 1933 and completed in May of 1937.

The Crash also took its toll on Grier's health, and in 1930, he suffered his first heart attack. Attended by nurses round-the-clock in his home, he recovered but remained under the care of two San Francisco physicians, Drs. Daniel W. Sooy, a surgeon, and Laird M. Morris, an internist, until his

---

40. From 1928 to 1929, Transamerica Corporation was formed as a holding company to absorb the assets of the Bank of Italy.

To acquire other banks through the exhange of stock, Transamerica held two California branch-banking systems, as well as a New York bank, two large insurance companies, and controlling interest in General Foods Corporation.

death five years later.[41]

After surviving a second heart attack in 1933, Grier sought a change of pace and tried unsuccessfully to exchange his yacht *ELOGRIER* and the Piedmont home for an operating fruit ranch, with considerable acreage, in Walnut Creek, California.

Compounding the trauma of illness and the '29 Crash, Grier was kidnapped and robbed by three men and a woman in downtown Sacramento in 1934. They forced him into a car near Seventh and J Streets, knocked him unconscious, took a diamond stickpin, other jewelry, and cash, and threw him from the car in Yolo County, near Sacramento. Neither the jewelry and money nor the kidnappers were ever found.

VISITING MAY GRIER BORMAN

Grier's children Bill and Eloyd were devoted to his sister May Grier Borman, who adored them. From 1928 to 1934, she regularly visited them in Piedmont, commuting by ferry from San Francisco to Oakland Mole depot, then boarding the Key Route electric train to 41st Street and Piedmont Avenue. There, she transferred to a streetcar that climbed up the wooded hills of Piedmont to the Griers' home at 107 Highland Avenue. The boys treasured her joyful visits and loving hugs, her amusing stories, games, and trinkets.

Bill and Eloyd were equally excited to visit their aunt May, uncle Charlie, cousin George Ann, and the Bormans' affectionate Irish terrier, Whiskers, in their San Francisco home near Golden Gate Park and the Pacific.

Their playful pet, a liver-colored mutt, was much loved by the boys. He accompanied May on her afternoon walks to market at nearby greengrocers on Balboa Street, went on fishing and camping trips, and slept in the basement in a wicker basket cushioned with old pillows and blankets.

George Ann played popular music on the family's upright piano and taught her cousins the scales and chords. She liked Irving Berlin's and Jerome Kern's compositions, George and Ira Gershwin's jazz harmonies, Harold Arlen's melodies, Cole Porter, Oscar Hammerstein II, and Lorenz

---

41. Both physicians had their offices in the medical-dental building at 490 Post Street. Dr. Sooy was in room 216; Dr. Morris, in room 644.

Hart. Many of these songs were popularized by Bing Crosby, although the most important indicator of popularity then was the weekly radio show "The Lucky Strike Hit Parade," to which George Ann and her cousins faithfully listened.

During these visits, May planned all manner of excursions to delight the children: picnics, rides on street and cable cars, ferryboats, and interurban electric trains (both the orange-colored Key Route and red-colored Southern Pacific in Oakland and East Bay), tours to the Ghiradelli chocolate factory, and visits to Playland-at-the-Beach, Fleishhacker Playfield and Zoological Gardens (now San Francisco Zoo), and toy departments of downtown stores.

The zoo was named after Herbert Fleishhacker, a San Francisco banker and former president of the San Francisco Park Commission who donated the pool and Mother's House, a resting place for mothers and their offspring. Located on 128 acres a block from the Pacific Ocean, the 1,000-animal zoo, patterned after Germany's renowned Hagenbeck Zoo, featured man-made streams, waterfalls, islands, cliffs, and caves—natural habitats separated from spectators by moats.

For the boys, Fleishhacker was paradise—a bucolic site of greenery where the smell of eucalyptus and pine always seemed to wash the air. They enjoyed the animals (especially the expressive apes, monkeys, and penguins) and loved to watch the feeding of the lions and tigers. They played on the swings and spiraling slides and built fortresses in the sand. They gleefully rode the carousel's colorful, hand-carved wooden horses while it turned to the lively sound of its band organ.[42] They rode ponies and the thrilling miniature railroad. An engineer, dressed in blue-and-white striped bib overalls and visor cap, sat in the diesel-powered locomotive and ran the train. After shouting "All aboard!" he sounded his whistle, started the engine, and the train would soon disappear from the view of people at the depot; chugging about the gardens and groves of tall eucalyptus, pine, and cedar trees, it passed through a tunnel and over a bridge before the whistle sounded its return to the station.

There also were picnics on the lawn and wading and swimming in the warmed saltwater of the outdoor pool for fifteen cents. When built in 1925, the pool was considered the largest in the world. Measuring 1,000 feet long and 150 feet wide, its depth ranged from three to fourteen feet, and it

---

42. The merry-go-round was constructed in 1925 by William H. Dentzel of Philadelphia, whose family was famous for producing intricate wood carvings of animals.

accommodated several thousand swimmers in its 6.5 million gallons of water.[43]

William Milton Grier, by this time a successful businessman in his fifties, was especially proud to be a father and to experience the childhood pleasures of his sons at a time in life when his career was well established.

GRIER AND FONTAINE, 1934–1935

Gold Mining in the Sierra Nevada

In 1934, Milt formed Grier and Fontaine with William R. Fontaine, a brilliant Oakland civil engineer and consultant who assisted Grier and Mead in constructing the Claremont tunnel.[44] Their venture was prospecting for gold in Placer County, California, where the company had taken leasehold options on acreage tracts near the towns of Loomis and Lincoln.

With his work now centered in this area, Grier leased the home in Piedmont, stored its furnishings with a company in Oakland, and moved his family to Sacramento, fifty miles away from his work site. Initially, they shared the home of Elo's parents Patrick and Julia Lannon, at 5314 J Street. Later, however, Milt and Elo lived in a motel in Loomis, while the boys remained with their grandparents. In September of 1934, they enrolled in El Dorado Elementary School, Bill in high first grade and Eloyd in kindergarten. They remember that during this period their father gave them vials of gold, after the crushed rock samples from his dredgings were assayed for gold content at laboratories in Sacramento.

On July 4, 1934, in celebration of Eloyd's fifth birthday, his father bought a variety of fireworks which he set off in front of the Lannons'

---

43. Opening on April 23, 1925, the pool was first used for the American Amateur Union (AAU) men's championships, where Johnny Weismuller won the four-day competition for his team, the Illinois Athletic Club.

On annual trips to San Francisco as an adult, Bill has enjoyed visiting the zoo and gardens, an oasis of serenity and nostalgia: strolling its lush glades and viewing its animals; watching mothers and their frolicking children; picnicking and reading by a pond; savoring its beauty and recapturing his boyhood play there under the loving gaze of his aunt May Grier Borman. He was saddened, though, at the removal of the miniature railway and the swimming pool, which had added such excitement to his adventures there.

44. William Fontaine lived in Oakland's Regillus Apartments at 244 Lakeside Drive, on Lake Merritt, and had an office in the nearby Ray Building, where Grier and Mead was headquartered.

Victorian home on tree-lined J Street. Family and friends enjoyed the display from ladder-back rockers and a swing on the second-floor pillared front porch, which was reached from the sidewalk by wide steps. The family also watched the State Fair's nightly fireworks in August from the Lannons' rear porch .

While living in Sacramento in the mid-thirties, the boys swam and picnicked during summer vacations at Southside Park, located on 6th and T Streets, and visited the zoo and miniature railway in William Land Park.

During 1934 and 1935, Grier traveled to San Francisco to see his doctors, conduct business, and be with his sister May, brother-in-law Charlie, and niece George Ann. The Bormans adored his visits. A good conversationalist, "Billy" (as May called him, or "Uncle Milt" to George Ann) entertained them with stories of his activities and family. He also took them to dinner at favorite restaurants and for cruises aboard his yacht *ELOGRIER*. (During this period, Charlie occasionally helped captain Garland Rotch in its maintenance.)

From May's home on October 3, 1934, Milt wrote a letter — the only one that has survived—to his wife Elo: "My dearest sweetheart: I was just leaving for downtown when your dear letter was handed to me...I was glad to hear from you. Mighty glad to know Eloyd is OK, and hope he is back in school now. I was very much pleased when I opened my grip to find everything so nicely arranged, just like you. Won't write more now, just wanted to answer as soon as your dear letter was received and before going downtown. All my love to the dearest girl in the world. Love and kisses to the boys and folks. I am, yours lovingly—Billy."

Grier and Fontaine Company continued gold prospecting until Milt succumbed to a third heart attack in Sacramento on December 8, 1935 at the age of fifty-seven. His ashes were placed near those of his father and mother, William John and Georgie, in the Oakland Columbarium near Piedmont.

William Milton Grier's untimely death left incomplete his promising gold exploration project in the Sierra Nevada. He left behind a young wife and two small boys of six and seven. But he left, too, a rich legacy of love and accomplishment that has inspired and brightened the lives of his family and friends to this day.

W.M. ("Milt") Grier, c. 1900

226

San Francisco, c. 1878 (Currier and Ives lithograph)

W.M. ("Milt") Grier, c. 1894

Above, first schoolhouse in Palermo, California, 1889; *below*, its replacement, 1904

228

California U.S. Volunteers' encampment at the Presidio, San Francisco
(*Courtesy of the California State Library*)

The S.S. *Puebla* leaves San Francisco Bay, en route to Manila, 1898
(*Courtesy of the California State Library*)

The burning of San Roque, under artillery fire, during the Spanish–American War and Philippine Insurrection
(Courtesy of the California State Library)

The S.S. *Sherman* steams into San Francisco Bay, August 24, 1899
(Courtesy of the California State Library)

San Francisco welcomes its returning heroes
(*Courtesy of the California Historical Society Library*)

To all Whom it May Concern:

Know ye, That William M. Grier, a Private of Battery "A", of the 1 Battalion Regiment of Heavy Artillery Cal U. S Volunteers, who was enrolled on the twentieth day of July, one thousand eight hundred and ninety-eight to serve two years, or during the war, is hereby DISCHARGED from the service of the UNITED STATES, by reason of Muster out of Battalion

* NO OBJECTION TO HIS REENLISTMENT IS KNOWN TO EXIST.

The said William M. Grier was born in San Francisco, in the State of California and when enrolled was 19 years of age, 5 feet 7 ½ inches high, White complexion, Grey eyes, Brown hair, and by occupation a Merchant

GIVEN at Presidio San Francisco Cal this twenty-first day of September 1899

Capt 1st Batt: H. A. O. USV.
Commanding the Battery.

Countersigned

John Robertson
1st Lieut 6th U. S. Infy.
Mustering Officer.

* To be erased should there be anything in the conduct or physical condition of the soldier rendering him unfit for the Army.
3—1276

Discharge certificate of Private William M. Grier from the California U.S. Volunteers (Spanish-American War and Philippine Insurrection), given at the Presidio in San Francisco, September 21, 1899 (three days before his twenty-first birthday)

232

Phoebe Hearst
(Courtesy of the California
State Library)

W.M. ("Milt") Grier at Homestake Mining Company,
Lead, South Dakota, October 1903

W.M. ("Milt") Grier and John Twohy in Washington State at the
North Bank railroad project along the Columbia River, 1908

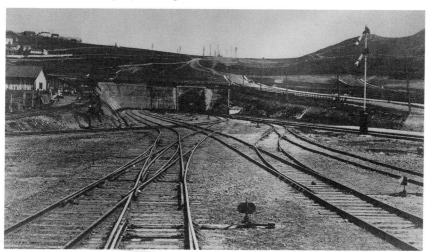

Bayshore Cutoff project in San Francisco, 1904-1907
(Courtesy of Southern Pacific Transportation Company)

Promenade of the Palace of Fine Arts, Panama-Pacific International
Exhibition, 1915
(*Courtesy of the California State Library*)

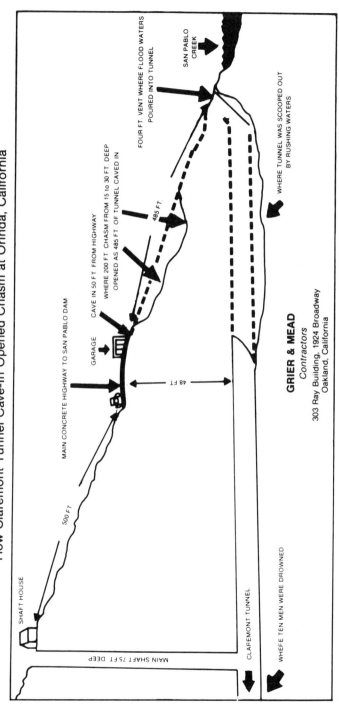

Claremont Tunnel Construction

In Orinda and Oakland, California, 1926-1930

How Claremont Tunnel Cave-In Opened Chasm at Orinda, California

SAN PABLO CREEK

FOUR FT. VENT WHERE FLOOD WATERS POURED INTO TUNNEL

WHERE TUNNEL WAS SCOOPED OUT BY RUSHING WATERS

485 FT.

CAVE IN 50 FT. FROM HIGHWAY

WHERE 200 FT. CHASM FROM 15 to 30 FT. DEEP OPENED AS 485 FT. OF TUNNEL CAVED IN

MAIN CONCRETE HIGHWAY TO SAN PABLO DAM

GARAGE

48 FT

500 FT

SHAFT HOUSE

MAIN SHAFT 75 FT DEEP

CLAFEMONT TUNNEL

WHERE TEN MEN WERE DROWNED

GRIER & MEAD

Contractors

303 Ray Building, 1924 Broadway
Oakland, California

Diagram shows location and effect of the cave-in which closed 485 feet of the Claremont tunnel's Orinda portal (dotted lines), after the tunnel was flooded by waters from San Pablo Creek on November 25, 1926. At the time of the cave-in, crews were searching for the bodies of the ten men drowned in the Thanksgiving flood. Above ground, the Mokelumne garage hangs precariously on the brink of a 200-foot chasm opened when the tunnel beneath collapsed.

236

W.M. ("Milt") Grier (*facing camera*) and Erickson
Petterson Grier Company equipment on site
during the Blue Canyon-Emigrant Gap,
California project in 1923

Winfield Scott Mead

W.M. ("Milt") Grier and W.S. Mead at the Orinda, California site
of the Claremont tunnel project, c. 1927

Milt and Elo honeymooned at the Ahwahnee Hotel in Yosemite National Park, when it opened in November 1927

Milt and Elo's first home, in Piedmont, California

W.M. ("Milt") Grier, c. 1927

Elo Lannon Grier, 1927

Left: Lannon sisters—Julia, Ferd, and Elo—at the Hotel Del Coronado, 1927

Below: Elo Lannon Grier in Piedmont, California, 1927

W.M. ("Milt") Grier, c. 1929

Bill Grier, c. 1929

Milt, Elo, and Bill Grier in 1929

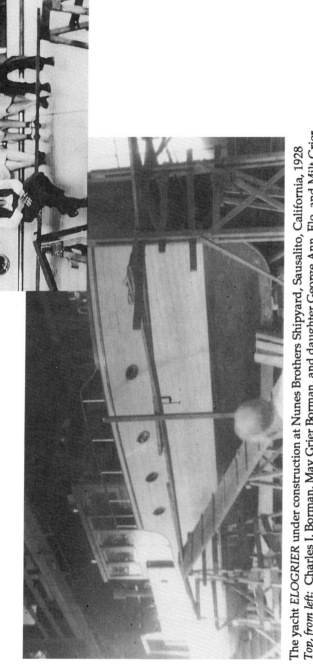

The yacht *ELOGRIER* under construction at Nunes Brothers Shipyard, Sausalito, California, 1928
Top, from left: Charles J. Borman, May Grier Borman, and daughter George Ann, Elo, and Milt Grier

244

Top: ELOGRIER, Sausalito, California, 1929
Below: ELOGRIER at St. Francis Yacht Club, San Francisco, 1929

W.M. ("Milt") Grier with niece George Ann
Borman and Wallace Hoover aboard the
ELOGRIER, in San Francisco Bay, 1931

The *ELOGRIER* in 1955, renamed the *EMMA-RON* by new owner Joseph Giuffre,
of San Francisco

246

Ray Lannon and Eloyd Grier

Bill and Eloyd Grier, 1933

W.M. ("Milt") Grier and his boys in
Piedmont, c. 1931

Eloyd Grier, Gerry Lannon, and Bill Grier at Lannon
grandparents' home, Sacramento, California, c. 1934

248

Bill Grier (*second row, extreme left*) at Frank C. Havens School, Piedmont, California, June 1934

Left: Milt and Elo Grier at Lannons' Sacramento home, 1927

Below: Bill Grier *(center)* on his fifth birthday, 1933, Piedmont, California

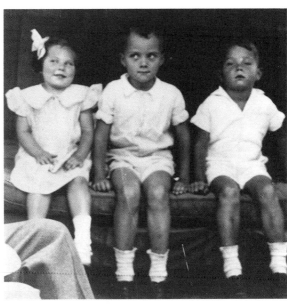

CHRONOLOGY OF ELO LANNON GRIER

1895	Born in Sacramento, California on September 26
1907	Graduates from John Marshall School in Sacramento
1910	Graduates from Mary Jane Watson Junior High School in Sacramento
1913	Graduates from St. Joseph Academy in Sacramento
1923	Meets William Milton Grier while working in Southern Pacific Railroad Company's Sacramento office
1927	Marries William M. Grier in Reno, Nevada on November 9; honeymoons at newly opened Ahwahnee Hotel, Yosemite National Park; moves into Piedmont, California home on November 19
1928	Son, William M. Grier, Jr., born in Oakland, California on September 23
1929	Son, Eloyd John Grier, born in San Francisco, California on July 4
1935	Husband dies in Sacramento on December 8; widowed at age forty
1936	Enrolls in Sacramento business school; works for California State Motor Vehicle Department, then joins John Deere Plow Company in San Francisco
1937–1939	With sons, lives first on Jackson Street, later on Clay Street in San Francisco
1940	Joins Fireman's Fund Insurance Company in marine insurance underwriting; learns to drive
1941	Moves to 888 31st Avenue in San Francisco during summer

1947	Returns to live in Piedmont home, with sons; continues with Fireman's Fund
1948	Eloyd moves to Pennsylvania in August
1952	Bill leaves home to join Air Force unit in Minneapolis, Minnesota in January
1953	Visits Bill in Washington, D.C. in June; travels with him to New York City
1955	Bill visits her in Piedmont during June
1958	Granddaughter, Shelby W. Grier, born in Harrisburg, Pennsylvania on April 6
1959	Grandson, William M. Grier 3d, born in New York City on November 11
1950s	Sells Piedmont home; moves to San Francisco; continues with Fireman's Fund
1960	Retires from Fireman's Fund on December 31 at age sixty-five; works part-time in San Francisco
1961	Bill and family visit her in San Francisco during May
1962	Buys and rents out home in Sacramento in October
1968	Retires; moves to Sacramento home on April 1
1987	Dies in Sacramento at age 91 on July 16

Elo Lannon Grier, 1927

14

ELO LANNON GRIER
1895–1987

Graceful and Plucky

The daughter of Irish natives Patrick and Julia McDermott Lannon, Elo was born in Sacramento, California on September 26, 1895. Like her four sisters and two brothers, she was educated in Sacramento's public and parochial schools—The John Marshall School, Mary Jane Watson Junior High School, and Saint Joseph Academy.

As a young woman, Elo worked as a secretary for the Southern Pacific Railroad Company, and it was in their Sacramento office that she met William Milton Grier, a prominent civil and railroad contractor, who was seventeen years her senior. They were married in Reno, Nevada four years later, on November 9, 1927 and immediately moved into a ten-room, Tudor-style home in Piedmont, California.

The Griers soon had two sons—William Milton, Jr., born on September 23, 1928 and Eloyd John, born on July 4, 1929. Both boys were baptized in Phoenix, Arizona in March 1930, while the family lived in their winter home on Camelback Road.

During the 1920s and 1930s, the family often entertained in their Piedmont home and on their yacht, *ELOGRIER*.

In 1934, when Milt founded a gold mining enterprise, Grier and Fontaine, they leased out their Piedmont home and moved to Sacramento, near the company's mining sites in Placer County.

Elo's husband, who had suffered a heart attack in 1930 and again in 1933, was struck by a third and fatal attack on December 8, 1935. He was fifty-seven years old. (See Part Four: 13)

Suddenly widowed at the age of forty, Elo became the source of support—both financial and moral—for her two young sons during the Great Depression years. Although buoyed by the love of her Lannon relatives and Borman in-laws, it was Elo's own resourcefulness, humor, energy, and resolve that carried the family through this trial.

After their father's funeral, Bill and Eloyd lived in Santa Maria, California with Elo's youngest sister Ferdy and her attorney husband Fred Shaeffer. (Fred had two children from a previous marriage: Marie, a student at the University of California at Berkeley, and Freddie, a student in the local high school.) There, the boys celebrated Christmas 1935 and attended elementary school from January to June 1936. Afterward, they returned to live with their Lannon grandparents in Sacramento and re-entered El Dorado Elementary School in September of that year.

En route from Santa Maria, Bill and Eloyd visited their mother and stayed with her older sister Marie and husband Walter Hall in their San Francisco apartment at 610 Leavenworth Street. Marie took them to Fisherman's Wharf, Crystal Palace market, her husband's optometry office in Weinstein's department store, and to Sacramento on an overnight trip aboard the *Delta Queen*—a riverboat with a large stern paddle wheel, richly paneled lounges, and three decks. The boys shared a room with portholes looking out on the water. (Shortly thereafter, the *Delta Queen* and its sister ship *Delta King* ceased operations on the Sacramento River after fifty years of service. The *Delta Queen* now plies the Ohio River from Cincinnati to New Orleans, and the *Delta King*, converted to a hotel and restaurant, is berthed on the Sacramento River at K Street, in Old Sacramento.)

CAREER

While settling her husband's estate and living with her parents, Elo enrolled in a Sacramento business school and worked for the California State Motor Vehicle Department. After Grier's estate was settled on May 7, 1936,[1] Elo accepted a secretarial and bookkeeping position with the John Deere Plow Company in San Francisco, at 424 Townsend Street. For a few weeks she resided with in-laws May and Charles Borman at 818 41st Avenue, then rented a downtown apartment and returned by train on weekends to the Lannons and her sons in Sacramento.

Always prudent, Elo lived within her salary, saved a portion of it, and

---

1. Grier's will had been drawn and signed on February 26, 1930 in San Francisco. Less than a week later, on March 3, in Phoenix, Arizona (Maricopa County), a codicil was added in which a $20,000 trust fund was established for Laura A. Watson, Grier's first wife. The executor of the trust was A.P. Giannini's Bank of Italy National Trust and Savings Association. Given Grier's financial state at his death, neither this trust nor those established for his second wife and children were put into effect.

The *ELOGRIER* was sold to Arthur E. Nystrom on November 2, 1936. During World War II, it was requisitioned by the War Shipping Administration. In 1947, the yacht was redocumented and renamed *JAN*; in 1956, it was purchased by Joseph A. Giuffre of 32 Hillsdale Avenue, Daly City, California, who renamed the vessel *EMA-RON* and, in 1961, added a 671 GNC diesel engine and flying bridge for fishing.

used credit sparingly. Her dress was stylish and conservative, complemented by hats and gloves. On evenings out, she favored suits or dark dresses, a pearl necklace, and fox or other furs. She patronized I. Magnin, City of Paris, White House, the Emporium, and Hale Brothers.

During the workweek, Elo rose and retired early. On the weekends, she liked dining out with her sons, friends, and dates, among them Emil Wilmunder. Before dinner, she enjoyed a bourbon highball, an old fashioned, or a Manhattan and after the meal, a brandy Alexander with coffee. She also enjoyed hosting dinner parties and seeing films and stage shows.

Elo managed the family home in Piedmont, which was first leased out in the summer of 1934 when her husband formed a partnership with W.R. Fontaine in Placer County (Grier and Fontaine). She negotiated leases, oversaw repairs, and kept the books. While there, Elo often visited and lunched with Piedmont friends—Annette Mead (widow of her husband's late partner), who lived a block east of the Griers; the Dreyers (founders of the ice cream company), who lived across Highland Avenue; the Cheathams (owners of the Sweet Shop in Piedmont); and the Merricks, next door neighbors on the corner.

SAN FRANCISCO YEARS, 1937–1947

From the time Elo settled in San Francisco in 1936 through 1937 when her sons moved there to be with her, she and the boys visited her family in Sacramento over weekends, taking the ferryboat to Oakland Mole where they transferred to Southern Pacific trains. Seeing her parents, brothers Joe and Raymond, cousins Deirdrie Knapp and Helen Flanagan, and old friends was always a pleasant respite from her responsibilities in San Francisco.

Over Thanksgiving week of 1936, Bill and Eloyd stayed in San Francisco with their aunt May, uncle Charlie, and cousin George Ann Borman. Arriving at the Ferry Building, the boys were met in the swirling crowd by George Ann and her Lux School classmate Carmen Aquado. In her family car, George Ann took them to lunch and a matinee performance at the Golden Gate Theatre, where they saw the Fred Astaire and Ginger Rogers film *Follow the Fleet* and a stage show.

Before returning to Sacramento, the boys enjoyed a host of activities in San Francisco. At Playland-at-the-Beach, they reveled in being by the ocean, in the carnival rides, arcade games, the small automobiles, the Big Dipper, and the Funhouse with its long undulating slides, round spinning platforms, mirrors, and mechanical laughing lady. They rollerskated and played "kick the can" with George Ann's friends: Wallace Hoover, his cousins Robert and Edith, Gloria Binns, Janet Leavitt, and George Ann's Lux School classmate Virginia ("Ginger") Klute from 682 39th Avenue. The boys also watched George Ann ride horseback and take equestrian instruction in Golden Gate Park, and, with friends Duane Harder and Billy Binns, they rode handmade coasters (whose wheels were automobile ball bearings) down 41st Avenue between Cabrillo and Fulton Streets.

Elo and her sons celebrated Christmas 1936 with the Lannons and their large family in Sacramento.[2] However, when the winter school term ended in Sacramento in January 1937, Elo decided to move to a first-floor walk-up apartment on Jackson Street in San Francisco, where Bill and Eloyd were enrolled in Spring Valley School, directly across from their apartment. Elo hired helpers to supervise her sons' after-school play and homework and to start dinner.

During the late afternoon, the boys listened to radio serials—"Dick Tracy," "Captain Midnight," "Jack Armstrong," and "Little Orphan Annie." On Saturday mornings in 1937 and 1938, they took tap-dancing and singing lessons at a studio on Market Street, near the Fox Theatre, performing to popular songs like "A-Tisket A-Tasket" and "Stop Beatin' Round the Mulberry Bush." Saturday afternoons were devoted to film matinees at one of the Polk Street theatres—the Royal or the Alhambra—which ran two features, a newsreel, a cartoon, and long-running serials, including "The Adventures of Wild Bill Hickok," all for a dime.

On Sunday mornings, Bill and Eloyd read the *San Francisco Examiner*'s sports and comics sections, then walked six blocks on Nob Hill to Episcopal services and Sunday school at Grace Cathedral. The Griers sometimes dined out on weekend evenings, with Elo's boyfriend Emil Wilmunder. The boys also accompanied Elo and Emil to the Saturday afternoon horse races at Bay Meadows and Tanforan, a short train ride south of the city. For Christmas in 1937, Elo gave her sons bicycles which they rode when they visited their aunt May. Billy Binns, a 41st Avenue friend, often rode with them around Golden Gate Park and the beach.

The Griers' family dentist at this time was Dr. Lew E. Wallace, a tall and genial man whose greeting was always a broad grin and a firm handshake. His office, across from the St. Francis Hotel in the Elkan Gunst building at 323 Geary Street, Room 708, overlooked Union Square. Dr. Wallace had

---

2.   All from California, the guests were Ferdinand Henrietta ("Ferdy") and her husband Fred Shaeffer from Santa Maria; Norma Winifred and Herb Pope Langton, from Berkeley; Mary Elizabeth ("Marie") and Walter George Hall, from San Francisco; Joseph Martin, Gerald ("Gerry") Joseph, and Wilhelmina ("Mina") Lannon, from Sacramento; and Raymond James Lannon, bachelor and youngest Lannon child, from Sacramento.

admired the boys' father, whom he treated from 1922 until Grier's death in 1935, and took a special interest in the boys' welfare. Bill's orthodontic work was done by Dr. Wallace from 1941 to '43.

Between 1937 and 1946, the Griers celebrated Christmas Eve at the Bormans' home. Presents were opened after dinner and Uncle Charlie later drove them about the city—to St. Francis Wood, Pacific Heights, and Marina districts— to see the colorfully lighted gardens and homes. Elo also hosted Thanksgiving and Christmas dinners and New Year's parties, as well.

SACRAMENTO SUMMERS

During their summer vacations in 1937 and 1938, Bill and Eloyd were at Tilly's Roost, a camp in the Santa Cruz mountains near Boulder Creek and Ben Lomond, California. The following three summers, the boys alternated six-week visits with their Lannon grandparents in Sacramento.

The summers with the Lannons were idyllic times for the boys. Bill remembers waking early to their crowing rooster. After a breakfast of rolled oats or cream of wheat, fruit, toast, and milk, the boys sometimes helped their grandfather Lannon feed the chickens and fetch eggs. Located inside a vine-covered, wire-fenced yard several hundred feet to the rear of the Lannon home, the chicken shed was reached from the back lawn by a path through a grape arbor and a cluster of quince, apple, cherry, and apricot trees.

To the side and rear of the shed were vegetable gardens. Some strawberries and fruits were stewed, then bottled, capped, and stored in the basement. The boys helped to cultivate and pick crops, mow lawns, and trim shrubs around their grandparents' Victorian home. Bill, using the Lannons' equipment, also developed a profitable lawn-cutting service with a number of the neighbors.

After lunch, the boys and their grandparents took naps. In the evenings, using a wall blackboard, their grandmother occasionally tested the boys with spelling and arithmetic exercises; though Bill and Eloyd disliked these sessions, they doubtlessly were salutary to their verbal and computing skills.

All was not work, however, during these summers with their grandparents. Bill and Eloyd took hikes with their grandfather to parks and along the levees of the Sacramento and American Rivers. They played on the El Dorado softball team, competing against other Sacramento playground teams, and enjoyed croquet, ping pong, and crafts. They went on group outings to the State Capitol and Sutter's Fort, picnicked and swam at

McKinley Park and the American River, and attended professional baseball games of the Sacramento Solons.

The boys also accompanied their grandmother on her "first of the month" bill-paying trips to downtown Sacramento, to the telephone company, Pacific Gas & Electric, and City Hall.

At the Public Market at 13th and J Streets, where many stores were gathered under one roof, Bill and Eloyd weighed themselves on the huge produce scales in the rear of the building. Then, for a nickel, they usually had a glass of buttermilk—all they could drink—at Henderson's.

While waiting for the home-bound streetcar in front of Country Maid Ice Cream on 12th and J Streets, their grandmother treated them to a milkshake or a cornucopia, as she called ice cream cones.

Bill and Eloyd went to movies at the Alhambra theatre, an exotic Egyptian-styled structure,with its long entryway of gardens and little bridges spanning the ponds and fountains. (Today, alas, "progress" has replaced this unique building with a Safeway supermarket.) Next door to the Alhambra, the boys could get cones at the Shasta ice cream shop.

Late in the summer, they went to the State Fair on Stockton Boulevard. There, they explored the Counties Building, with its animated exhibits depicting each county's choicest products, and the Flower Building, humid, fragrant, and breath-taking in its natural splendor. They were intrigued by the Machinery Building, where huge pumps forced water down a canal in the middle of the building; the mind readers; the organ grinders with their penny-grabbing monkeys; the souvenir hawkers; the nighttime horse show in all its grandeur; the midway, brightly lighted by its many rides; and the grandstand show, complete with dazzling fireworks which could also be seen from the Lannons' rear porch.

The boys also saw their older Sacramento cousins, who would later become public school teachers there: Wilma Henn, the only child of Elo's oldest sister Marie Lannon Henn (1893–1965), and Gerry Lannon, the only child of Elo's brother Joseph Lannon (1899–1955). Wilma, thirteen years older than Bill, occasionally took care of her Grier cousins during these summer visits. Gerry lived with his parents Joe and Mina at 820 41st Street. His father, a graduate of McGeorge School of Law, was a detective for the Sacramento County district attorney's office and a local real estate investor.

After dinner, the Lannons usually retired to their ladder-back rockers or hammock on their home's columned front porch, facing the cool north side. Patrick Lannon smoked his pipe as they read, enjoyed the evening's breezes, and entertained friends. At mid-evening, Julia Lannon served tea and dessert.

The Lannons' unmarried daughter, Julia Margaret (1897–1970), a registered nurse and supervisor of nurses at Sacramento County Hospital, lived with her parents and sometimes joined them in the evening, and their youngest child, Raymond James (1911–1945), a mechanical contractor, was also occasionally present. On other evenings, Julia Lannon took her grandsons on walks about the neighborhood, where she called on friends in their homes.

For the boys, summer in Sacramento was a treasured time. The city's cool and shady streets were sun-dappled by day, soft and beguiling at dusk, and beckoning and mysterious tunnels by night. Summer flowed as lazily as the Sacramento and American Rivers between their cottonwood-shaded banks at the west and north ends of town. Night came slowly, as the sounds of frogs and crickets dominated the air, and the fireflies winked along the darkening streets and trimmed lawns like a sky full of stars brought down to earth for the season.

ACTIVITIES

In 1939, the Griers moved two blocks away from Jackson Street to a larger, third-floor walk-up apartment on Clay Street. Part of the Griers' Piedmont home furniture was taken out of storage and used in both the Jackson and Clay Street apartments.

During 1939 and '40, the boys visited Treasure Island (the Golden Gate International Exposition) in San Francisco Bay—the world's fair of towers and pavilions. There, in 1940, they heard Republican presidential candidate Wendell Willkie make a campaign speech.

The boys were especially captivated by the marionette shows, with their magical stage sets and amusing plays, and the exciting miniature railway displays, featuring thousands of feet of multiple tracks for toy trains. They inspired Bill to build a portable puppet theatre in their Clay Street apartment and create his own marionettes, directing and producing *Hansel and Gretel* for the family and his Spring Valley School classmates. He also constructed an HO gauge train layout on large plywood panels in his aunt May's basement in San Francisco.

After school in 1940, Bill and Eloyd sold popular magazines door-to-door in their neighborhood and *Evening News* and *Call Bulletin* newspapers on street corners—Bill at Sacramento and Polk Streets, Eloyd at Hyde and Sutter.

After graduating from Spring Valley School in January 1940, Bill entered the seventh grade at Redding School, on Larkin and Pine Streets. Like Spring Valley, this school had a rich ethnic mix of Oriental, Italian, Portuguese, Hispanic, and Anglo students. Bill joined Boy Scout Troop 146, which met in the school auditorium on Friday evenings. Dallas Brock, later a San Francisco attorney, was a classmate and scout in Troop 125. He and

Bill belonged to the school's camera club and attended Sunday school at Grace Cathedral, where Dallas sang in the choir.[3] They also attended Camp C.C. More in the summertime.

One of Bill's football heroes at the time was Tom Harmon, an all-American single-wing tailback at the University of Michigan in 1940. Possibly Harmon's day of greatest glory came against Ohio State that year, in his final collegiate appearance. In the game at Columbus, he led the Wolverines to a 40-0 victory by running for three touchdowns, passing for two more, kicking four extra points, and averaging fifty yards with three punts. Bill saw him play in the East-West game on New Year's Day, 1941, in San Francisco's Kezar Stadium.

Eloyd entered Redding in February 1941. The boys, members of the school's traffic patrol, played on volleyball and soccer teams which competed against other city schools.

Elo's workweek during the pre-World War II years was five and one-half days—forty-four hours. When she joined Fireman's Fund Insurance Company in 1940, in marine underwriting, she no longer worked on Saturday mornings, cutting her schedule to thirty-seven and one-half hours.

That same year, tutored by her brother-in-law Charles Borman, Elo learned to drive a car, at age forty-four. When licensed, she bought a 1941 maroon-colored Chrysler New Yorker sedan, with "fluid drive" (the first automatic shift). As well as driving to work in downtown San Francisco and visiting family and friends, Elo and her family drove to Sacramento, Russian River, and to Hillsborough to visit her sister Norma and brother-in-law Herb Langton. Norma was a successful homebuilder in the Berkeley hills during the 1930s and early forties; Herb was a financial executive with a San Francisco steamship firm.[4] A cautious driver, Elo's slow pace on the highways sometimes caused anxieties for her sons, who, with gentle urging and humor, could usually induce her to increase her speed during these trips.

Because Elo's job in marine underwriting—insuring military ships—was essential to the war effort, she had a "B" gas rationing card, providing a greater monthly gasoline allowance than the three-gallons-a-week "A" card, but less than the "C" card. Nonetheless, it proved more than enough

---

3.   After reading Dallas's name in the Menlo School and College Directory, Bill contacted him and they lunched in April 1987 with friends at Fiore d'Italia in San Francisco.

4.   During World War II, when Norma operated a women's clothing shop at 1417 Burlingame Avenue in Burlingame, the Langtons moved to Hillsborough from their Berkeley hills home at 1020 Miller Avenue. In the 1950s, Norma subdivided land and built homes in Los Altos, where she and Herb occupied two houses, first at 301 and later at 261 Langton Avenue.

for her family needs.

CAMPING TRIPS, JOBS
1941–1947

In summer 1941, the Griers rented the second-floor flat at 888 31st Avenue, a few steps from Golden Gate Park. The following summer, Bill worked as an office boy in the financial district for Hinchman Rolph & Landis, insurance agents, at 345 Sansome Street, earning seventy-five dollars a month. And in 1941 and '42, Eloyd delivered the *Evening News* in Sutro Heights.

For a week over Labor Day 1941, Bill and Eloyd went fishing and camping near Mount Shasta and Mount Lassen with their aunt May, uncle Charlie, and cousin George Ann. The youngsters slept in portable canvas tents, while May and Charlie enjoyed the comfort of their autobed.Their meals were cooked over open fires and a portable gas stove. They packed their provisions on a burro and rode horseback, with a guide, to a remote log cabin complete with a fireplace and a front porch overlooking a lake, green meadows, and forests. In this tranquil setting, they hiked and fished from a rowboat, catching trout which were sauteed for breakfast and dinner. Charlie also shot a deer, which provided many venison meals that fall. This was one of several such outings in northern California, the redwoods, and Yosemite National Park that the Bormans and Grier boys made together in the thirties and forties.

In September 1941, Bill and Eloyd transferred to Presidio Junior High School. Both boys played intramural basketball and baseball. Eloyd was on the track team, running the 50- and 100-yard dashes and the 220-yard relays. During lunch period, Bill worked in the school cafeteria.

It was during this first year at Presidio that the boys and their classmates gathered in the school auditorium to hear President Roosevelt's radio address on December 8, 1941, declaring war on Japan.

After school, Bill, Eloyd, and neighborhood friends—Bill Degenhardt and his older brother John, the Cohn brothers, Monroe Johnson, Jack Anderson and his younger sister Jane—played touch football outside the Griers' flat on 31st Avenue.

Madeline and Grace Gilmore, who lived around the corner, were also frequent cohorts for Bill and Eloyd. The girls attended Sacred Heart School, a Catholic girls' school in Pacific Heights. Grace liked giving the Grier boys and others rides around Golden Gate Park in her dark blue, three-wheel motor scooter with sidecar passenger seat.[5]

During weekends between 1941 and 1943, Bill worked at Sutro Baths and Ice Rink, assigning lockers and dispensing towels for the pools or collecting tickets at the rink.

Built on a cliff overlooking the Pacific in 1896 by Adolph Sutro, the baths had six indoor swimming pools of both fresh and salt water, varying in size, depth, and temperature. Later, an ice rink was added. The Victorian glass-roofed structure also featured wide-tiered galleries and promenades, bordered with palm trees, tables, and chairs. Tragically, this unique building was destroyed by a fire in 1966.

From 1943 to '45, Bill and Eloyd delivered the *San Francisco Shopping News* to residences near their home on Wednesday afternoons and Saturday mornings; later, Eloyd became captain and administrator of several routes, supervising other carriers.

In 1943, Bill entered George Washington High School (GWHS), where he studied a college preparatory curriculum, lettered in basketball and played football,[6] and joined the Omega fraternity.

Bill was a substitute quarterback on the varsity football team in 1945, in coach Milt Axt's T formation.[7] Duane Harder, Bill and Eloyd's boyhood friend from 41st Avenue, played halfback. Some of the games were held in Washington's unique campus stadium. From there, one saw the majestic burnt-orange towers of the Golden Gate Bridge and the green hills of Marin County. Passing through the 30th Avenue entrances, one confronted a poignant epigram set in stone on the stadium wall: "Of all the victories the first and greatest for a man is to conquer himself. Plato." Games were also held in Kezar Stadium in Golden Gate Park, where college ball and the Shriners' East-West games were played.

From June of 1943 to July of 1945, Bill worked two days a week after school and on Saturday mornings in the shipping department of Ingram Laboratories, Inc., a small pharmaceutical firm located off Union Square at 278 Post Street. He and two other San Francisco high school students wrapped products for shipment; before closing, the packages were brought to the nearby post office in the White House department store.

5.　Their father William Gilmore, president of Gilmore Steel Corporation in San Francisco, was an avid polo player and owned land near Menlo School and College, which was sold to Menlo after his death in the 1960s.

6.　George Washington High School was the subject of a television report in San Francisco in the early 1980s—"The Kids at Washington High," produced by local station KOE—which outlined changes that had occurred there since 1955.

7.　Bill's T formation quarterback heroes were Stanford's Frankie Albert, Notre Dame's Angelo Bertelli and Johnny Lujack, and Chicago Bear's Sid Luckman.

During the summers between 1944 and 1948, Eloyd worked in San Francisco's Winterland Auditorium as head concessionaire, selling programs, novelties, and food items. The Ice Follies were staged at Winterland, and in time, he met and became friendly with some of the show's artists, including Russ Tuckey, a performer and transportation manager for the Follies.[8] Eloyd also worked evening events at Winterland throughout the school year.

In the fall of 1944, Bill withdrew $500 from his savings to buy a 1935 gray De Soto coupe, with rumble seat, from a dealer. His uncle Charlie Borman, after checking its condition, recommended its purchase; he also taught Bill how to drive and parallel park near the beach.

In July 1945, Bill resigned from Ingram Laboratories to begin work as an assistant groundskeeper at Kraft Foods in south San Francisco (where he cut and edged lawns, pruned trees, and watered the grounds) and as an office boy during his Christmas vacation in 1945.

Between 1944 and 1945, Bill also worked three evenings a week at Presidio Junior High School as a gym assistant to Josh S. Faulkner, director of physical education. Earning seventy-five cents an hour, he succeeded Jack Anderson, an older friend and basketball player at George Washington High School who later received both bachelor's and master's degrees in education from Stanford University. When Bill resigned a few weeks prior to graduating from GWHS in 1946, his brother succeeded him in the position, a job which Eloyd held until his own graduation in 1947.

On Saturday evenings, Bill and friends occasionally attended professional basketball games at San Francisco's Civic Auditorium or films, big band performances, and stage shows at the Golden Gate Theatre. Afterward, they stopped at cafes for sodas and desserts.

On balmy spring days, Bill, Eloyd, and their classmates went to China Beach in the stately Sea Cliff district, eight downhill blocks from school. The view from the cove-shaped beach encompassed the Golden Gate Bridge to the east, the headlands of Marin County to the north, and the Pacific Ocean to the west. There, the boys swam, played volleyball and touch football, and eyed and talked to the girls. On summer weekends, they sometimes went to Russian River, staying with friends in Guerneville or Monte Rio.

Graduating from George Washington High School in 1946, Bill then

---

8.   Russ Tuckey, a native of Harrisburg, Pennsylvania, had been a basketball star at Gettysburg College.

George T. Campbell, manager of Winterland, lived on 41st Avenue, a few doors south of Bill and Eloyd's aunt May Grier Borman. In earlier years, the boys had played with Campbell's two sons, who had a large electric train layout in their basement.

studied for a year at Menlo Junior College in nearby Menlo Park, while Eloyd enrolled at San Francisco State College following his high school graduation in 1947. (See Part Four: 15 and 16)

BACK TO PIEDMONT

Elo and her sons returned to live in their Piedmont home in the summer of 1947. Still with Fireman's Fund, Elo now commuted by train across the San Francisco-Oakland Bay Bridge to her office in the financial district.

The previous year, Elo had traded in her Chrysler for a De Soto sedan, and in 1949, she bought a De Soto coupe—her last automobile.

Although Elo had several savings accounts at other San Francisco banks, her checking account and safe deposit box were always with Wells Fargo Bank, in its imposing building at Grant Avenue and Market Street.

After moving back to Piedmont, Bill enrolled at the University of California at Berkeley, where he would earn a Bachelor of Arts in chemistry and zoology.

When Bill and Eloyd's Sacramento cousin Gerry Lannon attended St. Mary's College in nearby Moraga, California, he was a frequent guest at their Piedmont home. In the late 1940s, Bill and Gerry both dated students at Mills College, and Bill hosted parties in his mother's home. Later, Gerry took his Master of Arts in English and literature at the University of San Francisco.

BOYS LEAVE HOME

In August of 1948, Eloyd, unhappy and in conflict with his mother, decided to continue his education in the East. Urged by Russ Tuckey, an acquaintance from the Ice Follies and an alum from Gettysburg College, he moved to Harrisburg, Pennsylvania and attended York Collegiate Institute and then Gettysburg College.

Three years later, Elo, her brother Joseph Lannon, and family friends attended Bill's graduation from Berkeley in June 1951, followed by a reception hosted by Elo in her Piedmont home.

After Bill left home the following January to join his Air Force unit at Fort Snelling in Minneapolis, Elo continued to live in Piedmont and commute to her job in San Francisco. She took occasional vacations with friends to Carmel and Lake Tahoe and visited her sisters. During the workweek, she often dined out and attended shows with business friends.

In early June of 1953, Elo flew to Washington, D.C. to visit Bill, who was working as a passenger agent with United Airlines at National Airport. After a week of sightseeing there, she accompanied him to Manhattan for a brief holiday and saw him off on the S.S. *Stavangerfjord* as he sailed for Norway.

After study and travel abroad, Bill received a Master of Science degree from Columbia University Graduate School of Business in 1955. He then returned home to Piedmont for a six-week vacation before starting work in the finance training program of General Motors Overseas Operations in New York City.

During this period, his brother Eloyd was also establishing roots in the East. After attending college in Pennsylvania, he joined the Federal Bureau of Investigation in Washington, D.C. and subsequently entered the insurance business in Pennsylvania.

Elo's sons both married during the second half of the fifties, and by the end of the decade, she had two grandchildren, as well: Eloyd's daughter Shelby, born in 1958, and Bill's son William Milton Grier 3d, born one year later.

With her sons grown, married, and living in the East, Elo sold the large Piedmont home in the late 1950s and leased flats in San Francisco, both near Fireman's Fund Insurance Company's new complex at 3333 California Street.

RETIREMENT YEARS

After retiring in the fall of 1960 at age sixty-five, and too energetic to remain idle, Elo worked part-time in the offices of several downtown San Francisco firms, including the Fairmont Hotel. She now had time for friends and for visits with her three sisters and a brother-in-law: Marie Hall Henn, a widow, who lived in a San Francisco apartment at Leavenworth and Geary Streets; Norma and Herb Langton, who had moved in the 1950s from their Spanish colonial home in Hillsborough to Los Altos, where Norma, a contractor, had built a tract of homes; and her younger, divorced sister Ferd Shaeffer, an elementary school teacher in Sacramento.

In May of 1961, Elo's son Bill, daughter-in-law Joan Sears Grier, and one-and-a-half-year-old grandson Billy visited her for three weeks from Boston. Accompanied by Bill's cousin George Ann, Elo met them at the airport and that evening hosted a dinner party for friends and family, including George Ann and her husband Sam Palmer and Elo's older sister Marie.

Bill's UC-Berkeley friend Jay Martin, a San Francisco lawyer, gave a party for the Griers in his two-level apartment, with striking views of the Bay. The young Griers were also entertained in the Berkeley hills home of the Palmers—George Ann, Sam, and their children Catherine, Charles, and Kenneth. Bill's uncle Charlie Borman— George Ann's father—came over from San Francisco to see his nephew and family. En route to Carmel and Big Sur, Bill and his wife had lunch with Norma and Herb Langton in Menlo Park, near their Palo Alto financial consulting office.

After the Griers visited Lannon relatives in Sacramento (Bill's aunts Ferd Shaeffer and Julia Lannon; cousins Gerry Lannon and Wilma Henn Tamblyn; and Elo's cousin Deirdrie Knapp Berrigan, a music teacher and violinist with the Sacramento Symphony Orchestra), Bill and Joan toured Lake Tahoe and Reno, while grandmother Elo cared for young Billy. During Bill's years of residence in the East and in Denver, he annually visited his mother, family, and friends in California, sojourns of nostalgia and adventure that always exhilarated and refreshed him.

Anticipating retirement in Sacramento, near her sister Ferd Shaeffer, Elo bought a one-story, two-bedroom stucco home at 5400 H Street in October of 1962, which she rented out over five years. Then, after forty-one years in San Francisco and Piedmont, Elo, nearing seventy-three, moved into her Sacramento home in April 1968.

In her later years, Elo lived in a nursing home in Sacramento. She died there on July 16, 1987—two months and ten days short of her ninety-second birthday. She was buried in East Lawn Cemetery—where her parents and several of her brothers and sisters had been buried.

MEMORIES

Elo was kind, generous, tolerant, and scrupulously honest in thought and deed. As a young girl and mother, she was slight, pretty, bright-eyed, elfin, and gay. A brunette with a shapely figure—impulsive and flirtatious —she liked to dance and play the piano.

Yet behind the gaiety, a discernment and purposefulness directed her life—traits that became evident after her husband's death. And while her vanity never deserted her, neither did her wit and courage. Indeed, it was these qualities that shone luminously as she emerged from her personal loss in the Depression, and—alone—forged a successful career and raised her two sons.

After eight years of a privileged life as the wife of a well-to-do entrepreneur, the plucky Elo—through her subsequent struggle and hard-won triumph—taught her sons a timeless lesson: In adversity, you neither forsake humor nor complain nor give up; rather, you persevere, you endure, and by endurance the garland is won.

In a conversation with her cousin Bill in April of 1983, Elo's niece George Ann spoke of the phone call that came to her mother early in the morning of December 8, 1935—Elo's call, informing the Borman family of Uncle Milt's death. She recalled Elo's first year as a widow, when she had lived for a few weeks with George Ann and her parents while establishing her career in San Francisco. She remembered that Elo would rise in the pre-dawn darkness, well before the household, and catch the nearby Fulton streetcar heading downtown, where she breakfasted before going to work at John Deere Plow Company on Townsend Street.

During this dolorous time, Elo bore her burdens lightly. As she grappled valiantly with a new life and job and enlarged family responsibilities, her humor lifted the spirit of family and friends. George Ann had poignant memories of her aunt Elo's endearing ways—her cheerfulness and dignity in the face of ineffable sadness—which deeply touched the Bormans and drew them ever closer to her. "From such anguish and pathos," Bill has said, "I believe my soul was born."

Many years later, Bill recalled a day in 1937 when, as he sat on his aunt May's lap and giggled at her stories, she asked him if he could keep a promise. When he agreed, she whispered in his ear, "Promise me you'll never forget your mother." Quickly, he reassured her, and, indeed, over the next fifty years of his mother's long life, Bill would remain lovingly devoted to her.

In front of the P.J. Lannons' home in Sacramento, California, c. 1927—*at top:* Elo, *from left,* her mother, Julia, and youngest sister, Ferdie

Norma Lannon Langton,
(1902-1964)

Above: Langtons' Spanish-style home in
Berkeley hills, 1938
Below: Entrance to the Langtons' home at
1090 Miller Avenue. Norma and Herb
Langton were Elo's sister and brother-in-law

Herbert Pope Langton,
(1899-1963)

Eloyd and Bill Grier, c. 1937

Bill and Eloyd Grier, 1938

Elo Grier and her sons, Bill and Eloyd, c. 1940

Elo, Bill, and Eloyd Grier dining out in San Francisco with Emil Wilmunder, c. 1938

Right:
Elo's father
Patrick Joseph
Lannon, c. 1880s

Left: Elo's grandmother Mary
Elo Owens Lannon, c. 1850s
(Courtesy of James M. Knapp)

274

Bill Grier (*third row, third from left*) and his graduating class at Presidio Junior High School, 1943. *Top row, left to right:* Richard Mills, George Borelli, Robert Freeman, Walter Bent, Tom McGowan, Peter White, Jack Riskin, Frank Muller. *Third row:* Aubrey Behr, Albert Littman, Bill Grier, Tom Lane, Glenn Brown, Richard Silverman, Al Levy, Donald Erman, Teddy Sutter. *Second row:* Shirlee Hampton, Corinne Gale, Naomi Pinkus, Suzanne Gordon, Theone Funnemark, Laura Lee Spiro, Betty Knudsen, Geri Bleckman, Della Ranke, Pat Orr. *First row:* Lorraine Schultz, Violet Eshow, Erica Harvey, Jerry Taylor, Maxine Blumenthal, Leila Moss, Estelle Rando, Carol Schillaci, Jean Zebley.

Eloyd Grier (*second row, second from right*) and his graduating class at Presidio Junior High School, 1944. *Top row, left to right:* Robert Rosenberg, Adrian Foster, Richard Keegan, Robert Eckhoff, Robert Reyff, Robert Fitzhenry, Lawrence Lash. *Third row:* Robert Stagg, James King, Grover Cleveland, Donald Brinckman, Philip Hoehn (vice president), Victor Sawdon, Joseph Maleh, Jack Stein, Robert Garbarino, Robert Duncan. *Second row:* Ronald Sadick, Denny Ragan, Jacqueline Kemp, Roberta Parsons (class president), Mary Ann Davidson, Evelyn Miglian, Barbara Stone, Patricia Oliphant, Barbara Baumberger, Eloyd Grier, Truman McDaniel. *First row:* Anna Lekas, Natalie Blum, Jean Howell, Shirley Newton, Joanne Fitzmier, Mary Tosch, Julia Agustinovich, Marie McCollum (class secretary), Marlene Novak, Joyce Chavez, (class treasurer).

CHRONOLOGY OF WILLIAM M. GRIER, JR.

1928	Born in Oakland, California on September 23
1930	Baptized in Trinity Cathedral in Phoenix, Arizona on March 22
1933–1934	Attends Frank C. Havens School, Piedmont, California
1934	Moves to Sacramento, California; enrolls in El Dorado Elementary School
1935	Father, William M. Grier, Sr., dies in Sacramento on December 8
1935–1936	Lives in Santa Maria, California with aunt and uncle; attends elementary school there
1936	Returns to Sacramento and El Dorado Elementary School in June
1937	Moves to San Francisco, California; enrolls in Spring Valley School
1937–1938	Summers at Tilly's Roost Camp, Santa Cruz Mountains, California
1939–1940	Summers with Lannon grandparents in Sacramento; visits Golden Gate International Exposition (Treasure Island)
1940	Enters Redding School in San Francisco (junior high years) in January
1941	Works during summer for Hinchman Rolph & Landis in San Francisco; camps with Borman family near Mt. Shasta, California over Labor Day; transfers to Presidio Junior High School in San Francisco in September

1941–1943	Works part-time at Sutro Baths and Ice Rink
1943	Enters George Washington High School in San Francisco
1943–1945	Works part-time at Ingram Laboratories and as gym assistant at Presidio Junior High School
1945	Works at Kraft Foods during summer
1946	Graduates from George Washington High School; enters Menlo Junior College in Menlo Park, California; works at Yosemite National Park in August
1947	Returns to live in Piedmont home; enrolls in University of California at Berkeley
1948–1950	Works during summers at Lake Tahoe, at Hunt Foods, and at summer camp in Huntington Lake, California
1949	Joins Air National Guard, Alameda, California
1949–1951	Works as playground director for City of Oakland
1951	Graduates from University of California at Berkeley in June with B.A. in chemistry and zoology
1952	Joins California Air National Guard in January, on active duty in U.S. Air Force, Fort Snelling, Minneapolis, Minnesota
1953	Discharged from Air Force in February; moves to Washington, D.C. and works for United Airlines; studies on scholarship at the University of Oslo Summer School; travels in Scandinavia, Britain, and Europe; studies at the Institute of Touraine in October; travels in Europe over Christmas holidays
1953–1954	Studies at the Sorbonne
1954	Travels in Europe in spring and summer; enters Columbia University Graduate School of Business in New York City

1955	Receives M.S. from Columbia Graduate School of Business; visits family and friends in Piedmont and California; joins General Motors Overseas Operations in New York City
1959	Joins Previews, Inc. in New York City in spring; marries Joan Cecilia Sears in New York City on April 11; son, William M. Grier 3d, born in New York City on November 11; moves to Cambridge, Massachusetts; continues with Previews, Inc. in Boston in fall
1960	Forms Feature Arts, marketing museum art reproductions, books, and records
1962	Divorces Joan Sears Grier in November; forms real estate investment and management firm in Cambridge in December
1963–1969	Vacations in Europe and Mediterranean
1969	Joins Apache Corporation; relocates to New York City
1970	Joins Union League Club in New York City
1971	Vacations in England in May
1972	Vacations in Europe in February; marries Joan Grafmueller in Ketchum, Idaho on June 15
1972–1973	Lives in France; travels in Europe
1973	Visits East Africa in July; relocates to Denver, Colorado and founds Grier & Company in November
1974–1989	Vacations in the United States, Canada, and Mexico
1976	Begins publication of *Real Estate West* in June
1980	Grier & Company edits, designs, and produces *Walter Judd: Chronicles of a Statesman*

1987   Mother, Elo Lannon Grier, dies at age 91 in Sacramento on July 16

1989   Publishes *Grier of San Francisco: Builder in the West and His Family 1878–1988*

1991   Publishes *The Griers: Pioneers in America and Canada, 1816–1991*

William Milton Grier, Jr.
(1928–)

15

WILLIAM MILTON GRIER, JR.
1928–

Publisher, Investor, Biographer

The elder son of William Milton ("Milt") Grier, Sr. and Elo Lannon Grier, Bill was born on September 23, 1928 in Oakland, California. He and his family lived in nearby Piedmont, spending winters in Phoenix, Arizona, until Bill was five.

In 1934, when Milt formed Grier and Fontaine, a gold mining company in the Sierra Nevada, the family leased their Piedmont home, and Bill and his brother Eloyd lived with their Lannon grandparents in Sacramento until Milt's death in 1935. Following that, seven-year-old Bill stayed with an aunt and uncle in Santa Maria for half a year, then, from June 1936 until January 1937, he and Eloyd returned to the Lannons' home in Sacramento, where they were enrolled in El Dorado Elementary School.

The boys rejoined their mother Elo in San Francisco early in 1937, where they attended Spring Valley School, across from their Jackson Street apartment. Bill later went to Redding School, transferred to Presidio Junior High, and entered George Washington High School in 1943.

Elo, the sole support for her sons, held full-time jobs during these San Francisco years, and both boys had part-time jobs while in school. Bill sold and delivered papers, mowed lawns, and worked at Sutro Baths and Ice Rink, among other jobs. (See Part Four: 13 and 14)

After graduating from George Washington High School in 1946, Bill enrolled in Menlo School and Junior College, a small, private men's institution in Menlo Park, California. Entering Menlo with older, returning World War II veterans, Bill, a callow seventeen—more interested in sport than study—was now challenged by eager classmates and a demanding curriculum. Menlo awakened his curiosity and stirred his imagination; spurring scholarship, it marked the beginning of his becoming a student.

MENLO

At the time Bill enrolled, Menlo Junior College had 192 students, and its secondary boys' school, 151. On campus, he lived in Upper House and in College Hall.[1] He studied French with Holbrook Bonney; western civilization with Donovan D. Fischer; physics with Dr. William Pomeroy; and biology and psychology with Dr. Paul Hurd.

It was at Menlo that Bill began a lifelong friendship with John D. Russell, the distinguished director emeritus of the College and its School of Business Administration. A Stanford University alumnus and lawyer, Russell began teaching business law at Menlo in 1938. Several years later, while serving in the Navy during World War II, he received frequent letters from servicemen whom he had taught at Menlo—letters which helped to persuade him that his true metier lay not in law, but in education. He became convinced that he could affect more change, do more good, and, in turn, enjoy a more rewarding life through teaching. During his fifty-year tenure at Menlo, his able leadership and inspired teaching helped advance the school's academic excellence and enhance the lives of legions of its students. Since his official retirement in 1977, Russell (fondly known as "Judge") has kept an office at the school and continues to guide and encourage a second and third generation of Menlo students.

Over the years, he and Bill have exchanged a good many letters and postcards, and since 1947, Bill has received his self-designed Christmas and birthday cards with personal greetings. Throughout this period, Bill has benefited from Russell's counsel, admired his humane spirit and liberal temper, and cherished his friendship.[2] In a letter to Bill in 1984, Russell revealed his philosophy:

---

1.   Several of Bill's classmates were from Hawaii, alumni of Punahau School: Allan and Bob Clarke; Bob Gibson, now a Honolulu dentist; and Larry Doolittle, Bill's first roommate in Upper House. Other Upper House classmates were Chuck and Fritz von Geldern from Sacramento; Truman ("Tony") De Lap from Stockton, now an artist in Corona del Mar, California; Russell Hael; Chauncey G. Behrens, now an anesthesiologist; and the late Vern Purcell from Seattle. Classmates from physics were John Whipple; John Zeile, an environmental engineer with Ralph M. Parsons Company in Pasadena; Bill Sheridan; and Bob Lurie, real estate investor and owner of the San Francisco Giants.

2.   Bill and his wife Joan attended a reunion picnic at Menlo School and College on Sunday, October 13, 1985; while seeing Judge Russell and other friends, they were entertained by the Kingston Trio, Menlo alumni of the mid-fifties.

Don't worry about such things as memorials. Mine are living. My memories (memorial) and wealth consist of those special Bill Grier's,'my boys,' close friends through the years, whose progress and productivity give me continuing pride and satisfaction. I consider myself a very wealthy person in essentials for the good life, my assets being my former students ('my sons'), and my income consisting of pleasure from continuing communication and contact and pride from their achievements. I therefore do not need to be further honored while I live or memorialized after I die. One Bill Grier already honors me sufficiently by taking time and trouble to send me cards, letters, examples of his works, and a complimentary subscription to *Real Estate West*.

I have enjoyed a full life, forty-seven years of which were at Menlo where I have been able to participate in building a fine educational institution. I like to think that I have laid a constructive brick or two into the foundation of each of my boys, to help make their careers more significant and successful. Thus I have gained more than I have given in my Menlo relationship through the years.

Edgar Wise Weaver—"The Weav," as he was affectionately known—was a popular English professor at Menlo. Urbane, humorous, and tweedy, a pipe smoker and collector of jazz vocal recordings, he was dedicated to clear thinking and good writing.   In 1946, he was Upper House dorm counselor, whose suite was near Bill's room; prior to dinner, "The Weav's" sitting room was the place where Bill and his classmates gathered to enjoy conversation and music.

Other faculty acquaintances of Bill's were E. Hutson Hart (chemistry), Leon T. Loofbourow (history and literature), and president William E. Kratt.

ACTIVITIES

Bill played basketball at Menlo for coach Roy Hughes. Like the student body, the team was dominated by World War II veterans, several of whom were also graduates of George Washington High School: Bill Rose, Cliff Gerstner, Ken Berridge, Bob Durnal, and Harry Myers. Other teammates included Hank Needham, Byron VanAlstyne, Joe Greenbach, Harry Cusack (alumnus of Punahau School in Honolulu), Harry Morris (who became a three-star Air Force general), and Hobert Burns (former president of San Jose State University). After scoring well in early games, Bill was nicknamed "Points" Grier. "Points" also earned expense money by working as a bus boy at Menlo.

In August 1946, Bill worked as a bus boy with other college students in Camp Curry Company's dining room in Yosemite National Park. While there, he renewed his friendship with the vacationing Lloyd Leith, former GWHS basketball coach whom Bill had known briefly in 1943 before Lloyd entered the Navy. At Yosemite, Lloyd offered Bill the extra bed in his tent-cabin, which Bill used a few nights before moving to quarters provided by Camp Curry Company.

Working breakfast, lunch, and dinner six days a week, Bill's day began early, but he and the staff were free after lunch to rest or explore the park, hike, ride horseback, swim, fish, and raft on the Merced River. In the evenings, there were ranger talks and films, entertainment around the amphitheatre's campfire, and outdoor dancing to Bud Stone's band.[3]

BERKELEY

Bill transferred to the University of California at Berkeley in the fall of 1947 and earned a Bachelor of Arts degree in chemistry and zoology with the class of 1951. His chemistry professor was the renowned Dr. Joel H. Hildebrand, a scholar-teacher whose *Principles of Chemistry* was the text-book. A skier and environmentalist, manager of the U.S. Olympic ski team in 1936 and president of the Sierra Club in 1937, Hildebrand died at the age of 101 in 1983.

From Berkeley's tradition of academic excellence, of vigorous dissent and free speech—a university tolerant of a diversity of views and expressions—Bill developed a creativity and a love of the arts, a questioning mind, an independence of thought and action which have shaped his life.

While at Berkeley, Bill pledged Pi Kappa Alpha fraternity but chose not to become a member and lived at home in nearby Piedmont. Bill Hahn, Neville Rich, and Bill Bigelow, Bill's basketball teammates from GWHS, also attended UC-Berkeley, and both Hahn and Bigelow became members of Pi Kappa Alpha fraternity.[4]

On Thursday evenings during the school year, Bill attended San Francisco Symphony concerts, conducted by Pierre Monteux, in the War Memorial Opera House with Pi Kappa Alpha friends who had a box there.[5] The

---

3. Bud Stone lived in Piedmont and attended the University of California at Berkeley.

4. Bill and Diane Hahn have lived in Hawaii since the late 1950s; they visited Bill in Cambridge, Massachusetts in the sixties. Bill Bigelow, a golfer at UC-Berkeley, became a CPA.

5. In 1978, Davies Hall was built in San Francisco for its symphony orchestra. Pierre Monteux was the conductor when Bill attended Thursday evening concerts from 1947–1950.

group often dined together in San Francisco restaurants prior to these performances.

Bill and his friends also attended Saturday "Cal" football games at Memorial Stadium and the Cal vs. Northwestern Rose Bowl game in Pasadena, California on January 1, 1949. Under coach Lyn ("Pappy") Waldorf, the Golden Bears won the Pacific Coast Conference Championship in 1948, '49, and '50 and went to the Rose Bowl, though losing each time.

While working his way through UC-Berkeley, Bill held a variety of jobs. He worked as a bellboy at Homewood Lodge and Cottages on Lake Tahoe in the summer of 1948. The following year, he worked at Hunt Foods' cannery in Hayward, California, where he lived with his cousin George Ann and her husband Sam Palmer. (The young couple owned and operated Palmer's, a combined pharmacy and variety store on Main Street in Hayward.) Later that summer, Bill worked in the San Francisco warehouse of Schwabacher-Frey, stationers, rearranging inventory.

Bill was a playground director for the City of Oakland Recreation Department during the 1949–1951 school years, working from 3 to 6 p.m. on weekdays and all day on Saturdays.

On June 17, 1950, Bill was an usher in the wedding of Philip Amos Crane, Jr. and Rosemary ("Rary") Pratt in Fresno, California. Phil's brother Bruce served as best man, and his sister Barbara was an attendant. The other ushers were Dick Miller, Ray Smith, Jay Martin, Stanley Pratt, and Bill Nordlund. The reception was held at the Sunnyside Country Club.[6]

During the summer of 1950, Bill and Ray Berg, a UC-Berkeley classmate, worked as waiters at Huntington Lake Camp for Girls, some 100 miles northeast of Fresno.[7] (Ray had worked there the previous summer and persuaded Bill to apply in 1950.) The camp's owner and director was Marjorie Gay Walter (UC-Berkeley class of 1922). With one day off a week and every afternoon free, Bill, Ray, and other student workers swam, sailed, canoed, or rode horseback. In the evenings, they read, wrote letters, or played games—ping pong, darts, and shuffleboard—or danced in the nearby lodge.

---

6.   Rosemary's mother and stepfather were Maude and Roy Paehlig.

Phil and Bruce Crane were raised near Chicago in Hinsdale, Illinois. Bill's classmates at UC-Berkeley, they were members of Pi Kappa Alpha and have been his lifelong friends. In the summer of 1966, Bruce and his second wife Barbara ("Basia"), a Polish emigre, were Bill's guests in his home at 220 Harvard Steet in Cambridge, Massachusetts; together, they toured Nantucket and Cape Cod.

7.   Ray, an orthopedic surgeon, interned at St. Vincent's Hospital in Manhattan's Greenwich Village from 1956–1957.

MILITARY SERVICE, 1949–1953

In 1949, Bill joined the California Air National Guard in Alameda, California. The unit trained on Monday evenings and for two summer weeks at Hamilton Air Force Base in Marin County. Bill's unit was ordered to active duty in the summer of 1951 and later assigned to Fort Snelling in Minneapolis, Minnesota, where he joined them in February 1952.

After his discharge as a corporal one year later, Bill traveled east to tour Boston, New York City, Philadelphia, and Washington, D.C., where his brother Eloyd lived and worked for the FBI Identification Section. In Washington, Bill rented a third-floor room in a nineteenth-century brick home, across from George Washington University Law School, and worked as a passenger agent for United Airlines at National Airport.

STUDY AND TRAVEL ABROAD, 1953–1954

While on duty at Fort Snelling, Bill had applied and was interviewed for admission to the University of Oslo Summer School in Oslo, Norway, and in May 1953, he received notification in Washington that he had been accepted and granted a scholarship, funded by a Norwegian hydro-electric company.

Prior to his June departure for Norway, his mother Elo, visiting him for a week in Washington, accompanied him by train to New York City for a short holiday.

On June 16, from Pier 42 in the Hudson River, Bill said goodbye to his mother and boarded the Norwegian American Lines' S.S. *Stavangerfjord* for the ten-day voyage to Norway. He and his fellow students traveled tourist class, though they moved freely between cabin and first-class lounges to enjoy teas, dances, films, and concerts.

After breakfasts of smorgasbord and American dishes, the students attended Norwegian language and orientation classes. Afternoons were devoted to games, reading, swimming, relaxing in deck chairs, and getting to know the classmates who came from thirty-seven states.

On the eighth and ninth days of the trip (June 24 and 25), the ship stopped for a part of each day in the Norwegian cities of Bergen, Stavanger, and Kristiansand. (At each port, including New York, both the Norwegian national anthem, "*Ja, Vi Elsker*," and "The Star-Spangled Banner" were played.)

They arrived in Bergen just a few days past midsummer night, the longest day of the year—a magical time when the northern sun casts its glow upon the night sky. Bill and his classmates were charmed by the beauty of the old Hanseatic city, with its pointed, tile rooftops stretching to the sky over a busy fishing harbor and its magnificent fjord views. The portside market was filled with flower vendors, fishmongers, and fruit and vegetable merchants.

Bill visited Bergenhus Fortress and Hakon Hall, the Hanseatic Museum and Wharves, Fantoft Stave church, and "Troldhaugen," Edvard Grieg's home. In late afternoon, he rode the funicular railway to the top of Mount Floien, where a terraced restaurant offered dramatic views of the town, its fjord, and the surrounding mountains. With Bill were fellow students Jake Jacobson of Providence, Rhode Island; Dick Cameron of Durham, New Hampshire; Karl Trygve Gundersen of Boston; Clayton Willis of Green-wich, Connecticut; and others. Exhilarated by the setting and their arrival in Norway, they toasted their good fortune with several rounds of Norwegian beer, chatting away and singing songs.

UNIVERSITY OF OSLO

On June 26, the ship docked in Oslo harbor. The University of Oslo campus, located on a wooded hill near Holmenkollen ski area (site of the 1948 Winter Olympics), was a fifteen-minute ride by "trikk" (electric tram) from downtown Oslo. The six-week session offered courses in Norwegian and Scandinavian history, politics, literature (Henrik Ibsen, Sigrid Undset, August Strindberg), music (Grieg), and art (Vigeland, Munch). There were also lectures and debates by leaders of Norway's political parties and government.

The program included two, three-day weekend excursions in Norway. By train, bus, and the nineteenth-century sidewheeler paddle steamer *Skibladner* (skib means ship in Norwegian, pronounced "ship"), the group visited Lillehammer, Hamar, Aulestad, and Eidsvoll and crossed Lake Mjosa, Norway's largest lake. They went on bus to Rjukan via Drammen, Kongsberg, Rauland, Morgedal, Seljord, and Notodden.

On two other weekends, Bill, Jake, and Peter Steese were guests of Ragnhild ("Pusa") Strand at her parents' attractive country home in Aamot, Modum, a short train ride west of Oslo. Pusa's friend Margaret Thoraldson and her sister Tove were also there.[8]

---

8.   Pusa, a Norwegian scholarship student at the University of Maine (Orono), would later marry Karl Gundersen, a Boston native and Williams College alumnus; they met aboard the S.S. *Stavangerfjord* en route to Norway.

Bill shared a three-room suite in Blindern Hall with Jake, Peter, and Stuart Chase. Peter, a student at Houghton College, was a minister's son from Rochester, New York; Stuart later succeeded his father as headmaster at Eaglebrook School in Deerfield, Massachusetts. Karl Gundersen and Dick Cameron shared the adjoining room at the end of the second floor.

Stuart, Karl, and Dick had met their future wives aboard the S.S. *Stavangerfjord*, [9] while Bill met Nancy Stevens of San Francisco, an alumna of the University of California at Berkeley and an acquaintance of several of Bill's friends from both UC and Piedmont. [10]

At a Blindern reception the weekend before classes started, Bill also met Lila Linkey, a talented, blue-eyed brunette, who had grown up in San Mateo on the San Francisco Peninsula and studied at the University of California-Santa Barbara. She was spending the year with a Norwegian shipowning family. Their elegant home above Blindern, where Lila hosted several dinners, overlooked the city and its beautiful fjord. An accomplished guitarist and singer, she played and sang a moving rendition of Rodgers and Hart's "Blue Moon" to Bill and others at a student show and accompanied him to dances and other events.

Bill and his classmates also attended concerts and art exhibits, swam and played tennis, explored Oslo, and savored local cafes, including Blom, known as "The Artist's Restaurant." On July 4th, the U.S. Embassy hosted a reception for Americans in Oslo, and a month later, Bill and other scholarship recipients were feted by the Norwegian Shipowner Association at a sumptuous evening buffet, with string ensemble, in the penthouse of "Redernes Hus," the shipowners' building overlooking Oslo's harbor.

THE CONTINENT AND ENGLAND

After successfully completing their examinations, receiving certificates, and attending a farewell dinner at Blindern on August 8, Bill and Karl Gundersen took a train to mid-Norway, near the Jotunheimen Mountains, the mythical home of the Nordic gods. (According to legend, Peer

---

9.   Stuart met Edmonia Johnson, from Bedford, Virginia and Randolph-Macon Woman's College, while at the University of Oslo. Dick Cameron, a geologist from the University of New Hampshire, also met his wife Dorothy ("Dottie") Loew at the school; she was a student at the University of Indiana.

10.   Nancy A. Stevens had resigned a job in San Francisco to attend the University of Oslo and travel that summer. In June 1955, following his graduation from Columbia University Graduate School of Business, Bill dined with Nancy in San Francisco.

Gynt flew over the ridge here on his reindeer.) They spent several days at the old seacoast city of Trondheim, visiting the medieval Nidaros Cathedral, which is considered one of Scandinavia's most notable architectural masterpieces. They also stayed a few nights at "Sellanraa" in the Rondane Mountains, the summer home of Karl's American cousin Elizabeth Gundersen, who had married Norwegian doctor Harold Somerfeldt and settled in Norway. They also spent a night with Karl's uncle Borge Gundersen, who owned and operated a profitable farm, harvesting timber in Flisa, near the Swedish border.

Bill and Karl flew to Stockholm, where they remained for four days. They then went by train to southern Sweden, stopping for a night and a day at Sweden's colorful amusement park, Lisberg, and at various beaches before boarding a ferry to Denmark. While in Copenhagen, Bill and Karl lived in a youth hostel, savored smorgasbord in the elegant garden of the Royal Library, rode the trams, and walked about the city. They enjoyed Tivoli Gardens' cafes, concerts, entertainment, and nightly fireworks. They also visited Hans Christian Andersen's home in Odense and toured the Royal Palace, museum, waterfront (Nyhavn), and Carlsberg brewery. Before leaving, they went by train to Elsinore Castle, and, with spirits undampened by wet weather, they admired its ramparts and communed with Hamlet's ghost.

From Copenhagen, they took the train to Hamburg, Germany for a two-day visit, then proceeded to Amsterdam. There, they stayed in a small hotel near the station, rode canal boats, went to museums, and saw many of Rembrandt's paintings, including "Night Watch." After a visit to The Hague and Rotterdam, Bill and Karl went on to Brussels, Ghent, Bruges, and Ostend in Belgium, then sailed across the channel to England.

In the summer of 1953, there was still evidence of World War II bombings around London, particularly near St. Paul's Cathedral, which was miraculously spared. Traveling in England and Europe at this time was a bargain for Americans—and especially for Bill, an impecunious student-adventurer!

While in London, Bill and Karl attended the theatre, and at a performance of Ibsen's *A Doll's House*, they met Clayton Willis, a fellow Oslo summer alum who was visiting friends and inquiring about admission to Oxford University.

Karl returned to the University of Oslo after a few days in London, to fly to Boston and his final year at Williams College. Renting a third-floor bedroom in a townhouse near Paddington train station, Bill and Clayton spent three weeks touring London and the English countryside. They visited museums and Fleet Street bookstores. They rode double-decker buses, trains, the underground, and boats on the Thames. They strolled through Kew Gardens and Regent's Park (known as Queen Mary's Garden) and the romantic St. James Park, with its sinuous lake, dreamy willows, and fountains. They also toured Eton School and its playing fields, Windsor Castle, and Oxford University.

Bill and Clayton flew to Paris for a few days in early September, then took a train to Montpellier, France, where they lived in a hotel near downtown and the University of Montpellier. From there, they toured Nimes, Arles, and Avignon and attended Sunday afternoon bullfights.

INSTITUTE OF TOURAINE

At the end of September, Bill boarded a train for Tours, where he enrolled in a French language course at the Institute of Touraine, housed in an elegant eighteenth-century home with marble stairways, marquetry floors, and a walled garden.

He rented a third-floor room in the home of the Jacob family at 13 rue de Vinci, a few blocks from school.[11] Here, Col. and Mrs. Jacob, Bill, and two other students—a young Italian foreign service officer and a Swedish postal executive—were served exceptional lunches and dinners, and their lively conversations improved Bill's French. At mid-evening, their maid brought trays of tea, toast, butter, and jelly to the guests' rooms; Bill usually shared this time with the genial Swede.

The Institute of Touraine's morning course was conducted entirely in French, covering grammar, reading, writing, and oral responses to their instructors' questions. In the afternoons, Bill and his friends sometimes bicycled about Tours or along the Loire River and the countryside, visiting chateaux and the Vouvray wine cellars; they also went to museums and cafes. On Saturday evenings, they attended the opera at the baroque opera house in Tours, after which they met other students for drinks in nearby cafes.

The Institute had students of all ages and nationalities. Bill became a close friend of Cecilia Larson, a native of Oslo, whose father was the publisher of *Dagbladet,* a Norwegian newspaper. Cecilia's French host family repared to their attractive country home on the weekends. Bill, a guest there with others on two Sunday afternoons, enjoyed fine wines amidst much bonhommie, gaiety, and grand luncheons.

---

11.   Colonel Jacob, a St. Cyr graduate (the West Point of France), was retired, having served in World War II, Algeria, and French Indochina. In April 1973, when Bill and his second wife Joan were living in Tours, they visited the Jacobs' home and its new owner (the Jacobs had died) and lived in Tours with Mrs. Jacob's sister Madame Maupa.

SORBONNE

At the end of October, Bill departed for Paris, where he enrolled at the Sorbonne in a French language and civilization course for foreign students. He found a fourth-floor walk-up room in a Left Bank hotel on rue Monsieur Le Prince, near Boulevard San Michel, the Sorbonne, and Luxembourg Gardens. Bill's classmates included Richard Wright, the black American author whose books, *Black Boy* and *Native Son*, Bill had read and admired in high school. They saw each other at popular Left Bank cafes, where Bill also met the American writer James Baldwin.

During this period in Paris, the dollar was so strong that Americans could live comfortably on $15 to $20 a week. Receiving $110 a month from the G.I. Bill of Rights, Bill availed himself fully of Paris's cultural life, attending the theatre, opera, ballet, concerts, films, and museums at low student rates.

Bill, Dermott Doyle, Clayton Willis, and others often attended receptions at the American Cathedral on Sunday evenings. On one occasion, they met U.S. Senator William Benton's family, including his three adopted children—Louise, Helen, and John—who were attending a preparatory school in Paris.[12] On Sunday afternoons, Bill sometimes took in plays at the Odeon or went to Montmartre to hear singers and comedians.

Over the Christmas holiday, Bill traveled with John Emmerich (from McComb, Mississippi) and his wife Celia in their Renault sedan, touring Luxembourg, Germany, Austria, and Switzerland. On Christmas Day, they walked and dined in Heidelberg, and after driving through Bavaria, Garmisch, and Berchtesgaden, they celebrated New Year's Eve in an Austrian inn, singing and dancing until dawn. Bill and the Emmerichs returned to Paris by way of Liechtenstein, Zurich, and Basle.

Over Easter vacation in 1954, Bill and Dermott Doyle hitched a ride on a vegetable truck from Les Halles market in Paris to the Riviera, then proceeded by bus and train along the French and Italian Rivieras to Pisa, Florence, and Rome, where they saw Louise, Helen, and John Benton and their parents.

Desiring to return to Paris by plane, Senator Benton engaged Bill and Dermott to drive his family's large black Citroen sedan back to Paris,

---

12. After his unsuccessful campaign for election to the U.S. Senate from Connecticut, William Benton had taken his family to Paris for a year, 1953–1954.

He and Chester Bowles, Yale classmates, founded Benton & Bowles, the advertising agency, in 1929. Later, he acquired and published the *Encyclopedia Britannica*.

expenses paid. Accepting with alacrity, they returned to Paris in style, touring Venice, the Italian lakes, Locarno, Lugano, Geneva, Zurich, and Basle while en route. Back in Paris, spring greeted them with greening trees, blossoming flowers, and chestnuts.

SPAIN, PORTUGAL, AND GIBRALTAR

At the end of June 1954, having completed classes at the Sorbonne, Bill and another American toured Bordeaux, Biarritz, and the lovely beaches of the Cote d'Argent before taking the train through the Pyrenees to San Sebastian, Spain, on the Atlantic Ocean.

In July, they were in Pamplona for the annual fete—the running of the bulls—and the bullfights and life in the cafes which Ernest Hemingway recorded in *The Sun Also Rises*. They then traveled to Barcelona and the islands of Majorca and Ibiza before returning to mainland Spain at Valencia and journeying by bus to Madrid. After several days in the capital, they boarded an overnight express train to Lisbon, where they toured the city, Estoril, and nearby towns. Returning to Spain, they stopped in Seville, Cordova, Granada (the Alhambra), and finally the Andalusian city of Malaga on the Mediterranean. After his American friend returned to Portland, Oregon, Bill lived in Malaga for three weeks with a Swedish family whose villa was a short trolley ride east of town.

After lunch and a siesta, Bill, the Swedish family, and their guests swam in the Mediterranean, relaxed, and read on the beach. He enjoyed Spanish food (particularly paella) and watching performances of Spanish folk dances. After visiting Gibraltar and Morocco, Bill returned to the United States by ship from Algeciras, Spain, with a port call at Halifax, Nova Scotia en route to New York City.

COLUMBIA

In September 1954, Bill entered Columbia University Graduate School of Business, where he completed a Master of Science degree in 1955. While there, he lived in John Jay Hall, sharing a two-room suite with Jim Syrett, Gene Dimet, and Tosiharu Terashiki, a Japanese scholarship student who was an officer with Sumitomo Corporation in Tokyo. There, Bill also met John Watts, who was studying for his Ph.D. in economics. Both men earned

A's in international economics and remained friends until Watts's death in March of 1988.[13]

During his year at Columbia, Bill worked part-time in the university's Career Placement Office. In the spring semester, he was elected president of the Business School's Foreign Trade Association and subsequently planned activities, arranged for speakers, and conducted dinner programs in John Jay Hall.

EARLY CAREER, 1955

Following his 1955 graduation, Bill accepted a finance trainee position with General Motors Overseas Operations in New York City, starting in accounting.[14] The goal in three to five years was a promotion to treasurer or finance manager at a GM foreign manufacturing or assembly plant.

During this period, Bill shared an apartment on Riverside Drive and 107th Street with Columbia friends Jim Syrett and Arthur Kimball. When Jim married in 1957, Bill and Arthur leased a fifth-floor apartment in a townhouse off Fifth Avenue at 9 East 84th Street.

In early 1956, another Columbia colleague, Norman Allan, then with Compton Advertising Agency, had the foresight to buy eight tickets to the opening night's performance of *My Fair Lady*. Thus, Norman, Bill, and other friends were present at the musical's Broadway debut on March 16, 1956. Afterward, they celebrated over drinks at Sardi's and listened to the reading of the New York newspaper critics' rave reviews. The *World-Telegram and Sun* called it "the biggest thing of the century in musical theatre."[15]

Unsatisfied with the financial work at GM, Bill resigned in spring 1959

---

13.   In Tokyo, Terashiki lived at 24 Kagegaoka-cho, Shibuya-Ku. He received his B.A. in 1944 from Keio University in Tokyo. Syrett, from Rock Island, Illinois, received his B.A. from Augustana College. Gene Dimet, a Miami University (Ohio) graduate, grew up in Niagara Falls, New York.

John Watts, from Norman, Oklahoma, held a B.A. from the University of Minnesota, an M.A. from the University of Pennsylvania, and a Ph.D. in economics from Columbia University. John taught economics at the University of Rhode Island, Michigan State University, Brooklyn College, St. John's University, and Iona College. A bachelor, Dr. Watts lived in a Greenwich Village apartment at 135 Waverly Place in Manhattan from the late 1950s until his death there of a heart attack on March 16, 1988.

14.   Bill was one of four men selected for GM's program. The others were James P. Thompson, Bill's classmate at Columbia who came from Georgia; a graduate of the Amos Tuck School of Business at Dartmouth College; and a Harvard Business School alumnus.

15.   *World-Telegram and Sun*, 17 March 1956.

and accepted a real estate sales position with Previews, Inc., an international real estate marketing firm in Manhattan, at 49 East 53rd Street, and other offices across the United States and Europe.[16] In this post, Bill inspected and evaluated large residential, commercial, and farm properties in New York, New England, and eastern Canada; sold the firm's marketing service to owners; prepared property reports covering saleability, highest and best use, and value; and assisted brokers in property promotions and negotiating sales. The service required a retainer fee to cover advertising, brochure and newsletter preparations, mailings, owner and broker consultations, and sale negotiations.

FIRST MARRIAGE, 1959

On April 11, 1959, Bill married Joan Cecilia Sears of Devon, Connecticut. The Manhattan ceremony was held in the "Little Church Around the Corner"—the Episcopal Church of Transfiguration. George S. Banks, Jr., a GM associate and an alumnus of University of Pennsylvania's Wharton School, was best man; Mrs. Ronald F. Dobson was matron of honor. A reception was held in the Library Suite of Manhattan's St. Regis Hotel. In addition to family members, Dr. John Watts, James P. Thompson, Wayne W. Hartley (a GM associate from Seattle and the University of Washington), and Louise H. Benton attended.

Joan was born on July 3, 1935 in Bridgeport, Connecticut, the only child of David and Edna Sears (Sesarsky). She graduated from Mary Burnham School in Northhampton, Massachusetts and received her Bachelor of Arts degree in 1957 from Skidmore College in Saratoga, New York. At the time of her marriage, she was working in the investment department of the Bank of New York.

A son, William Milton Grier 3d, was born to the couple in Manhattan on November 11, 1959 in the Harkness Pavilion of Columbia University Presbyterian Hospital.

16. Ten of Bill's GMOO associates gave him a farewell luncheon at the New York Athletic Club on Central Park South in April 1959.

CAMBRIDGE, MASSACHUSETTS, 1959

Later that year, the Griers moved to Cambridge, Massachusetts, where Bill worked for the Boston office of Previews, Inc. and had responsibility for operations in New England, eastern Canada, the Canadian Maritime Provinces, and Bermuda. In time, he became a manager and an officer of the firm.

In 1960, while in Cambridge, Bill also formed Feature Arts, a mail-order business which marketed museum reproductions of well-known paintings, sculpture, and antique jewelry, as well as art books and records. The business was closed in 1962.

DIVORCE, 1962

In November 1962, the Griers were divorced, and a prolonged dispute over custody of their son Billy ensued.[17] Angered by the divorce, which Bill had sought, Joan refused to allow him weekend or vacation custody, despite repeated court orders over the next six years. Consequently, Bill was able to see his son only once or twice a month on Saturdays or after school, driving four hours from Boston to the boy's home in Weston, Connecticut.

After each court order issued between 1962 and 1968 reaffirming Bill's custody rights, Joan immediately filed motions to modify those orders, thereby thwarting any solution.

For Bill, it was anguishing to have his son periodically taken out of school to appear in court, where, sometimes in tears, he submitted to questioning by attorneys and judges. To spare his son further agony, and distraught over Joan's intransigence and the futility of litigation, Bill suggested that Joan and her second husband, Dr. Edward Keelan, adopt young Billy, a proposal which she promptly rejected. To end the debilitating impasse, Bill reluctantly agreed, when his son was nine in 1968, to forego weekend and vacation custody until the boy was older. He continued day visitations, and Joan agreed to support Billy and provide for his education through college.

---

17.   Joan, who had custody of young Billy, then lived with her family in Devon, Connecticut while teaching school in nearby Bridgeport from 1961–1962.

The following year, she married Dr. Edward Keelan, a Dublin-educated psychiatrist who had emigrated to Westport, Connecticut, where he later established a practice. They had a son, David, in 1966 and lived in Weston, Connecticut. In the late 1970s, Dr. Keelan, a manic-depressive, had a mental breakdown, which was exacerbated by financial reverses and the loss of their home.

After Bill's move to Manhattan in 1970, his son spent one weekend with him there, but Joan refused to permit such visits in the future, claiming the boy suffered "separation anxiety"—an argument that was repeatedly rejected by the court. When Billy entered his teenage years, his father again attempted to arrange for overnight visitations, as well as longer stays during his son's school vacations. Joan, however, remained opposed, unwilling to cooperate throughout Billy's high school years.

In fall 1973, when Billy was fourteen, his father and stepmother moved to Denver, and thereafter they saw each other in the East over Christmas holidays.

It was not until Billy's senior year in college that Joan began to relent a bit. Regrettably, by then both father and son were effectively deprived of any normal relationship—a loss they carry with them today.

REAL ESTATE INVESTMENT

Shortly after his divorce in 1962, Bill formed a real estate investment and management firm, while continuing in his position with Previews, Inc. From 1962 to 1970, his firm acquired, renovated, and managed six Cambridge apartment buildings; all were three-story, frame walk-ups in Central Square, between Harvard University and Massachusetts Institute of Technology. The first acquisition was a six-unit structure on Western Avenue, a half block from the Charles River, where Bill occupied a unit until purchasing a three-story Victorian with mansard roof at 220 Harvard Street; he lived in this house from 1964 to 1969. At that time, Boston area real estate was greatly undervalued. With urban renewal and Harvard's real estate development in Cambridge during this period, the value of Bill's holdings appreciated substantially. Their gain was realized when Bill sold his properties in the late sixties and early 1970.

Over the Christmas holidays during this period, Bill usually visited his family in San Francisco and friends in Los Angeles. Every spring, from 1963 to 1969, he vacationed for three weeks in Europe, primarily in northern Italy, southern France, Switzerland, Austria, and Germany. In spring 1967, he went to Italy, Yugoslavia, Greece, and Turkey; from Venice, he sailed aboard a Yugoslav ship for five days along the Dalmatian Coast, stopping for visits in Trieste, Dubrovnik, and other cities before arriving in Greece. After a week on the mainland of Greece, Bill took a cruise to the Aegean Islands, Istanbul, the Bosphorus, the Dardanelles, and the western coast of Turkey, including Ephesus.

RETURN TO NEW YORK CITY, 1969

At the end of 1969, Grier returned to New York City and worked in investment sales with Apache Corporation, a New York Stock Exchange firm with headquarters in Minneapolis. In this post, Bill sold tax-sheltered, limited partnerships in oil and gas and real estate to high-income individuals. During this period, he also became a member of the Union League Club at 38 East 37th Street, where he entertained clients and friends, played squash, and used the library.

Unfortunately, the proliferation of oil and gas tax-shelter programs being marketed in the late sixties caused increased competition which, along with a bear market in 1971, forced Apache to phase out its offices. Bill, therefore, left the firm with the intention of acquiring or founding a business.

TRAVEL ABROAD, 1971–1972

In May 1971, Bill vacationed in England, crossing the Atlantic on the S.S. *France*, on the next to last voyage of the venerable French ship. Aboard, he met British actress Hermione Gingold and accompanied her to a rerun of her winning role in "Gigi" in the ship's theatre. From Southhampton, he drove through Thomas Hardy's West Country and the Cotswolds. In Bideford, he bought a George III mahogany flap table and four nineteenth-century mahogany dining chairs from J. Collins and Son; the furniture was shipped to New York City, with three oil paintings purchased in London galleries. Branching out from London, he visited Cambridge, Canterbury, and Winston Churchill's home, "Chartwell," in Kent. During the last week of his holiday, Bill was joined in London by Joan Grafmueller, who was visiting a classmate from Ethel Walker School— Elaine Domingues Rawlinson (Lady Peter Rawlinson), whose husband was then serving as attorney general in Prime Minister Edward Heath's cabinet.

The following February, Bill went to Europe for three weeks, visiting Turkish friends in Munich, Germany; skiing in San Anton, Austria and San Moritz, Switzerland; then sightseeing in Madrid, where he visited the Prado and, in a gallery in the capital, bought two paintings; and finally, touring Lisbon and nearby Estoril and Cascais.

SECOND MARRIAGE

On June 15, 1972, Bill married Joan Grafmueller in Ketchum, Idaho, next to Sun Valley. The ceremony took place in the home of Presbyterian minister Curtis M. Page, where the windows and terrace overlooked Mt. Baldy and Sun Valley's downhill ski runs, a deep green at the time.

Prior to their wedding, Bill and Joan had traveled through the Black Hills of South Dakota, visiting the Homestake Mining Company and seeing the statue of Bill's great-uncle Thomas Johnston ("T.J.") Grier, Homestake's superintendent for thirty years, in Lead, South Dakota. The couple had also traveled to Yellowstone and Grand Teton National Parks and to Helena, Montana.

The newlyweds flew from Boise, Idaho to Portland, Oregon after the ceremony. Following a few days of sightseeing there, they rented a car and drove along the Oregon and California coasts, past the redwoods to San Francisco and Sacramento, where they visited Bill's family. Later, they drove to Monterey, Carmel, and Big Sur, then proceeded south along Coastal Highway One to William Randolph Hearst's estate, "San Simeon," and to Brentwood, where they were the guests of Bruce and Barbara Crane. A two-week holiday in Mexico City followed, with visits to Oaxaca and Acapulco.

Bill and Joan had met in Manhattan in November of 1968 through Nadia Von Hurt, a mutual friend in Cambridge, Massachusetts. A native of New York City, Joan was born on September 21, 1935 in Columbia University Presbyterian Hospital, the only child of Charles Edward and Barbara Rose Grafmueller (nee Brownlee). When she was three-and-a-half, her mother died of a brain tumor in Scarsdale, New York, on August 28, 1939. Barbara was the daughter of Dr. Harris Fenton Brownlee and Adelaide Dennis of Danbury, Connecticut. Her maternal grandparents were Mr. and Mrs. Martin L. Dennis. [18]

Until the age of ten, Joan lived in Scarsdale, New York; Danbury, Connecticut; and Grosse Pointe, Michigan with her father, her stepmother Edith Colby de Rham, and her stepsister and stepbrother, Edie and Charlie. In 1945, the Grafmuellers moved to Greenwich, Connecticut, where Joan graduated from Greenwich Country Day School four years later. In 1953, she graduated from the Ethel Walker School in Simsbury, Connecticut.

Following three years at Sweet Briar College in Lynchburg, Virginia

---

18.   Joan's mother, Barbara Rose, was educated at Miss Porter's School, Farmington, Connecticut, and Finch College in New York City. Her Dennis ancestors—among the first settlers of Newark, New Jersey—donated the Dennis Library in Newton, New Jersey.

(1953–1956), Joan settled in New York City, where she worked at *Look* magazine for eight and a half years as an assistant to the director of personnel and ran a training program for thirty-seven editorial trainees. Later, Joan worked for Rock Resorts and the JDR III Fund (John D. Rockefeller III's personal investments); Young & Rubicam advertising agency; and, until 1972, as an executive secretary for Doubleday & Company.

FRANCE AND EAST AFRICA

When Bill's financing to purchase a business fell through in September of 1972, the Griers decided to take a year off. They spent that year in France, studying the language, traveling extensively, and considering a relocation from Manhattan to the West upon their return. After buying an Audi in Germany, they lived in Aix-en-Provence from November 1972 to March 1973 and in Tours, deep in the chateaux country of the Loire Valley, from May to August 1973. They studied French at the University of Aix-en-Provence and at the Institute of Touraine and traveled in France, Italy, Switzerland, Germany, and Austria. From Tours, they also visited Joan's cousin Barbara Bolton and her French husband Jerome Gratry in Paris and toured Brittany and Normandy as well.

In July, inoculated and properly outfitted, Bill left Joan behind in Tours and took a trip to East Africa, visiting Kenya, Tanzania, and the islands of Zanzibar and Pemba. He flew to Nairobi, Kenya with eighteen French professionals; armed with sleeping bags and a restless spirit of adventure, the group and an Indian guide toured Kenya and Tanzania game reserves in two Volkswagen vans. They saw Nairobi National Park, the Masai Mara, Serengeti National Park, the Olduvai Gorge, and Seronera.

Roughing it, the group slept in huts, in a museum, in the workers' quarters at parks, and in modest hotels. They swam and bathed in streams and lakes, often with a vista of Mount Kilimanjaro as a backdrop. They retired early each evening and rose with the sun, as a crease of orange transformed the night into shrimp-colored hues of dawn.

From the Serengeti, Bill and his companions spent a day at the Ngorongoro Crater, a spectacular caldera. Perched on the crater's edge, the Ngorongoro Wildlife Lodge had a view of the crater's floor some 2,000 feet below. At the center was a large alkali lake of a dazzling jade color, accented by thousands of pink-winged flamingos, crowned cranes, and storks with neck pouches.

En route from Serengeti to Ngorongoro, the group surmounted the Great Rift Valley wall and saw Masai herdsmen guiding their cattle along. After ten days in the vans, they then traveled by Tanzania's trains and buses to visit an agricultural research center and a model Tanzanian community, as well as Dar-es-Salaam, the capital, where Bill bought a dozen primitive (naive) oil paintings.

After a two-day visit in Zanzibar and a brief stop on the island of Pemba, they flew to Mombasa, Kenya. There, Bill visited his great-uncle Thomas Johnston Grier's stepdaughter—Margaret Eliza ("Madge") Christie (nee Ferrie). The widow of James Carron Christie, a Scot who had been the Queen's counsel in Kenya for almost fifty years, Madge was born in Scotland and had settled in Africa after her marriage on October 7, 1924 in her mother's Los Angeles home at 1675 Buckingham Road, Lafayette Square.

Over lunches, dinners, and teas in her comfortable house near the Indian Ocean, Madge recalled many events, people, and places from the past: her early years in Edinburgh and the Black Hills of South Dakota; her stepfather T.J. Grier and her mother Mary Jane Grier (nee Palethorpe); her student days at Lead High School and Columbia University; her life in Los Angeles after T.J.'s death in 1914; and her friendship with Phoebe Hearst. She spoke of her brother James William Ferrie, her half sister Evangeline Victoria ("Muddie") Grier, and her three Grier half brothers—Tommy, Lisgar, and Ormonde. She reminisced about Homestake Mining Company and the times when she had been a guest in Phoebe Hearst's California residences, "Hacienda" and "Wyntoon." Madge also gave Bill several family papers and photos.

In her English Ford, Madge drove Bill around Mombasa's large port, its downtown and residential areas, and nearby shorefront resorts. She entertained him at the elegant Mombasa Club, with its view of lush gardens and the Indian Ocean. Bill also met Madge's daughter and son-in-law, Jean and Ian Mills, who were vacationing at a resort to the north of Mombasa.

Bill had been corresponding with Madge for more than a year before his 1973 visit. Mildred Fielder, the author of *Homestake Gold*, had referred him first to Madge's half sister Muddie Grier (Mrs. Edwin Nelsen) in Sausalito, California; Muddie, in turn, urged Bill to contact Madge. For Bill, meeting her in July of 1973 was like meeting an old friend.

DENVER

When the Griers returned to New York in August of 1973, they decided to relocate in Colorado. After arranging their affairs in early October, they began a leisurely drive west, stopping to visit Gettysburg, Charlottesville, Great Smoky Mountains National Park, Knoxville, Memphis, Oklahoma City, Santa Fe, Taos, Colorado Springs, and Boulder on the way.

Arriving in Denver in November, the Griers rented an apartment, and soon after, Bill leased an office suite in the Empire Building in downtown Denver. Here, he founded Grier & Company, a management consulting, marketing, and publishing firm.

The following July, the Griers purchased one side of a duplex at 443 Marion Street—an attached, 1904 two-story brick house near the Denver Country Club, where they reside today.

GRIER & COMPANY
Real Estate West

During the early months in Denver, Grier & Company prepared executive resumes, corporate reports, brochures, and advertising, while Bill researched starting a commercial real estate trade newspaper. In June 1976, that concept became a reality with the publication of the first monthly issue of *Real Estate West*.

Now in its sixteenth year, the paper covers news of income-producing real estate development, financing, leasing, sales, and investment from the Midwest to the Pacific Coast and includes a *California Real Estate* section. In addition to city reviews and special features, the tabloid paper reports on the office, multi-family, shopping center, and industrial markets. Subscribers are developers, investors, brokers, building owners, officers of financial institutions, and corporate real estate executives.

In 1980, Grier & Company edited, designed, and produced a 432-page book, *Walter Judd: Chronicles of a Statesman*, for the Center for Science, Technology, and Political Thought in Boulder, Colorado. Bill and his staff worked on the project with Professor Edward J. Rozek, the Center's founder and director, a Polish emigre, Harvard University Ph.D., and political science professor at the University of Colorado.

In the summer of 1984, Grier & Company relocated to a larger downtown Denver office at 909 17th Street, Suite 607; in November 1988, the firm occupied a corner suite at 444 17th Street, Suite 918, a few steps from the Brown Palace hotel; and in August 1991, the firm moved to 825 East Speer Boulevard, Suite 300, a short stroll from Bill's home.

INVESTOR

When Bill sold, at a profit, his apartment properties in Cambridge, Massachusetts in the late sixties and 1970, he invested the proceeds in corporate stocks, thereby launching a secondary career as an investor that has continued for two decades.

Initially a short-term trader and speculator, he sometimes bought stock on margin and on broker recommendations with little, if any, evaluation of a company's stock price in relation to its assets and earning power. This strategy, steadily eroding his portfolio's value, soon led Bill to reappraise his approach. He began to view a share of stock as a part-interest in a business, rather than a speculative medium, to stress business values instead of stock market values.

In analyzing the methods of money management, Bill was soon drawn to the basic value approach of Benjamin Graham, the esteemed professor of investments at Columbia University Graduate School of Business, father of modern security analysis, and founder of the Wall Street firm of Graham-Newman. In 1934, he and colleague David L. Dodd published their pioneering text, *Security Analysis.* In 1949, Graham also published *The Intelligent Investor.* (As a student at Columbia, Bill's emphasis was on foreign trade; therefore, he did not take their courses. However, his roommate Jim Syrett, a finance major, had talked enthusiastically about them.)

Successful investing, Graham said, requires patience and discipline; stocks should be bought with the curt calculation we apply to prices at the grocery store, not with the hopes and dreams we bring to the gambling casino. He also believed that emotion, whims, and changes of fancy in the market sometimes caused specific stocks to sell for less than their true value.

In developing a portfolio, he wanted companies with more equity than debt, stocks priced at or below net current asset value (current assets minus current liabilities and debt). He would buy such bargains among various companies and industries for diversification and safety. Thus, the key was to buy stocks selling at low prices relative to current earnings, to apply Graham's test of assets divided by liabilities to determine how much real value existed.

Since Bill began to practice Graham's principles in 1974, he has had rewarding results—buying undervalued companies for the long term.

OTHER INTERESTS

Since the late seventies, Joan Grier has designed and produced sachets and lingerie for Bergdorf Goodman, Lord & Taylor, I. Magnin, and D. Porthault, Inc., the French linen firm.

In the summers, the Griers have vacationed in Nantucket, Maine, and Vermont. In August 1979, they sailed for several days with Bill's Montreal cousin, David Grier, on his sloop on Lake Champlain. At other times, they have been guests of Joan's Cleveland cousins, the Boltons, in Prouts Neck, Maine. From 1980 to 1984, for a month each year, the Griers rented homes in Nantucket, Massachusetts. In spring 1984, they explored the old houses, plantations, and gardens of Charleston and Savannah.

The Griers visited Bill's mother each year until her death in 1987 and saw his family in San Francisco and Sacramento. Since settling in Denver in 1973, they have traveled extensively in the West, including trips to Taos, Santa Fe, Portland, Seattle, and Victoria and Vancouver, British Columbia. They have also alternated Christmas-New Year's vacations with both of their families—Bill's in California and Joan's in Connecticut. While visiting the Grafmuellers, the Griers have sometimes rented apartments in Manhattan.

WILLIAM MILTON GRIER 3d
(b. November 11, 1959)

The only child of William Milton, Jr. and Joan Sears Grier, young Billy spent his first two years in Cambridge, Massachusetts. In May of 1961, he and his parents visited his grandmother Elo Grier in San Francisco, his great-aunt Ferdy Lannon Shaeffer in Sacramento, and his Palmer cousins—Cathy, Charles, and Kenneth—in Berkeley.

Following his parents' divorce in November 1962, Billy and his mother shared the home of her parents, David and Edna Sears, in Devon, Connecticut.

Billy's mother remarried in 1963, and in 1966, she and her second husband, Dr. Edward Keelan, had a son, David, some seven years Billy's junior. The family first lived in Westport, Connecticut, where Dr. Keelan had a psychiatric practice. In the mid-sixties, they bought a home in Weston, Connecticut, where they lived until the late 1970s.

Billy attended public schools in Milford, Westport, and Weston until the fourth grade. From 1968 until his graduation in June 1977, he attended Greens Farms Academy, a private school in Greens Farms, Connecticut.

The following September, Billy enrolled in the freshman class of Rollins College in Winter Park, Florida. In his sophomore year, however, he transferred to Colgate University in Hamilton, New York, where he majored in fine arts and was on the university's tennis team. During his college summers, he worked as an assistant tennis pro at clubs in Connecticut, including Wee Burn Country Club in Darien.

Billy was awarded a B.A. in fine arts from Colgate in May of 1981, and his father and stepmother attended the commencement ceremonies. In a letter sent to Billy shortly before graduation, Bill shared with his son three quotes. He wrote of Adlai Stevenson's caveat to the 1954 graduating class at Princeton University—"Don't forget when you leave why you came"— and his wise assessment that "what a man knows at fifty that he didn't know at twenty is, for the most part, uncommunicable. The knowledge he has acquired with age is not the knowledge of formulas, or forms or words, but of people, places, actions—a knowledge not gained of words but of touch, sight, sound, victories, failures, sleeplessness, devotion, love—the human experiences and emotions of this earth and of oneself and other men; and perhaps, too, a little reverence for things you cannot see." And lastly, Bill passed on the advice of Henry James to his graduating niece: "Be kind to people, be kind, be kind...."

After receiving his degree, Billy continued to work as a tennis pro at clubs in Connecticut's Fairfield County. Two years later, he accepted a sales position with a Manhattan firm that organized tennis tournaments in New York and Florida, assisting in marketing and selling sponsorships to corporations. Later, in Manhattan, he became an independent broker in commodity futures, a trader of the United States dollar in world currency markets.

Bill Grier outside the family's home in Piedmont, California, 1947

Above: Bill Grier and "Judge" John D. Russell at Grier & Company, Denver, August 1985

Below: Entrance to Menlo School and College, c. 1946, Menlo Park, California

Menlo College 1946 basketball team—*seated, from left*: Harry Myers, Bill Grier, Hobey Burns, Dick Brooke, John Cadrett, Harry Morris, and Al Werry; *standing, from left*: Bob Durnal, Bob Levy, Ken Berridge, Bill Rose, Cliff Gerstner, Hank Needham, Harry Cusack, and Coach Roy Hughes

Crane-Pratt wedding reception, June 17, 1950, Sunnyside Country Club, Fresno, California—*from left*: Jay Martin, Richard Miller, Bill Grier, Bruce Crane, Stanley Pratt, Jr., Ray Smith, and Bill Nordlund.

The Grier-Sears wedding reception at St. Regis Hotel in New York City, April 11, 1959—*top:* Louise H. Benton and Bill Grier; *below, from left*, Wayne Hartley, Bill and Joan Sears Grier, Mr. and Mrs. Ronald Dobson, and James Thompson

Above: Bill Grier, newly elected president, and Alvin Cohen, outgoing president, Foreign Trade Association, Columbia Business School, January 1955

Above: Bill Grier and son Billy at six weeks and at one-and-a-half years

310

Right: Bill Grier, Sun Valley, Idaho, New Year's Day, 1966

Below, from left: Bill Grier, Basia and Bruce Crane, Joan G. Grier, Carmel-by-the-Sea, California, December 1981

Top: Billy (age 3-1/2), Old Saybrook, Connecticut, 1963

Below left: Bill and Billy Grier (age 7), November 1966

Below right: Billy (age 1-1/2) at Karl Gundersen's home, Newton, Massachusetts, 1961
(Courtesy of Karl T. Gundersen)

312

Above left: Karl and Pusa Gundersen in Bill Grier's home,
220 Harvard Street, Cambridge, Massachusetts
(February 1965)

Above right: Bill in Tours, France, June 1973

Below: Gundersen family home, Rangeley, Maine, July 17, 1965,
from left, Karl Gundersen, Pat Dennehy, Bill Grier, Pusa Gundersen,
Ray Dennehy, Betsy Marble *(back to camera)*

Right: Bill Grier and Peter Crane,
June 1970

Below: Bill Grier and Bruce Crane,
chez Crane, Falkirk Lane,
Brentwood, California, 1967

Right: Joan Grafmueller, c. 1965

Below, from left: Joan Grafmueller Grier, along Oregon coast, on honeymoon, June 1972; Joan and Bill Grier after their wedding in Ketchum, Idaho, June 15, 1972

Above, from left: Joan Grafmueller in Redding, Connecticut, c. 1937; her grandmother and mother, Adelaide and Barbara Rose Brownlee, Easthampton, New York, 1919

Below: Joan with father and mother, Scarsdale, New York, c. 1937

On Rearing Children From Crib To College

October 1970 60¢

PARENTS'

MAGAZINE & BETTER FAMILY LIVING

More than 2,100,000 Circulation

**Must We
Legislate
Family Size?**

**The Middle
Years of
Childhood**

**First Baby
in the House**

**Hidden
Handicaps to
Learning**

Billy Grier on the cover of *Parent's* magazine in October 1970

Right: Billy Grier receiving his Bachelor of Arts degree from Colgate University, May 31, 1981

Below, from left: Billy, Joan, and Bill Grier, 1972

318

Left: Joan Grafmueller Grier, c. 1982

Below: Griers' home, 443 Marion Street, Denver, Colorado, 1990

CALIFORNIA REAL ESTATE NEWS (Section B)

Minneapolis/ St. Paul P. A7	Hotel Management P. A11	Denver/Aurora Colorado P. A17

Real Estate West

THE JOURNAL OF
COMMERCIAL &
INVESTMENT PROPERTY

PUBLISHED BY GRIER & COMPANY

VOL. 14, NO.8   APRIL 1990

Albuquerque

Arts Center Planned For Downtown

Hit by lower oil prices and a depressed mining industry and concerned about cuts in defense spending, Albuquerque is working to revitalize its downtown, stimulate convention business and attract new industry.

Recently the City Council decided to put a new performing arts center on vacant land adjacent to Civic Plaza. The ground parking garage will be

The decision to build the arts center downtown was controversial. Development pieces are coming together there, but the city's uptown urban center competes for public investment.

Downtown's 35 buildings contain 2.35 million sq. ft. of office space (not counting the Beta West building) Uptown's 48 buildings offer 1.82 million sq. ft.

Office Vacancy Rate
At 23% In 1989

renovated late this year. Beta West, a Denver subsidiary of U.S. West, also in Denver, will complete its 350,000-sq.-ft. office building next month on the Civic Plaza and will open an adjacent 405-room Hyatt Regency Hotel in August. A convention center to which 106,000 sq. ft. is being added will open this fall with 718 parking spaces. It will increase exhibit and meeting space by 40% and permit meetings of up to 5,000 delegates.

To complement both its downtown and convention centers, the city doubled the capacity of the airport, to 22 gates, in 1989. Dennis Campbell, director of sales for the Albuquerque Convention and Visitors Bureau, said bookings extending to the year 2000 increased by 158% in the last six months of 1989.

In the fourth quarter of 1989, the vacancy rate for both areas was about 23%. Developers in the uptown area—about five miles northeast of downtown—clamored for the city to choose their sites for the arts center. But the city's own planners and citizens groups strongly supported downtown.

While the location issue was settled in November, the arts center's size is uncertain. Some Councilors, nervous about revenue shortfalls, want to trim its $64 million price tag. A proposal to reduce the number of theaters from three to one has been rejected. Until the cost and size questions are settled, the search for an executive director will be suspended, and city planners do not expect to meet the scheduled completion date of 1994. Δ

TEXAS BRIEF

San Antonio's first "Power Center" was recently announced at McCullough and Loop 410. Wade-Gribble Commercial Real Estate of San Antonio and American General Realty Investment Corp. of Houston plan to develop a 175,420-sq.-ft. retail shopping center in San Antonio. Located across from North Star Mall, the "power center" will be anchored by Phar-Mor Drug and Office Depot, both new to the San Antonio market. To be completed this fall, the $15 million center will be called The Pavilions at North Star.

Continued on Page A10

Downtown Seattle

$16 Million Condominium Project

Rendering of One Pacific Tower, new condominium planned in Seattle

A $16 million, 70-unit condominium project-the first major new condominium proposed since the early 1980's-is being planned for a downtown site by the Hammond-Pacific Development Co.

The plans call for a 26-story tower, called One Pacific Tower, at 2000 First Avenue and Virginia St. in the Denny Regrade area.

Officials hope that the condominium attracts more residential complexes to the neighborhood, which abuts the downtown core. If that happened, people would be able to live, work, dine and attend cultural activities there. In the last two years, 753 rental apartments have been built downtown and, as the effects of radical changes in 1984 in the municipal code became increasingly manifest, 3,700 new units have either gone into construction or into the approval process.

One-bedroom units will be 1,150 sq. ft., two-bedrooms 1,550 sq. ft. and three-bedrooms 2,250 sq. ft., each with a den. There will be a health spa and groundfloor shops.

Continued on Page A10

Las Vegas Laboratory Under Way

Architectural rendering of Lockheed Analytical Laboratory which Chanen Construction Co. was selected by Howard Hughes Properties, Inc. to construct. The facility is located at the Hughes Airport Center in Las Vegas, Nevada. Construction has started on the 32,000 sq. ft. environmental analysis lab which will be used to analyze environmental samples and support remote sensing and monitoring contracts with the U.S. Environmental Protection Agency.

Portland, Oregon

Sunset Corridor Continues Growth
Land Sales Up 289%

Land sales in the Sunset Corridor soared 289% and principal-user development increased 34% in the 9,000-acre site, according to the Sunset Corridor Association.

In addition to land sales and principal-user development, retail development, speculative development and multifamily housing showed increases. The only declining area was industrial space leasing.

"The development totals were buoyed by the continued interest of Japanese high-technology firms in both new facilities and expansions.

Several local firms, moreover, also grew substantially and expanded their facilities or built larger headquarters," said Betty Atteberry, executive director of the association.

The inventory of end-user development—buildings built for the use of a specific company—increased by 1.18 million sq. ft. to a total of 3.48 million sq. ft. Speculative development—buildings built to be leased, grew by 215,000 sq. ft. to 2.71 million sq. ft.

1989's biggest project is Nike Inc.'s

Continued on Page A16

INSIDE

Regular Departments

Special Section

April 1990 issue of *Real Estate West* (Vol. 14, No. 8)

Right: Bill Grier at Bruce Crane's home, Kentfield, California, April 1988

Below left: Basia Crane, Bill Grier, and Marlene Delong in the gardens of Filoli, Woodside, California, April 1988

Below right: Joan Grier in Filoli gardens, April 1989

Top: Bill Grier in Pacific Heights, San Francisco, March 28, 1990

Below, from left: Basia Crane, Philip A. Crane, Jr., and Joan G. Grier at the Olympic Club, San Francisco, April 2, 1990

322

FETE FOR THE SHAH

From left: Shah Pahlavi II, Joan and Bill Grier

Bill and Joan and Professor Edward J. Rozek hosted a dinner for 100 Coloradans at the Denver Country Club, April 5, 1991, in honor of His Majesty Reza Shah II of Iran. The 30-year-old heir apparent to Iran's Peacock Throne was visiting the state at the behest of University of Colorado Professor Rozek and his Institute for Comparative Politics and Ideologies in Boulder, Colorado. Joan has served on its board for twelve years.

From left: Professor Edward J. Rozek and Joan Grier

From left: Bill Grier
and Ahmad
Ghoreishi, Iranian
prime minister
in exile

Right: Joan Grier at Basque
Cultural Center, San Francisco,
March 30, 1990

From left: Bruce Crane, Bill Grier, and Philip A. Crane, Jr. in the
Olympic Club Library, San Francisco, April 2, 1990

Eloyd John Grier in 1934

CHRONOLOGY OF ELOYD JOHN GRIER

1929	Born in San Francisco, California on July 4
1930	Baptized in Trinity Cathedral in Phoenix, Arizona on March 22
1934	Moves to Sacramento, California; enrolls in El Dorado Elementary School
1935	Father, William M. Grier, Sr., dies in Sacramento on December 8
1935–1936	Lives in Santa Maria, California with aunt and uncle
1936	Returns to Sacramento and El Dorado Elementary School in June
1937	Moves to San Francisco; enrolls in Spring Valley School
1937–1938	Summers at Tilly's Roost Camp, Santa Cruz Mountains, California
1939–1940	Summers with Lannon grandparents in Sacramento; visits Golden Gate International Exposition (Treasure Island)
1941	Enters Redding School in San Francisco in February; camps with Borman family near Mt. Shasta, California over Labor Day; transfers to Presidio Junior High School in San Francisco in September
1944–1948	Works summers at Winterland Auditorium in San Francisco
1944	Enters George Washington High School in San Francisco
1947	Returns to live in Piedmont home; graduates from George Washington High School; enters San Francisco State College

1948	Completes freshman and half of sophomore year; moves to Harrisburg, Pennsylvania in August; attends York Collegiate Institute
1949	Attends Gettysburg College in Harrisburg
1950	Joins FBI in Washington, D.C. as fingerprint trainee in January
1950–1952	Serves in U.S. Army Military Police, in West Germany; graduates from intelligence school with superior commendation
1952	Discharged from Army, returns to FBI while studying Spanish and law at George Washington University in Washington, D.C.
1956	Marries Patricia Warrington Bender in Valley Forge, Pennsylvania on September 1
1957	Joins John Hancock Life Insurance Company in Harrisburg in January
1958	Daughter, Shelby Warrington Grier, born in Harrisburg on April 6
1959	Promoted to assistant district manager; relocates to Jacksonville, Florida
1962	Becomes assistant district manager for Hancock's Tampa, Florida office
1966	Made district manager for Hancock's Atlanta, Georgia office
1968	Resigns from Hancock; relocates to West Chester, Pennsylvania where he buys and operates a delicatessen near West Chester University
1983	Retires in March

1984	Divorces Patricia Bender Grier
1987	Mother, Elo Lannon Grier, dies at age 91 in Sacramento on July 16
1988	Daughter Shelby marries Brian Marc Mackrides in September
1989	Grandson, Kyle Brian Mackrides, born on December 7
1991	Continues to live in West Chester; enjoys weekends and summers of boating at waterfront home in Chestertown, Maryland

Eloyd Grier in 1947

16

ELOYD JOHN GRIER
1929–

Entrepreneur and Boater

Born in San Francisco on July 4, 1929, Eloyd was the second son of William Milton Grier, Sr. and Elo Lannon Grier. He lived in Piedmont, California until the age of five, then spent a year in Sacramento, where he attended kindergarten at El Dorado Elementary School.

Eloyd was six years old when his father died in 1935. He and his brother Bill then lived briefly in Santa Maria, California, before returning to Sacramento and the home of their maternal grandparents, Patrick and Julia Lannon. In 1937, the boys settled in San Francisco with their mother, who had begun a career in business.

During his years in San Francisco (1937–1947), Eloyd attended Spring Valley and Redding Elementary Schools, Presidio Junior High, and George Washington High School. After school and over vacations, he held a number of jobs, one of which was head concessionaire at Winterland auditorium. (See Part Four: 13 and 14)

Eloyd would remain in his native California until the age of nineteen. After graduating from George Washington High School in 1947, he studied for one-and-a-half years at San Francisco State College (later named San Francisco State University), while living with his family in Piedmont. During this period, Eloyd, unhappy at home, began to consider continuing his education in the East.

Russ Tuckey, a Gettysburg College alumnus and member of the Ice Follies, had been encouraging Eloyd to attend his alma mater in Pennsylvania. Anxious for a change in his life, Eloyd moved to Harrisburg, Pennsylvania in late summer of 1948, where he attended York Collegiate Institute for one semester and became president of the YMCA and the Linguistics Society. The following year, he completed three semesters at Gettysburg College and joined Sigma Chi fraternity.

FBI, 1950

In January 1950, Eloyd accepted an appointment as a fingerprint trainee in the Technical Section of the Identification Division of the Federal Bureau of Investigation (FBI) in Washington, D.C. That fall, however, he was drafted into the Army, and after basic training at Fort Knox, Kentucky and eight weeks of military police (MP) school at Camp Gordon, Georgia, he was promoted to corporal and transferred to West Germany, where he served as a military policeman aboard passenger trains. He later graduated from intelligence school with a superior commendation. Following his honorable discharge in late 1952 at Indiantown Gap, Pennsylvania, Eloyd returned to the FBI as a fingerprint classifier, while studying Spanish and law in the evenings at George Washington University.

MARRIAGE AND CAREER

While with the FBI, he met his future wife, Patricia ("Pat") Warrington Bender; they were married on September 1, 1956 in the Valley Forge Memorial Chapel, Valley Forge, Pennsylvania. The daughter of J. Herbert and Laura Warrington Bender, Pat was born on November 27, 1934 in West Chester, Pennsylvania.

With his marriage, Eloyd also made a career change, becoming a sales agent with John Hancock Life Insurance Company in Harrisburg, Pennsylvania in January 1957. There, a daughter, Shelby Warrington, was born to the Griers on April 6, 1958 at Polyclinic Hospital. A second child, a son, died in infancy. Eloyd was promoted to assistant district manager and relocated to Jacksonville, Florida in 1959. Three years later, he became assistant district manager in the firm's Tampa office, where his district ranked thirty-seventh nationally. By 1966, he had risen to district manager and supervised forty-eight sales agents in the Atlanta, Georgia office until 1968. During his tenure with Hancock, Eloyd rose to top management and sales in each of his districts, becoming a member of the company's prestigious Regional and President's Clubs. When he resigned in 1968, his southeastern district ranked twelfth in national sales.

ENTREPRENEUR, 1969–1983

Despite his success with Hancock, Eloyd, like his father before him, yearned to be an independent businessman—an entrepreneur. Hence, after a family trip to California that included a visit to his native San Francisco, Eloyd and his family settled in West Chester, Pennsylvania, where he purchased a delicatessen one block from West Chester University. He successfully operated this business for fourteen years—from April 1969 to March 1983, when he retired.

Eloyd and Pat were divorced in 1984. Today, they both continue to live in West Chester, where Pat works for John Harland Company. On weekends and in summers, Eloyd enjoys his waterfront vacation home in Chestertown on Maryland's eastern shore.

SHELBY GRIER MACKRIDES
(b. April 6, 1958)

Shelby Warrington Grier, Eloyd and Patricia's surviving child, received her early schooling at St. John's Episcopal School in Tampa, Florida and in Atlanta, Georgia and graduated from Henderson High School in West Chester, where she was an honor roll student, a cheerleader, and a member of the school's ski club, varsity track, and gymnastics teams.

Shelby received a Bachelor of Arts in Spanish and English, with honors, in June of 1980 from Allegheny College in Meadville, Pennsylvania. During college, she was an Alden Scholar and a member of Alpha Chi Omega sorority. She also received an award for excellence in Spanish from the National Conference of Foreign Language Teachers and was named best Spanish student for 1980. In her junior year, she studied at the University of Madrid; as a senior, she tutored Spanish, was an assistant in the language laboratory, and, with a third-class operator's license, worked for the college radio station, WARC.

After graduation, Shelby was a bilingual executive secretary for Pennsylvania State Export Corporation, then became an administrative assistant in Plymouth Meeting, Pennsylvania with Woodward-Clyde Consultants, engineers with extensive Latin American business. In 1985, she became personnel manager for a health care firm in Bryn Mawr, Pennsylvania, while studying in the evenings for an M.B.A. at Villanova College. Shelby also served as a financial advisor to her sorority, Alpha Chi Omega (Zeta Tau Chapter), and as secretary of the Pi Pi Alumnae Chapter while attending Villanova.

In September 1988, Shelby married Brian Marc Mackrides. Her husband, the son of former Philadelphia Eagles football player Dr. William Mackrides and his wife, holds a degree in geology from Bucknell University and a civil engineering degree from Drexel University. He is a project manager with R.M. Shoemaker Company in Princeton, New Jersey. Living in Newtown, Pennsylvania, the couple has two children: son Kyle Brian born December 7, 1989 and daughter Kyrstin Warrington born August 19, 1991.

Shelby Grier
(Courtesy of Eloyd J. Grier)

Shelby G. and Brian M. Mackrides at their September 1988 wedding in Chadds Ford, Pennsylvania
(*Courtesy of Shelby Grier Mackrides*)

PART FIVE

ALBERT GRIER
BRANCH

THE GRIER FAMILY

Genealogical Trees of Anne M. Grier
(Mrs. A. Gilbert Fell) and C. Denham Grier

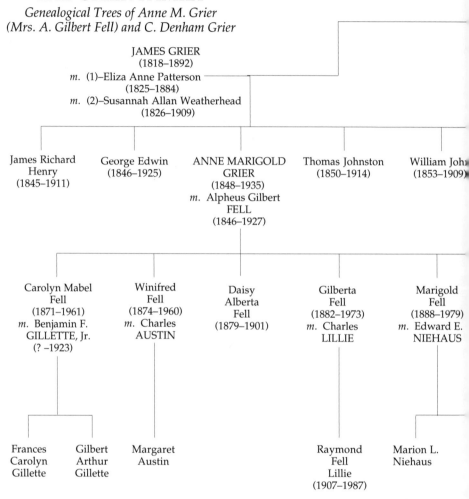

JAMES GRIER
(1818–1892)

m. (1)–Eliza Anne Patterson
(1825–1884)
m. (2)–Susannah Allan Weatherhead
(1826–1909)

James Richard
Henry
(1845–1911)

George Edwin
(1846–1925)

ANNE MARIGOLD
GRIER
(1848–1935)
m. Alpheus Gilbert
FELL
(1846–1927)

Thomas Johnston
(1850–1914)

William John
(1853–1909)

Carolyn Mabel
Fell
(1871–1961)
m. Benjamin F.
GILLETTE, Jr.
(? –1923)

Winifred
Fell
(1874–1960)
m. Charles
AUSTIN

Daisy
Alberta
Fell
(1879–1901)

Gilberta
Fell
(1882–1973)
m. Charles
LILLIE

Marigold
Fell
(1888–1979)
m. Edward E.
NIEHAUS

Frances
Carolyn
Gillette

Gilbert
Arthur
Gillette

Margaret
Austin

Raymond
Fell
Lillie
(1907–1987)

Marion L.
Niehaus

Name changed to Marigold in next generation.
**Daughter died in infancy.*
***Couple has chosen to remain unmarried.*

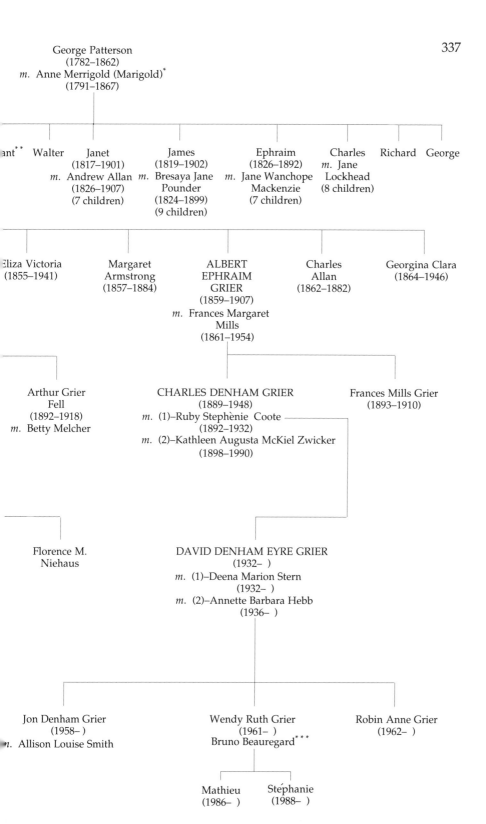

CHRONOLOGY OF ALBERT E. GRIER

1859	Born in Iroquois, Ontario on July 28
1876	Graduates from Iroquois High School
1879–1880	Attends Toronto's Osgoode Hall Law School
1881–1883	Emigrates to the American West; works as lawyer in Lawrence, Black Hills of the Dakota Territory; moves to Denver, Colorado and works as law clerk
1884	Marries Frances Margaret Mills on April 28 in Denver
1888	Admitted to the Colorado Bar on May 4
1889	Son, Charles Denham, born on October 1
1893	Daughter, Frances Mills, born September 13
1907	Dies of tuberculosis on October 28; buried at Fairmount Cemetery in Denver

Albert Ephraim Grier (age 40) and son Charles Denham (age 9) in 1899

17

ALBERT E. GRIER
1859–1907

Denver Attorney

While a number of the second-generation Griers established careers in mining, railroads, and real estate, Albert Ephraim Grier expressed an interest in the law from an early age. Educated in Canada, he practiced law in Denver, Colorado, where he also married and raised two children.

EARLY YEARS

The eighth child of James and Eliza Grier, Albert was born on July 28, 1859, in Iroquois, Ontario. While attending public school there, he worked for his father in the post office, as had his brothers and sisters before him.

In 1879, he and his younger brother Charles Allan (1862–1882) were admitted to Toronto's Osgoode Hall, the oldest law school in North America. After a year of study, Albert left Toronto to visit his brother Thomas Johnston ("T.J."), a bookkeeper for the Homestake Mining Company in Lead, South Dakota.

Inspired by the examples of his older brothers William John and T.J. and his sister Anne Marigold, Albert soon emigrated to the United States. He first worked as a lawyer in Lawrence in the Black Hills of the Dakota Territory, then settled in Denver, Colorado in 1882, initially working as a law clerk.

Known as the Queen City of the Plains, Denver was a booming agricultural and mining center in the 1880s—just the place for a young and ambitious man like Albert. The somewhat primitive conditions of the previous decade had given way to many improvements in the city's streets and buildings, and in 1881, an impressive railway station, Union Depot, was built almost entirely of Colorado stone. The construction of a Roman rotunda-style state capitol with Corinthian columns followed in 1886. Meanwhile, the business and residential districts were also growing. The nearby Central City Opera House attracted famous singers and sizable crowds, and later in the century, residents had access to live drama at Elitch Gardens Theatre and to western-style entertainment in Buffalo Bill's Wild West show.

CAREER AND FAMILY

On April 28, 1884, Albert married Frances Margaret Mills, the daughter of a leading retail merchant in Iroquois. The wedding took place in Denver at St. John's Episcopal Church of the Wilderness, a Victorian-Romanesque church located on 20th and Welton Streets.[1] Frances's father, Cephas Mills, attended the ceremony, as did Albert's sister and brother-in-law, Anne and Gilbert Fell, and his parents, James and Eliza Grier, who were returning to Canada after a trip across the western states. The newlyweds purchased a one-and-a-half-story house at 1237 Corona Street, in the Capitol Hill area of Denver.

Albert Grier was admitted to the Colorado Bar on May 4, 1888. During his legal career, he was counsel for several Denver firms, including the Denver Gas & Electric Light Company (predecessor of today's Public Service Company of Colorado) and the Rollins Investment Company, with downtown offices in both the Essex and Ernest & Cranmer buildings, just east of Union Depot.

Albert and Frances had two children: Charles Denham, born on October 1, 1889 and Frances ("Franny") Mills, born on September 13, 1893. Both children attended nearby Corona Elementary School, on 9th and Corona.

Early in the 1900s, tragedy struck the Grier family when Albert Ephraim died of tuberculosis at age forty-eight on October 28, 1907, in his Corona Street home; he was buried in Denver's Fairmount Cemetery. Shortly thereafter, Frances and her children moved to 1283 Lafayette Street. Just three years later, daughter Franny succumbed to typhoid fever on November 2, 1910; she was buried next to her father.

Deeply saddened by the untimely loss of both her husband and daughter, Frances came to depend heavily upon her son, Denham, with whom she spent most of the many remaining years of her life.

An alumnus of the Colorado School of Mines five-year professional curriculum (B.A., 1912) and the University of Washington (M.A., 1918), Denham's career in mining and metallurgical engineering took him to Seattle, to New York City, and, eventually, to Johannesburg, South Africa. His mother shared his home in each city, and for several years after

---

1.   This church was destroyed by fire in 1903.

Denham's first wife, Ruby Coote, died in childbirth, Frances cared for her young grandson, David.

Frances outlived her son, who died in South Africa in 1948. She, David, and Denham's second wife, Kathleen Zwicker, returned to North America in 1949, staying briefly in New York City before settling in Montreal, Canada. Frances died at the age of ninety-three in Vancouver, British Columbia on May 31, 1954.

St. John's Episcopal Church in the Wilderness, Denver, Colorado, c. 1880s
(Courtesy of the Denver Public Library Western History Department)

Osgoode Hall (oldest law school in North America, founded in 1797), Toronto,
Ontario *(Sketch by architect Col. F.W. Cumberland, 1857)*

Denham Grier in August 1890

346

CHRONOLOGY OF CHARLES DENHAM GRIER

1889	Born in Denver, Colorado, on October 1
1907	Graduates from Denver's Manual High School in June; father dies on October 28
1912	Graduates from the Colorado School of Mines with a Bachelor of Arts in engineering metallurgy in June
1912–1915 Silver	Works at Homestake Mining Company in Lead, South Dakota, at Northern Nevada Mines Development Company in Tuscarora, Nevada, and at Pittsburgh-Peak Gold Mining Company in Blair, Nevada
1915	Joins Alaska Treadwell Gold Mining Company in Treadwell, Alaska as an accountant and chemist; becomes member of American Institute of Mining and Metallurgical Engineering
1918	Receives a Master of Science in metallurgy from University of Washington in Seattle; serves as a second lieutenant in the U.S. Army Corp of Engineers
1919	Returns to Seattle and becomes a Fellow in Metallurgy at University of Washington's College of Mines; publishes "Electrometallurgical and Electrochemical Industry in the State of Washington" and "The Electric Furnace Laboratory of the Bureau of Mines"
1920–1922	Works as sales engineer for New Jersey Zinc Company in New York City
1923–1924	Works at American Cyanamid Company, in New York City offices
1924	Publishes "Falls Which Rival Niagara" in *The Aero Brand*, magazine of American Cyanamid Company

1925	Transfers to Johannesburg, Transvaal, as director of American Cyanamid Company's interests through its agents, Fraser & Chalmers (SA), Ltd.; becomes member of Chemical, Metallurgical and Mining Society of South Africa
1927	Marries Ruby Stephenie Coote on February 26
1932	Son, David Denham Eyre Grier, born on April 12; wife dies in childbirth
1937	Marries Kathleen Augusta McKiel Zwicker on April 3; appointed chairman and managing director of South African Cyanamid Company, Ltd.
1920s–1940s	Travels extensively in Africa, Europe, and North America
1948	Dies at his residence on Pallinghurst Road, in Parktown, South Africa at age fifty-nine

C. Denham Grier, c. 1934

18

CHARLES DENHAM GRIER
1889–1948

An International Mining Career

Like several of the Griers who preceded him, Denham's life and career were shaped by his interest in mining and metallurgical engineering. His work took him not only to the East and West Coasts of the United States, as well as Alaska, but eventually halfway around the world to Johannesburg, South Africa, where he settled permanently.

EDUCATION

The son of Albert Ephraim Grier, an attorney, and his wife Frances Margaret Mills, Denham was born in Denver, Colorado on October 1, 1889. His sister Frances ("Franny") Mills Grier was born four years later. Both children attended the Corona Elementary School, located just three blocks from their home at 1237 Corona.[1]

Denham graduated from Manual High School, at 1700 E. 28th Avenue, in June of 1907. Several months later, on October 28, he lost his father to tuberculosis.[2] Thus, at the age of eighteen, Denham became the head of the household and was to prove a great source of strength to his mother. Indeed, their relationship grew even closer when, on November 2, 1910, his sister Franny, still a teenager, died of typhoid fever.

After high school, Denham was accepted as an engineering student by the Colorado School of Mines in Golden, Colorado. There, he completed a five-year professional curriculum leading to a Bachelor of Arts degree in engineering metallurgy, which he received in June 1912.

---

1. Among their classmates were Frances Ryan, future wife of Lowell Thomas; Mamie Doud, who later became Mrs. Dwight D. Eisenhower; and Clara Mitchell, who married Henry Cruger Van Schaack, founder, in the early 1900s, of Van Schaack and Company, a leading Colorado real estate brokerage firm.

2. After Albert's death, the family moved to 1283 Lafayette Street in Denver.

Denham's first professional position was with the Homestake Mining Company in Lead, South Dakota, where his uncle T.J. Grier served as superintendent. T.J. hired Denham to do mill work in Homestake's ore-processing plants, which used a cyanamide flotation process. In Lead for about a year, Denham stayed with his aunt Mary Jane and uncle T.J. and his six cousins, as he had done during visits while still a student.[3]

After Homestake, he worked in the plants of Northern Nevada Mines Development Company in Tuscarora, Nevada and in those of Pittsburgh-Silver Peak Gold Mining Company in Blair, Nevada.

In 1915, Denham was an accountant and chemist with Alaska Treadwell Gold Mining Company in Treadwell, Alaska, doing all the firm's chemical analysis. A subsequent promotion increased his administrative, financial, and metallurgical responsibilities. He also became a member of the American Institute of Mining and Metallurgical Engineering.[4]

Between 1917 and 1918, Denham studied in a graduate program in metallurgy at the University of Washington in Seattle, receiving a Master of Science degree on June 17, 1918. His thesis, entitled "Electrometallurgical and Electrochemical Industry in the State of Washington," was published in the university's Engineering Experiment Station Bulletin of March 1919.

While in graduate school, Denham shared his Seattle home at 4552 Brooklyn Avenue with his mother, who would live in his other homes—in the United States and South Africa—until his death.

Following graduation, Grier was commissioned a second lieutenant in the U.S. Army Corp of Engineers. His six-month tour of duty, which included recruit training, engineer officers' training camp, and construction work, was served in the States. He was mustered out shortly after the November 11 signing of the armistice ending World War I.

EARLY CAREER

Denham returned in 1919 to Seattle, where he became a Fellow in Metallurgy under a cooperative agreement between the University of

---

3.   His cousins included the four children T.J. and Mary Jane had together—Evangeline Victoria ("Muddie"), T.J., Jr. ("Tommy"), Ormonde Palethorpe, and Lisgar Patterson—and Mary Jane's two children from a previous marriage—Margaret Eliza ("Madge") and James William Ferrie.

4.   Denham was also a life-long member of the American Institute of Mining, Metallurgical and Petroleum Engineers, as well as a member of the Chemical, Metallurgical and Mining Society of South Africa.

Washington's College of Mines and the U.S. Bureau of Mines. His work involved experiments in the chemical and electro-metallurgical fields. One project, for example, was the development of a process for the recovery of tin from tin cans—a recycling technique that would help to overcome shortages of tin that had developed during the recent war years.

Later that year, Denham's article on "The Electric Furnace Laboratory of the Bureau of Mines" was published in *Chemical and Metallurgical Engineering*'s October 29 issue.

Between 1920 and 1922, Denham was a sales engineer for the New Jersey Zinc Company in New York City. He and his mother lived in a Manhattan apartment during this time. In 1923, he accepted a position with American Cyanamid Company, the employer he was to serve until his death in 1948. He worked for two years in Cyanamid's New York office before being transferred to Johannesburg, Transvaal, South Africa in 1925. There, he became the director of American Cyanamid's South African operations, which began trading through its agents Fraser and Chalmers (SA) Ltd. In 1937, Denham was appointed chairman of the board and managing director for the firm's newly created subsidiary, South African Cyanamid Company Ltd., which was formed to build a factory at Witbank, Transvaal to produce cyanide for the Witwatersrand gold mines.

FAMILY

On many occasions during his long residence in South Africa, Denham took business and vacation trips to England, Canada, the United States, and the firm's New York headquarters. He also traveled widely in southern Africa, making sales and service calls to clients in the mining and citrus-growing businesses. Along the way, he met Ruby Stephenie Coote, a young woman from Armagh in Northern Ireland.[5] They were married on February 26, 1927. A son, David Denham Eyre Grier, was born on April 12, 1932. Tragically, Ruby died in childbirth. Denham's mother Frances Margaret,

---

5.   Ruby's mother was Mary Emilie Wolfe, the eldest daughter of the Venerable John Charles Wolfe, archdeacon of Cloger, Ireland. One of the Wolfes of Fornaght (an estate on what is now the border between Ireland and Ulster), he is reputed to have been a descendant of the General Wolfe who died—and gained fame—on the plains of Abraham at Quebec. Mary Emilie married Albert Augustus Eyre Coote, the youngest son of the late Major Coote, on August 9, 1882. The couple produced eleven children (remarkable, since Mary Emilie also acted as manager of the Armagh Savings Bank). Ruby Stephenie's sisters included Violet, Sylvia, Emmy (twin of brother Tom), Olive (known as Polly, and Ruby's twin), Beatrice, Claire, and Grace. Her brothers were Albert, Tom, and Eyre.

then seventy-one, cared for her newborn grandson.

In August of 1933, while on another trip, Denham met his second wife, Kathleen Augusta McKiel Zwicker. The shipboard romance started on the trip from England to North America (Kathleen was returning to Canada from a European vacation) and continued by correspondence.

Kathleen, a native of Lunenburg, Nova Scotia, was nine years younger than Denham, having been born on April 20, 1898. She attended school in her home town, a small fishing village on Canada's eastern coast,[6] and upon graduation from high school, attended Ladies' College in Halifax, where she received a teacher's certificate in violin and voice.[7] After teaching music in Lunenburg, Kathleen traveled to Montreal, Quebec to enter the nurses' training program of the Royal Victoria Hospital. She received her cap, pin, and graduation certificate in April 1926.

Kathleen began her medical career as a scrub nurse in the Royal Victoria's main operating room. In 1928, she was chosen by neurosurgeon Dr. Wilder Penfield to become his personal surgical nurse. When Dr. Penfield founded the Montreal Neurological Institute in 1934 and a special building was erected to house it, Kathleen became the chief neurosurgical nurse there, in charge of the operating room nursing staff, while continuing as Dr. Penfield's scrub nurse. She remained in this role until she left Canada in February 1937 to marry Denham in South Africa.[8]

They were married on April 3, 1937, in the Anglican St. George's Church

---

6.   Lunenburg, Nova Scotia, originally settled by a group of emigrants from Germany, is well known (along with Gloucester, Massachusetts) as the home of the graceful "salt-banker" cod fishing schooners in the early twentieth century. The most famous of these was the *Bluenose*, which is commemorated on the Canadian ten-cent piece and by a modern replica, the *Bluenose II*, which now has Halifax as its home port. William Norman Zwicker, Kathleen's father, was a member of the syndicate which owned the original *Bluenose*, and he had a share in Zwicker & Company, the town's largest shipowning, trading, and fishing company at that time.

7.   Kathleen was in Halifax in 1917 at the time of the great explosion in which thousands died and many were injured. It resulted from a collision and fire involving a fully loaded munitions ship in Halifax harbor and was the largest man-made explosion in history until the detonation of the atomic bomb at the end of World War II. Witnessing it and the resulting injuries no doubt strengthened Kathleen's determination to become a nurse.

8.   Dr. Wilder Penfield was an American who moved to Canada and worked at the Royal Victoria Hospital. He gained worldwide fame for his pioneering work in neurosurgery and brain research. One of his best-known discoveries was that mild electrical stimulation of a specific spot in the brain of a conscious patient triggered a "replay"—with sight, sound, and smell—of a particular past experience. Kathleen Zwicker was present, assisting Dr. Penfield, when this was first observed. Dr. Penfield later wrote a book entitled *No Man Alone* in which he recalled Kathleen as an expert operating room nurse.

in the Johannesburg suburb of Parktown, not far from the new house at 11 Pallinghurst Road that Denham had bought for his family.

David, just under five when his father remarried, soon developed a close relationship with his stepmother. He was their only child.

The relationship between Kathleen and her mother-in-law, however, did not develop such warmth. Frances, feeling threatened with the new mistress of the house—her son's new wife and her grandson's new mother— would invoke the memory of Ruby, creating a subtle rivalry between the revered memory of David's mother and the reality of his stepmother. Kathleen, however, was understanding and self-confident and avoided open dispute.

Kathleen and Denham were an especially close and happy couple. In addition to maintaining their home together and actively entertaining, they traveled widely in Africa, as well as in Britain, Europe, the United States, and Canada. They kept a map marked with the track of each trip taken in southern Africa, and when Denham had a business trip in South Africa, Rhodesia, or other African countries, they would see if it would include parts of the continent Kathleen had yet to visit. If it did, she would usually accompany him, and they would sightsee along the way. Some of these trips turned into great adventures, as the couple was stranded by rains and flooding rivers in remote settlements.

TRAVEL

Not all of Denham's adventures, however, occurred on trips that he took with Kathleen. One particularly noteworthy incident took place in the early 1930s, prior to their marriage. In those days, an Imperial Airways "flying boat service"—one of the early long-distance air services—ran from London to South Africa by way of Marseilles, Athens, Cairo, and Central Africa. On a return trip from the United States, Denham was aboard one of these flying boats when it crash-landed on a river in the Central African bush. An experienced and resourceful camper and woodsman, Denham apparently played a leading role in providing a degree of comfort and security to the stranded passengers and crew until the party was eventually rescued.

A second adventure, in late 1937, revolved around Denham's knowledge of and skill with cyanide products. Sodium cyanide was at that time shipped to South Africa (by American Cyanamid in the United States and by Imperial Chemical Industries in Great Britain) in steel containers similar to today's fifty-gallon oil drums. A ship carrying one of these batches apparently encountered extremely bad weather, and the dangerous cargo shifted in the hold. When the ship docked, it became apparent that a drum had ruptured and mixed with water en route, thereby creating deadly hydrocyanic acid gas (HCn). Someone had to go down into the hold to remove the drum so that the area could be ventilated and the cargo removed. Charles Denham Grier was the expert called in, and he completed the job without mishap, despite considerable danger.

Most of Denham and Kathleen's travels in Africa were sales and service trips to South African Cyanamid's customers—mines which used cyanide for extracting gold or other metals from ore or citrus groves which used it for fumigating their trees to eliminate pests. And as Denham's responsibilities with the company grew more weighty, Kathleen became a valued assistant.

After the outbreak of World War II in 1939, the company found it had to supply cyanide to the entire southern African market, since Imperial Chemical Industries in England devoted all its attention to war production and stopped shipping the product to South Africa. The resulting increase in South African Cyanamid's business placed an even heavier load on Denham, as many of his key assistants joined the armed services, leaving him with a much-reduced management staff. The workload undoubtedly contributed to a substantial deterioration in his health and probably shortened his life.

In 1938 and again in 1944, Denham, Kathleen, and young David made two trips to North America. The first trip via Great Britain was relatively uneventful; the wartime voyage, however, was a considerable adventure. On the first leg of this trip, the family boarded a neutral Argentinian ship in Cape Town in early June 1944. For twenty-one days, the small 3,500-ton ship plowed through the notoriously rough seas of the South Atlantic's "Roaring Forties" before docking in Buenos Aires. The Griers then took a Pan American DC-3 across the Andes Mountains to Chile, up the western coast of South America, and across the Caribbean to Miami.

They returned to South Africa via a Portuguese ship, setting sail for Lisbon from Philadelphia on March 10, 1945. They were forced to wait for some weeks in Lisbon—then a hotbed of spies, both Allied and Axis—before proceeding south to Cape Town.

The journey from Johannesburg to the United States and Canada in mid-1944 was an arduous one, and Kathleen's nursing skills were called upon not only because Denham's health was already damaged (one of the trip's purposes was medical testing in the States), but because both Denham and David contracted pneumonia and were admitted, one after the other, to a hospital in Buenos Aires. To make matters worse, the Argentinian authorities, sympathetic to the Germans in World War II and hostile to

British subjects, refused, at first, to permit Kathleen to disembark from the ship, for she was traveling on a Canadian passport. Denham, by dint of bribery and string-pulling, managed to extract her from this predicament some days after the ship docked, sneaking her off the ship—sans luggage—in a rowboat. (Her suitcases were later retrieved.)

The return to South Africa, via Lisbon, came to a conclusion on VE Day, May 8, 1945, when the ship arrived in Cape Town harbor. There were no porters or taxis available, as the whole town was celebrating the Allied victory, but the Griers boarded a train for Johannesburg and home.

Denham was an enthusiastic and expert amateur photographer, who exhibited in salon competitions and garnered a number of prizes. He was active in the Johannesburg Camera Club, lecturing from time to time on the art and science of photography. With his training in chemistry, he processed his own negatives and prints and was an early experimenter with the development of color photography. His favorite photographic subjects included the region's native peoples, the spectacular South African scenery, the historical architecture of the Cape province, and, of course, Africa's remarkable wildlife.

DENHAM'S DEATH, 1948

During the last six months of his life, Denham suffered from nephritis, complicated later by liver failure and several mild strokes. Again, Kathleen's nursing background was of immeasurable value. There was a doctors' strike at the time, so Kathleen hired a special-duty nurse to help her as she, herself, cared for Denham day and night during his last weeks. Charles Denham Grier died in the family home on December 2, 1948, at the age of fifty-nine.

On February 10, 1949, the Board of Directors of the South African Cyanamid Company Ltd. recorded the following minute: "The chairman referred to the great loss the company had sustained in the death of Mr. Charles Denham Grier who had been Chairman of the Board and managing director of the company since its incorporation on March 10, 1937. Mr. Grier's wide experience had contributed materially to the successful progress of the company, and his loss would be one which would be very keenly felt by the company as well as by the members of the board personally."

After selling the house in Parktown, Kathleen, seventeen-year-old David, and "Granny" Frances Margaret returned to Canada. They arrived by ship in New York on August 12, 1949 and then proceeded by train to Canada. There, Kathleen and David settled in Montreal, while Frances took up residence in Vancouver, where a nephew on the Mills side of the family lived.[9] Kathleen resumed work as a nurse at the Royal Victoria Hospital and, after a short period of refreshing and updating her knowledge, taught neurosurgical techniques to graduate nurses who came for that purpose to the now-famous Montreal Neurological Institute. One of the most challenging and difficult phases of her career came in the 1950s, when she was asked to set up and run a special operating room at the Royal Victoria devoted to treating the victims of illegal, back-street abortions.

On August 11, 1990, Kathleen died in Montreal at the age of 92. In her later years, she had moved from the family home (at 186 Simcoe Avenue in the Town of Mount Royal) and lived in a senior citizens' residence. She greatly enjoyed the visits of her son David, her grandchildren, and her great-grandchildren and often reminisced fondly about her life and adventures halfway across the world in South Africa.

---

9.   By this time, eighty-four-year-old Frances was confined to a wheelchair. She moved into a senior citizens' residence in Vancouver, where she died on May 31, 1954.

Denham Grier, choirboy at St. John's Episcopal Church
in Denver, Easter 1899

Denham Grier, c. 1905

Denham Grier (age 29) during
service in the U.S. Army Corps
of Engineers, 1918

Ruby Stephenie Coote Grier

Kathleen Augusta McKiel Zwicker Grier

360

Denham Grier in South Africa, c. 1930s

Kathleen and Denham Grier on their wedding day, April 3, 1937

Shipboard snapshot of C. Denham Grier, taken in August 1933 on the transatlantic trip on which he met Kathleen A. McKiel Zwicker

C. Denham Grier, an avid and practiced photographer

CHRONOLOGY OF DAVID DENHAM EYRE GRIER

1932	Born in Johannesburg, South Africa, on April 12; mother, Ruby Coote Grier, dies in childbirth
1940–1945	Attends Ridge Preparatory School in Johannesburg
1945–1948	Attends King Edward VII School in Johannesburg
1948	Enters electrical engineering program at University of Witwatersrand in Johannesburg; father, Charles Denham Grier, dies on December 2
1949	Moves to Montreal, Canada with stepmother, Kathleen Zwicker Grier; studies at McGill University
1953	Granted a Bachelor of Arts in English and philosophy from McGill University; receives Ford Foundation scholarship to study at University of Mysore, India; enters master's degree program at McGill University
1954	Works as reporter for the Montreal *Gazette*
1955	Marries Deena Marion Stern on May 24; becomes editor of two trade magazines
1956	Joins DuPont of Canada, Ltd.
1958	Son, Jon Denham, born in Montreal on January 20
1959	Joins *Weekend Magazine* as copy editor
1961	Daughter, Wendy Ruth, born in Montreal on June 24; returns to DuPont as manager of communications and community relations
1962	Daughter, Robin Anne, born in Montreal on December 5
1967	Joins Royal Bank of Canada to establish public relations department

1970s	Serves as vice president of Canadian Public Relations Society and president of CPRS Quebec chapter; divorced from first wife
1980	Named vice president and chief advisor on government and corporate affairs at Royal Bank of Canada
1983	Moves to Toronto
1984	Marries Annette Barbara Hebb on March 3
1990	Stepmother, Kathleen Z. Grier, dies in Montreal at age 92

David D.E. Grier (1932–)

19

DAVID D.E. GRIER
1932–

Corporate and Public Affairs Executive

The first Grier born outside North America since his great-grandfather
James, David Denham Eyre Grier was born on April 12, 1932 in Johannesburg, South Africa, the only child of Charles Denham and Ruby Stephenie Grier (nee Coote).

EARLY YEARS

David never knew his mother, for she died in childbirth. He was raised
first by his grandmother Frances Margaret Mills Grier and then, from the
age of five, by his father's second wife, Kathleen Augusta McKiel Zwicker.
The family home was located at 11 Pallinghurst Road in Parktown, South
Africa.

David was educated in Johannesburg through high school. He attended
the Ridge Preparatory School from 1940 to '45 and the King Edward VII
School from 1945 to '48. Upon graduation, he entered an electrical engineering program at the University of Witwatersrand in Johannesburg. However, six months after his father's death on December 2, 1948, David left at
mid-year to return to Canada with his stepmother and grandmother.

MCGILL, STUDY IN INDIA

Settling in Montreal, David continued his studies at McGill University.
He changed his major from pre-science/engineering to English and philosophy and received his Bachelor of Arts degree in the spring of 1953.
While at McGill, David was editor-in-chief of the *McGill Daily*, the school
newspaper, where his writing won the Bracken award for the best editorials
in a Canadian student paper. He also held vacation and part-time jobs in
summer theatre and as a technician at a local radio station.

Following his graduation, David received a Ford Foundation scholarship to attend a six-week seminar at the University of Mysore, India. The seminar was organized by the World University Service and concerned "The Human Implications of Development Planning." Three weeks of planned travel in India and West Pakistan followed the seminar, and the participants then had two additional weeks of independent "tourist" travel. After a stopover in Paris and London, David returned to Montreal and a master's program in comparative religion at McGill.

CAREER AND MARRIAGE

After a year of graduate work, David left school in 1954 to become a reporter for Montreal's morning daily paper, the *Gazette*. That October, he became assistant editor of McGill's Graduate Society alumni magazine and designed direct mail fund-raising materials for the university, as well.

On May 24, 1955—Victoria Day—David married Deena Marion Stern, a McGill classmate, in Montreal. They had three children, all born in Montreal: Jon Denham, Wendy Ruth, and Robin Anne.

In November of 1955, David became the editor of two monthly trade magazines, one for women's-wear and one for children's-wear. The following year, tiring of the newspaper business, he joined Du Pont of Canada, Ltd., where he edited the employee paper and prepared product publicity on plastics, textile fibers, and explosives. David left Du Pont in February of 1959 to become a copy editor for *Weekend Magazine*, a national supplement in Canada similar to America's *Parade*. In time, he advanced to the number two position on the desk.

David returned to Du Pont in September of 1961, when he was hired to explore the use of radio, television, and film in Du Pont's public relations efforts. As manager of employee communications and community relations, he subsequently wrote, directed, produced, and edited a number of successful industrial films and appeared on many radio and television programs on behalf of the company.

David left Du Pont in April of 1967 to establish a public relations department for the Royal Bank of Canada, the country's largest bank and the fourth largest bank in North America. After supervising the department for ten years, he became an advisor to the bank's top management and in 1980 was named vice president and chief advisor on government and corporate affairs. The Royal Bank transferred him to Toronto in 1983, where he became vice president, Public Affairs, and later vice president and special advisor, Corporate Affairs. In this position, he advises senior management in such policy areas as social responsibility and ethical management, corporate philanthropy, and the environment.

Following are some excerpts from a speech by David on ethical dilemmas in business, delivered on September 19, 1989 to the Canadian Centre for Ethics and Corporate Policy in Toronto:

When Graham Tucker asked me to speak in this luncheon series, he wanted me to talk about what it is like to be the "vice-president of ethics" of a corporation. Well, I can tell you I was absolutely horrified at that, for a number of reasons.

First is simply that is not what I am, in title, in qualifications, or in function. Nor would I presume to so lofty a role. Indeed, I would suggest that just as the Chief Executive Officer of E.I. du Pont de Nemours recently identified himself as that company's "chief environmental officer," the CEO of every corporation is inevitably and inescapably that corporation's "chief ethics officer."

Second, I can think of no more impossibly heavy—and unrealistic—responsibility for a single person. Surely, every person in an organization, in a corporation, in business generally, in life, is making ethical decisions every day. They may not be thinking explicitly about it, but they are doing it. One is reminded of the "bourgeois gentihomme" who was surprised to discover he was speaking "prose." No, ethics cannot be assigned to a particular department or a particular officer. Ethics is everyone's business and everyone's responsibility. If war is too important to be left to the generals, ethics is too important to be assigned or delegated to one department, one discipline, or one manager. Other than a corporation's CEO, no one person can be "in charge of" ethics.

... Good public relations is "Doing Right—and Getting Credit For It." Where the discipline has sometimes failed in managing its own reputation is where practitioners have failed to understand that you can't properly do the second part—get credit—if the organization isn't in fact doing the first—doing what is right. Whitewash jobs have a habit of washing off in the rain.

...I worry when we seem to be saying that the prime reason we should be ethical in business is because it will be conducive to business success. Business exists to serve society, not the other way around. Let's get our sense of priorities straight.

Surely we should be seeking to behave ethically because that is the way to fulfill our potential as human beings; because that is the way to have a better society to live in; even because there is a spiritual imperative to seek virtue. The role of ethics as a promoter of long-term business success is a real one, but not a sufficient or necessary rationale for good ethical behavior. If we don't recognize and face up to this, I think we in business will get into trouble as soon as we come up against a situation where the costs of good ethics seem to outweigh the economic benefits.

...We in business seem to be beloved of the phrase "the profit motive." And in system terms, there is no doubt it is a powerfully creative force for the efficient allocation of resources and the creation of wealth.

But, it seems to me, we should remember that the phrase was invented by 19th-Century socialists as an *attack* on business and the narrowminded pursuit of money to the exclusion of all other obligations and considerations.

...Profit, in my view, is a necessary but not sufficent condition for the continuing conduct of business. It is also, of course, a handy way of keeping score, and I suspect this is one reason why it is so often thought of as purpose. The media cover business in much the same way they cover sports, as if it were all, and only, about winning and losing. As a result the public—and business people themselves—come to think of it as a game.

It is not a game. Business involves real people's lives, and deeply affects the human welfare of communities and nations. I think the media do us all a tragic disservice when they treat business as sport, and business people do us an equally tragic disservice when they approach their work as "gamesmanship." In my observation, much unethical practice springs from this misconception of what business is about.

I rather like what the CEO of Quaker Oats once said about profits. He said that making a profit is to a business what eating is to a human being. It is absolutely necessary; if you don't eat, you die. But very few of us would consider eating to be the purpose of human life. Indeed, we would consider it a bizarre aberration for someone to contend seriously that we live solely to eat. Yet business people often and routinely say, and seem to believe, that the purpose of business activity is solely to make a profit.

* * *

On January 24, 1990, David addressed the Conference Board of Canada Council of Public Affairs Executives on "The Corporation and Ethics." His introductory remarks follow:

As the last decade of the century overtakes us, public interest in ethics is at a historic high. There is a tremendous upwelling of public and media interest and concern about the ethics of our institutions, and of those managing them.

As members of the public, we read about government leaks, patronage, electoral financing improprieties and so on, and we become cynical about the ethics of those in government. As church members, we follow dramatic revelations about wrongdoing by church officials—whether they be TV evangelists or priests charged with the care of children. Here in Ontario we follow the news of a judicial enquiry into the misuse of funds in a charitable foundation. And on the business pages, we learn of insider trading, of illegal toxic waste disposal, of unsafe products, of kickbacks and bribery in corporate purchasing—you name it. And we watch fictional movies like *Wall Street* and wonder about the integrity of the real-life capital markets.

Is the world going to hell in a handbasket, are ethical standards diving to a new low? Probably not. There is little evidence that people in business today—or in politics, for that matter—are greatly more ethical or unethical than their forebears. Does the new interest in ethics and the current increase in discussion of the subject indicate a radical change in the standards of behaviour and expectations being applied by the public? I doubt that the change is a radical one, but I do think that the standards of behaviour being set, and the expectations of the public, are becoming more stringent, primarily because of increased attention and knowledge on the part of the public.

The major difference, I think, is in the availability of information, in communication. The difference is closer scrutiny. The goldfish bowl we work in is more transparent than it has ever been, and institutional activities are under a more powerful microscope than ever before. The global village is getting smaller, and there has been a substantial leap in the quantity and depth—though not always in the quality—of investigative reporting and critical journalistic inquiry into business activity. Moreover, the electronic media now give us a closer and more dramatic look at the results of business and political decisions. Whatever the reasons, there is no doubt that there is a significant increase in public concern about ethical behaviour in all of our institutions, particularly including business.

* * *

Separated from Deena in 1976 and later divorced, David married Annette Barbara Hebb, a Montreal social worker and expert in children's learning disabilities, on March 3, 1984. By coincidence, Annette had been born and raised in Lunenburg, Nova Scotia, the same fishing town from which his stepmother Kathleen had come.

OTHER INTERESTS

David has been a member of the Canadian Public Relations Society (CPRS) since October of 1969 and received his accreditation in 1973. From 1972 to 1974, he served as the organization's vice president and from 1974 to 1975, as president of the Quebec chapter. On several occasions, he received an Award of Excellence from the CPRS for public relations projects executed on behalf of his employer. He is currently a director of CPRS (Toronto).

An avid sailor, David owned a twenty-five-foot sloop, which he moored on Lake Champlain near Essex, New York. Many summer week ends were spent sailing there, and today he and his wife Annette enjoy winter holidays sailing in the Caribbean, as well as keeping a twenty-seven-foot sloop on Ontario's Georgian Bay, some 100 miles north of Toronto, where the couple now resides.

CHILDREN

Jon Grier

Jon Denham Grier was born in Montreal on January 20, 1958. He graduated from Montreal's Westhill High School in 1975. A music major, he attended Vanier College in Montreal from 1976 to 1978 and Dawson College New School from 1978 to 1979. He also studied at the Guitar Institute of Technology in Hollywood, California from 1979 to 1980. After playing guitar and singing in his own rock band, with engagements across Canada, and working at a world-class recording studio in Morin Heights, Quebec, near Montreal, he is now working as a musician and computer music programmer in San Francisco, California. On December 29, 1987, in Montreal, he married Allison Louise Smith, a native Californian and divorcee with a six-year-old son, Justin. The couple was divorced in 1990.

Wendy Grier

David Grier's second child, Wendy Ruth, was born in Montreal on June 24, 1961. After graduating from Montreal's Westmount High School in 1978, Wendy continued her studies at Dawson College New School. Today, she is studying early childhood education at Montreal's Concordia University and is the mother of two: Mathieu, born April 10, 1986, and Stephanie, born July 7, 1988. Their father, Wendy's "boy next door" Bruno Beauregard, a professional photographer, operates his own studio in Montreal.

Robin Grier

The youngest of David Grier's children, Robin Anne, was born in Montreal on December 5, 1962. A Westmount High School alumna (1979) and fine arts graduate from Montreal's Dawson College (1981), she is now studying architecture at the University of Waterloo, in Kitchener-Waterloo, Ontario.

Denham and David Grier, c. 1942
(Courtesy of David Grier)

Denham and David Grier outside
their home in Parktown, South
Africa
(Courtesy of David Grier)

372

Ruby Stephenie Coote Grier (Mrs. C. Denham Grier), c. 1930

Denham, Kathleen, and David Grier disembark at dock in Cape Town harbor, South Africa, on VE Day, May 8, 1945, from their 1944-1945 trip to the U.S. and Canada. (*Courtesy of David Grier*)

Wendy Grier and Bill Grier on dock at Essex,
New York, August 1979
(Photographed by Bill Grier)

David Grier sailing with Ellen Coolidge on Lake
Champlain, August 1979
(Photographed by Bill Grier)

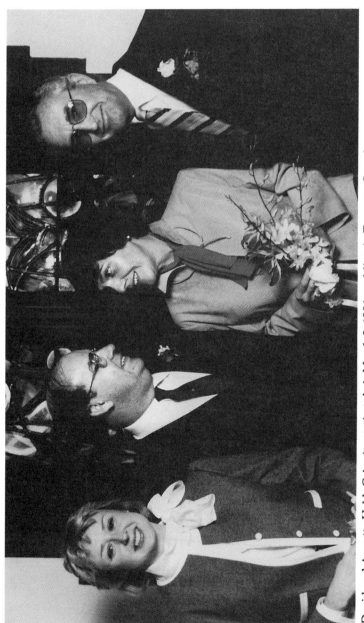

David and Annette Hebb Grier (center) at their March 3, 1984 wedding in Toronto, Canada
(*Courtesy of David Grier*)

PART SIX

OTHER GRIERS
IN NORTH AMERICA

Robert Cooper Grier (1794–1870)
(*Courtesy of Dickinson College*)

20

ROBERT COOPER GRIER
1794–1870

Supreme Court Justice

Robert Cooper Grier served as an associate justice of the United States Supreme Court for nearly a quarter of a century. During his tenure on the nation's highest bench, he presided through years of national crises and issued opinions on matters of great and far-reaching import—slavery, embargo, war, and subsequent reconstuction.

A Jacksonian Democrat, Grier was a staunch Unionist throughout the war years and would serve through the administrations of eight presidents, from Polk to Grant.

Grier was born in Cumberland County, Pennsylvania on March 5, 1794, the eldest of eleven children born to Presbyterian minister Isaac Grier and his wife Elizabeth Cooper Grier. After a rigorous, classical education under his father's tutelage, he entered Dickinson College as a junior in 1811 and graduated one year later at age eighteen. He embarked on a teaching career at his alma mater but was soon called upon to assist his father, principal of an academy in Northumberland, Pennsylvania. When Isaac Grier died two years later, twenty-one-year-old Robert succeeded him as head of this academy; he also taught Latin, Greek, chemistry, astronomy, and mathematics. Simultaneously, he studied law with a local attorney. In 1817, he was admitted to the bar and launched what would become a very prosperous legal practice in nearby Bloomsburg and, later, in Danville, Pennsylvania.

Grier was thirty-five when, in 1829, he married Isabelle Rose, the daughter of a wealthy Scot named John Rose who had emigrated to the States in 1798.

Four years later, Robert Grier became presiding judge for Allegheny County's district court, an office he would hold for thirteen years. During this period, his reputation as a scholarly, candid, and able jurist became firmly established in Pennsylvania legal circles.

His finest moment, however, came in 1846 when he was nominated to the Supreme Court by President James K. Polk; the U.S. Senate unanimously confirmed his nomination on August 5.

During his service on the Supreme Court, Grier rendered opinions on such pivotal matters as the *Dred Scott* case, the *Prize* cases, and *United States v. Hanway* (commonly known as the "Christiana Riot and Treason Trial")— all outgrowths of the sectional conflicts surrounding the Civil War. He is credited with identifying and responding to the central issues that would lead to war long before the nation's division in 1861 and played a significant role in the ultimate preservation of the Union.

In 1867, Grier's formerly robust health began to decline, and three years later, on February 1, 1870, he decided to retire from the bench. He died shortly thereafter, at the age of seventy-six, in Philadelphia.

21

DAVID PERKINS GRIER
1836–1891

General of the Army and Businessman

David Perkins Grier began his brief but illustrious military career at the age of twenty-four, when he organized a group of friends to fight in the 8th Missouri Volunteer Infantry during the Civil War. Within four years, he had served valiantly in many important campaigns throughout the South and rapidly rose through the chain of command to become a brigadier general.

Born in Danville, Pennsylvania on December 26, 1836, David was the second son of John Cooper Grier (1808–1891) and Elizabeth Perkins Grier (1813–1892).[1] The family moved to Peoria, Illinois in 1851, living at 207 Perry Street. John ran a packing business and later established the Grier Grain Company. His son David was working with him in this business when the Civil War erupted.

Young Grier began his service in the Union army as a captain in the 8th Missouri Volunteer Infantry. He took part in the Fort Henry and Fort Donelson campaigns and in the battles of Corinth and Shiloh. Commissioned colonel of the 77th Illinois Volunteer Infantry in 1862, Grier was in a number of battles, including Chickasaw Bluffs, Arkansas; Vicksburg, Mississippi; Sabine Cross Roads, Louisiana; and Spanish Fort and Mobile, Alabama.

By the age of twenty-six, Grier was acting commander of a brigade in the Vicksburg campaign; two years later, he led all the land forces on Dauphin Island in Alabama, as well as on the peninsula surrounding Fort Morgan. When commissioned brigadier general on March 26, 1865, Grier took command of the 1st Brigade of the 3rd Division of the 13th Army Corps in the campaign against Mobile.

In the midst of the war years—on September 17, 1863—David, then a colonel serving in Mississippi, had returned to Peoria on a brief furlough to marry Anna McKinney in "the most colorful and romantic wedding of the

---

1. John Cooper Grier was the brother of Robert Cooper Grier (1794–1870), U.S. associate Supreme Court justice (q.v.), and Brigadier General William Nicholson Grier (1813–1885).

nineteenth century in Peoria."[2] The wedding was held in the McKinney home, 109 North Madison Avenue, Peoria.

When the war ended, David and his brother Robert established the Grier and Company grain business in their hometown. They proved to be skilled entrepreneurs, and their business thrived. In short order, David built Peoria's first grain elevator, organized the permanent Peoria Board of Trade in 1870, and formed the city's first chamber of commerce five years later.

As his business grew, grain depots were opened in other cities and other states, and in 1881, Grier and his family moved to St. Louis, Missouri. However, financial misfortune awaited him there: He soon lost his substantial fortune and was unable to recover these losses before his untimely death at age fifty-four.

At his death, David P. Grier's seven children ranged in age from twenty-five to ten. They were: Smith McKinney Grier (1866–1908), John Perkins Grier (1868–1939), William Reynolds Grier (1869–1951), Margaret Grier (1872–?), Ralph Cooper Grier (1875–1940), David Perkins Grier, Jr. (1878–1947), and Annie McKinney Grier (1881–1940).

He was buried in Springdale Cemetery, Peoria. Dr. John Grier Hibben, a nephew and later president of Princeton University, presided.

General D.P. Grier's paternal ancestors were of Scottish-Irish origin. They settled in Shippensburg and Chambersburg, Pennsylvania early in the eighteenth century. Among the earliest were Thomas Grier (d. 1798) and the Reverend Robert Cooper, D.D. (1732–1805).

JOHN P. GRIER
1868–1939

General David P. Grier's son John, a partner in the brokerage firm of Charles D. Barney and Company, which became Smith, Barney and Company in 1938, was a member of the New York Stock Exchange.

In 1911, his friend Henry Clay Frick had him sit for a life-sized portrait

---

2.   Ann Todd Rubey, Florence Isabelle Stacy, and Herbert Ridgeway Collins, *The Todds of Virginia* (Dispatch Publishing House, 1913).

by artist Lois Swan, which Frick presented as a birthday gift to Grier's mother, in St. Louis.

Harry Payne Whitney named his most famous racehorse, *John P. Grier*, after his friend; at Aqueduct in 1920, the horse gave *Man O' War* his hardest run. The stallion died at age twenty-seven on December 28, 1943, having sired $2 million worth of winners, including champions *Boojum, High Jack*, and *Jack High*.

After retiring from his firm in 1924, John P. Grier made a number of tours abroad, several of which were as a guest of William K. Vanderbilt aboard his yacht, *Ara*. Vanderbilt later published an illustrated log of his 1924 voyage.

Grier contributed funds to Princeton University Library's Benjamin Strong collection on foreign public finance in 1930. His first cousin, Dr. John Grier Hibben (1861-1933), was associated with Princeton almost all of his life, from his student days to his term as its president from 1912 until 1932, when he retired.

John P. Grier died a bachelor on August 9, 1939, in his home at 550 Park Avenue in New York City. He was buried there in Woodlawn Cemetery.

Sir Edmund Wyly Grier (self-portrait, 1914)

22

SIR EDMUND WYLY GRIER
1862–1957

Portrait Painter

One of Canada's premier portrait artists, Sir Edmund Wyly Grier was born in Melbourne, Australia on November 26, 1862. He was fourteen years old when his family moved to Upper Canada, after a period of residence in Bristol, England.

Wyly graduated from Toronto's Upper Canada College before returning with his family to England—first, to the seaside town of Weston-Super-Mare, where his father had a thriving medical practice, and later, in 1879, to London, where Wyly could pursue his art studies.

In London, he studied under painter and engraver Alphonse Legros at the Slade School of Art. Within three years, Wyly's studies took him to Rome and the Scuola Libera; his evenings during this period were spent working in clay and wax at the British Academy.

At the urging of sculptor Alfred Gilbert, Wyly next traveled to Paris, studying at the Academie Julian under Tony Robert-Fleury and Bourguereau. His work there soon earned him a reputation as an exceptionally talented student, as well as recognition in a number of competitions.

By 1891, Wyly had returned to Canada, setting up a studio in Toronto and concentrating on portraiture. Just two years later, he was elected an associate of the Royal Canadian Academy (ARCA).

Wyly painted his first commissioned portrait in 1888, and over the next fifty-nine years, until his retirement at age eighty-five, he would capture on canvas many of his country's most famous personages—government leaders, business scions, judges, and journalists.

In 1895, Wyly was elected to the Royal Canadian Academy and, one year later, was made a member of the Ontario Society of Artists. He would serve as president in both these prestigious groups: a five-year term with the OSA in the early part of the twentieth century, followed by a decade as president of the Royal Canadian Academy, beginning in 1929.

In addition to his dedication to art, Wyly was a military enthusiast and served in the Royal Canadian artillery from 1897 to 1903. By the end of his tour of duty, he was a major in command of the 9th Field Battery.

In later years, as his reputation and standing in the artistic world grew, Wyly lectured widely and contributed to art journals as both writer and editor.

He received an honorary Doctor of Civil Law degree from the University of Bishop's College in 1934. The following year, on the recommendation of the Canadian government, he was knighted.

Wyly and his wife, an accomplished pianist from the Dickson family of Niagara-on-the-Lake, had three sons and two daughters: Crawford G.M. Grier, Edmund Geoffrey Grier, John E. Grier, Stella Grier Gould, and Mrs. V.W. Scully. Son Edmund (1900–1965) became a well-known artist in his own right and was elected to the Royal Canadian Academy in 1943.

23

DR. LEMUEL G. GRIER
1831–1887

Founder of The Grier School

In 1853, a group of central Pennsylvania residents, concerned about the lack of educational opportunities for young girls in their area, established a modest, one-building school on half an acre of land in Tyrone, Pennsylvania. Four years later, Dr. Lemuel Gulliver Grier purchased these simple facilities and welcomed six female students to the first class of the institution that would become The Grier School.

Today, well over a century later, the school thrives on a 300-acre campus, whose rolling hills are graced with trees planted in Lemuel's day. Some 150 boarding students—coming from more than twenty states and a dozen foreign countries—are enrolled in the school's college preparatory curriculum. Among the extensive facilities are a 10,000-volume library, a new gymnasium, a computer resource center, a gymnastics and dance building, and, for the equestrians at Grier, stables, both indoor and outdoor riding rings, and a hunt course.

The son of John and Harriet Hinkle Grier, Lemuel received his bachelor's, master's, and honorary Ph.D. degrees from Lafayette College. He married Sara Boileau in April of 1857—the year he founded The Grier School.

Lemuel was succeeded as head of the school by three consecutive generations of Griers. Upon his death in 1887, his son, Dr. Alvan R. Grier, took the reins, passing them on in 1932 to his own son, Thomas C. Grier, who, like Alvan himself, held a degree from Princeton. Throughout his administration, Thomas was assisted by his wife; when he died in 1965, she continued as head of the school until her son—today's director Douglas A. Grier—took control in 1968, after finishing his studies at Princeton and the University of Michigan.

Harry D.M. Grier (1914-1972)

24

HARRY D.M. GRIER
1914–1972

Art Museum Director

Another member of the Grier family with close ties to the art world was Harry Dobson Miller Grier, who served as director of the renowned Frick Collection in New York City from 1964 until his death in 1972.

Born in Philadelphia on January 23, 1914, Grier received a degree in architecture from Pennsylvania State University in 1935 and subsequently did graduate work in art and archeology at Princeton, where, in 1937, he served as a field assistant on an expedition to Antioch. He also studied as a Carnegie Fellow in both Paris and New York.

Prior to the outbreak of World War II, Grier was a lecturer and assistant to the dean in the Department of Education of the Metropolitan Museum of Art in New York City. He then served with the Army Counter-Intelligence Corps in Europe. At the end of the war, Grier, a major, was acting chief of the monuments, fine arts, and archives section of the U.S. military government office in Berlin for one year. In this post, he secured the first agreement between the four occupying powers for restitution of art works stolen during the war years.

Back in the States, Grier was named assistant director of the Minneapolis Institute of Arts and, in 1951, assistant to the director of The Frick Collection. Grier became the institution's third director upon the retirement of Franklin M. Biebel in 1964. During his tenure, he wrote the introduction to *Masterpieces of The Frick Collection* and supervised the acquisition of a number of important works, including Peter Brueghel's *Three Soldiers*, *Portrait of Man* by Hans Memling, and *Madonna and Child* by Gentile da Fabriano.

His professional affiliations included a term as president of the Association of Art Museum Directors. He was also a trustee of the International Exhibitions Foundation and the Amon Carter Museum of Western Art and a director of the America-Italy Society and the American Friends of Attingham, a summer school in England.

Herbert E. Grier (1911–   )

25

HERBERT E. GRIER
1911–

Scientist and Entrepreneur

A graduate of the Massachusetts Institute of Technology, Herbert Grier was a founding partner and the first president of EG&G, Inc., a nationally known corporation that supplies engineering and technical management services to U.S. governmental agencies.

Grier moved from his native Chicago to Brooklyn, New York at the age of ten and graduated from Brooklyn Technical High School in 1928. He went on to MIT, where he received a bachelor's degree in 1933 and a master's degree in electrical engineering in 1934. In 1967, he was awarded an honorary Doctor of Science degree from the University of Nevada at Las Vegas.

In the 1930s, Grier and his partners, Harold Edgerton and Kenneth Germeshausen, refined ultra-high-speed photography and stroboscopic and flash lighting techniques that were first used in night aerial reconnaissance by U.S. forces in World War II.

Grier also conducted research in atomic weaponry for the Manhattan Engineering District and the Atomic Energy Commission in the 1940s. After he and his partners incorporated their business in 1947, he was appointed president and continued in that position for seven years.

In 1953, he supervised company scientists involved in the AEC's nuclear operations at the Nevada Test Site. He also served as president and chairman of the board of Reynolds Electrical and Engineering Company, Inc. (a major contractor to the AEC in the 1960s and '70s) and as president of CER Geonuclear Corporation.

After retiring from EG&G in 1976, Grier continued to serve on its board of directors until 1983; he also was a director of AVX Corporation and chairman of both TACAN Aerospace Corporation and Sunburst Energy Systems.

Grier has served as chairman of the NASA Aerospace Safety Advisory Panel and consultant to NASA's Shuttle Operations Strategic Planning Group.

He has held many patents and published numerous works in the fields of high-speed lighting, nuclear explosives, and weapon design. Grier is also the recipient of awards: the National Medal of Science (1989), NASA

Distinguished Service (1985), NASA Public Service (1981), NASA Group Achievement (1985 and 1981), the Presidential Certificate of Appreciation (1971), and a Commendation of the President (1948).

BIBLIOGRAPHY

The author's documents, photographs, and memorabilia and a computer disk of this text are available in the William Milton Grier Collection at The Bancroft Library, University of California at Berkeley.

BOOKS

Bancroft, Hubert H. *A History of California.* San Francisco: History Co., 1886–1890.

Bjorge, Guy Norman. *The Homestake Enterprise in the Black Hills of South Dakota.* New York: Newcomen Society of England, American Branch, 1947.

A Brief Historical Sketch of the California Heavy Artillery, U.S.V., and the Operations of Batteries A and D in the Philippine Islands. San Francisco: Patriotic Publishing Co., 1898.

Bronson, William. *The Earth Shook —The Sky Burned.* New York: Doubleday & Co., 1959.

Brown, John Henry. *Reminiscences and Incidents of the Early Days of San Francisco.* San Francisco: Grabhorn Press, 1933.

Burgess, Gelett. *Bayside Bohemia.* San Francisco: Book Club of California, 1954.

Burlingame, San Mateo, Hillsborough, and Millbrae City Directories. San Mateo, California: Coast Directory Co., 1946–1947.

California's Tribute to the Nation. San Francisco: Patriotic Publishing Co., 1898.

De Russailh, Albert Benard. *Last Adventure.* San Francisco: The Westgate Press, 1931.

Faust, Karl Irving. *Campaigning in the Philippines.* San Francisco: Hicks-Judd Co., 1899.

Fielder, Mildred. *The Treasure of Homestake Gold*. Aberdeen, South Dakota, 1970.

First to the Front: First California U.S. Volunteers. San Francisco: Patriotic Publishing Co., 1898.

Flight of the Eagle. San Francisco: Patriotic Publishing Co., 1898.

Hafen, LeRoy R. and Ann. *The Colorado Story: A History.* Denver: Old West Publishing Co., 1953.

Harkness, John Graham. *Starmont, Dundas and Glengarry: A History, 1784–1945.* Ottawa: Mutual Press, Ltd., 1946.

Hittell, John S. *A History of San Francisco.* San Francisco: A.L. Bancroft & Co., 1878.

Homestake Opera House and Recreation Building. Lead, South Dakota: Lead City Fine Arts Association, 1985.

Husted's Oakland, Berkeley and Alameda Directories. Oakland, California: Polk-Husted Directory Co., 1908–1934.

Irwin, Will. *The City That Was.* New York: W.B. Huebsch, 1906.

James, Marquis and Bessie R. *Biography of a Bank : The Story of Bank of America N.T. & S.A.* New York: Harper Bros., 1954.

Kipling, Rudyard. *Rudyard Kipling's Letters from San Francisco.* San Francisco: Colt Press, 1949.

Langley's San Francisco Directories. San Francisco: Directory Publishing Co., 1878–1888, 1899–1929.

Levison, J.B. *Memories for My Family.* San Francisco: privately printed, 1933.

Lewis, Oscar and Hall, Carroll D. *Bonanza Inn, America's First Luxury Hotel.* New York: Alfred A. Knopf, 1939.

Maybeck, Bernard R. *Palace of Fine Arts and Lagoon.* San Francisco: Paul Elder & Co., 1915.

Moodie, Susannah. *Roughing It in the Bush: Or, Forest Life in Canada.* 1852. Reprint edition. Toronto: Bell & Cockburn, 1913.

Osbourne, Katharine D. *Robert Louis Stevenson in California.* Chicago: A.C. McClurg & Co., 1911.

Portland City Directories. Portland, Oregon: R.L. Polk & Co., 1906–1921.

Prieto, Guillermo. *San Francisco in the Seventies.* San Francisco: John Henry Nash, 1938.

Reedy, William Marion. *The City That Has Fallen.* San Francisco: Book Club of California, 1933.

Rennie, James Alan. *The Scottish People.* New York: Hutchinson & Co., Ltd., 1960.

Sacramento City and County Directories. San Francisco: McKenney Directory Co., 1888–1935.

Shapiro, Nat, ed. *Popular Music, 1930–1939: An Annotated Index of American Popular Songs.* New York: Adrian Press, 1964–1973.

South Dakota: Deluxe Supplement to the History of Dakota Territory. Chicago: S.J. Clarke Publishing, 1915.

Stetson, James B. *San Francisco During the Eventful Days of April, 1906.* San Francisco: privately printed, 1906.

Stevens, John Grier. *The Descendants of John Grier with Histories of Allied Families: A Biographical and Genealogical Record.* Baltimore: privately printed,1964.

Writers' Program of the Work Projects Administration in Northern California. *San Francisco: The Bay and Its Cities.* 2d rev. ed. New York: Hastings House Publishers, 1947.

MAGAZINES

Dana, Marshall N. "The Celilo Canal—Its Origin—Its Building and Meaning." *Oregon Historical Society Quarterly*, June 1915.

DeNeffe, Frederick M. "The Mysterious Shoe-String Railroad." *Oregon Historical Society Quarterly*, September 1956.

Dope Bucket: The Spokane, Portland and Seattle's Golden Jubilee Issue (a publication of the Spokane, Portland and Seattle Railroad Company), March 1958.

Dope Bucket: The Spokane, Portland and Seattle's Gold Spike Issue (a publication of the Spokane, Portland and Seattle Railroad Company), 1961.

George, M.C. "Address Delivered at Dedication of Grand Ronde Military Block House at Dayton City Park, Oregon, Aug. 23, 1912." *Oregon Historical Society Quarterly*, March 1914.

McCall, E. Kimbark. "The Growth of a City." *Oregon Historical Society Quarterly* (n.d.).

Merk, Frederick. *History of the Westward Movement.* New York: A. Knopf, 1978.

Mills, Randall V. "Prineville's Municipal Railroad in Central Oregon." *Oregon Historical Society Quarterly*, September 1941.

Official Journal of the British North America Philatelic Society, September 1965.

Rutherford, Frank. "Palermo Chronicles." *The Palermo Progress*, October 17, 1890. Reprinted in Butte County (California) Historical Society's *Diggin's*, Fall 1974.

Stindt, Fred A. "Peninsular Service: The Story of the Southern Pacific Commuter Trains." *Western Railroader* 20 (1957).

Teal, Joseph N. "Address of Joseph N. Teal." *Oregon Historical Society Quarterly*, June 1915.

Utley, Robert Marshall. *The Last Days of the Sioux Nation.* New Haven, Connecticut: Yale University Press, 1963.

NEWSPAPERS

Bathurst (Ontario) *Courier.* October 29, 1852; July 25, 1862; May 17, 1867.

Brockville (Ontario) *Times.* May 11, 1892; April 11, 1908.

CalReport: A Newspaper for Selected Alumni and Friends of the University of California in Berkeley, November 1987.

Lead (South Dakota) *Daily Call.* September 23, 25, 26, and 28, 1914; September 28, 1916.

Los Angeles Daily Times. December 7, 1921.

Los Angeles Times. February 13, 1983; April 18, 1984; September 12, 1947.

Montreal Daily Standard. September 28, 1925.

Montreal Gazette. November 26, 1946.

Montreal Standard. May 6, 1911.

New York World-Telegram and Sun. March 17, 1956.

Oakland (California) *Post Enquirer.* November 26, 1926.

Oakland (California) *Tribune.* December 3, 1967.

Ogden (Utah) *Daily Standard.* June 30, 1910.

San Francisco Call. April 18, 1906.

San Francisco Chronicle. August 25, 26, and 27, 1899; April 18, 1906.

San Francisco Daily News. April 18, 1906.

San Francisco Examiner. April 19, 1906.

NAME INDEX

SUBJECT INDEX

REFERENCES TO ILLUSTRATIONS ARE PRINTED IN BOLDFACE TYPE.